THE BUSINESS OF PSYCHOTHERAPY

THE BUSINESS OF PSYCHOTHERAPY

PRIVATE PRACTICE ADMINISTRATION FOR
THERAPISTS, COUNSELORS, AND SOCIAL WORKERS

ROBERT L. BARKER

COLUMBIA UNIVERSITY PRESS
NEW YORK 1982

Library of Congress Cataloging in Publication Data

Barker, Robert L.
The business of psychotherapy.

Bibliography: p.
Includes index.
1. Psychotherapy—Practice. I. Title. [DNLM:
1. Psychotherapy. 2. Private practice—Organ. WM 21
B255b]
RC465.5.B37   616.89′14′068   82-1307
ISBN 0-231-05438-6   AACR2

Columbia University Press
New York   Guildford, Surrey

Clothbound editions of Columbia University Press books are Smyth-sewn
and printed on permanent and durable acid-free paper.

TO KARL DEREK HAWVER, M.D.

My friend and partner in the
business of psychotherapy

CONTENTS

PREFACE

Iɴ the summer of 1969, Karl Derek Hawver, to whom this book is dedicated, and I made an important decision about our careers. We were then military officers and our service obligations were just concluding. Derek planned a future in intensive clinical psychiatry and psychoanalysis while I intended to concentrate on family and marital therapy. At first, neither of us was sure what the best setting would be in which to pursue our interests. We considered careers in hospitals, government, universities, social agencies, the military. Of course, we gave considerable thought to private practice too. Working for ourselves seemed to be one way of helping people while limiting the frustrations of employment in bureaucratic organizations. But we knew we would face problems. We had very limited financial resources for opening a private office, since we were paying off loans for our professional training and we had young families to support. We weren't even sure we liked the idea of being businessmen, which is essentially what private practitioners are. The business model didn't exactly conform to our prejudices about how people in need could best be helped. Our most immediate obstacle was our lack of knowledge about how to manage a business. Though we were confident about our professional training and practice skills, our experience in operating a business was minimal. However, this last shortcoming was one we could remedy. We could learn everything possible before committing ourselves. We could talk with those who were successful in private practice, benefit from their experiences, and avoid the pitfalls they had encountered.

After we had agreed to open an office together we sought the advice of the most successful and affluent private psychotherapy practitioner that we knew of. Our consultant invited us to his home-office for a meeting. It was located in a very expensive neighborhood, and his house seemed to be an ideal place in which to live and practice. His facilities were tasteful and elegant, obviously the product of careful planning. He was justifiably proud of his surroundings and told us that we too could be in such a position in a relatively short time. He spent the next several hours with us, answering our questions, offering practical suggestions, warning us about the hazards we would face, and showing us how we could combine the goals of providing good service for our clients and a comfortable livelihood for ourselves.

Throughout his discourse, one central theme prevailed: use sound business principles in the management of the practice. Be honest and honorable, he stressed, but don't hesitate to confront clients with their financial obligations. Get bills to them before the first of the month so that they will pay for the therapy first. Hand them the bills in person. Ask them about payment if they are even a day behind. Don't permit them to wait for insurance reimbursement checks to come in before they pay. Don't get carried away with free service or reduced fee therapy. Get plenty of insurance, and take every precaution possible to avoid malpractice suits. Invest the proceeds wisely so as to reduce income taxes. Combine home and office so that some living and housing expenses can be minimized. Hire top-notch clerical help and financial advisers. Establish the office in a good neighborhood, and decorate it with high-quality accessories so that clients don't feel they are involved in a shoddy operation. Give the office an impressive title with an institutional sound to attract more "customers." Promote the service, just as any other good business people would do.

Our minds were reeling when we left the consultant's home. His advice wasn't at all what we had in mind for our office. We wanted to help people. We weren't interested in wealth, or in placing more emphasis on business practices than on professional ones. We would do it our way. We would locate our office where the need was, rather than where the money was. We would provide a service to the community. We would offer free consultation to civic groups, and would never turn away the needy. We would see some clients for less than full fee and would not be so zealous about getting clients to pay. We wanted the relationships we had with clients to be based on mutual trust rather than primarily on financial considerations.

So we didn't pay much heed to our consultant's suggestions. At first, the only idea of his we did use was to give our office an institutional name. We called ourselves "The Potomac Psychiatric Center." We leased space in a modest apartment complex in a blue-collar suburb of Washington, D.C. We furnished our consulting offices in a comfortable but less than opulent manner, and virtually ignored our waiting room. The latter had in it some old, unused furniture from our homes—a $30 couch we bought at a garage sale, an old table and lamp from my basement, and two wicker chairs and a large scatter rug from Derek's attic. Our wives prepared our bills and letters, since we had no secretary, reception desk, or typewriter. We were casual about conveying to our clients that they had to pay their bills on time and often forgiving when they failed to pay at all.

Our innocence about the business side of private practice was short lived. Before long we realized that our consultant's ideas had had considerable merit. Our naiveté was not fatal because two of our decisions proved to be good ones. We found that our choice of location was wise because our services were actually in great demand there. Our decision to provide free community service gave us considerable visibility to those who refer clients. In a few months our schedules were filled. But it took longer for our practices to become viable careers. We gave away too much of our time. We were too casual about our billing procedures. We tried to economize in places that created inefficiencies. We made some false starts in our economic planning. Naturally we found ourselves remembering the consultant's suggestions. We dusted off the notes we had taken in his home and began to apply them with sincere enthusiasm. We hired a good secretary, employed interior decorators to redo our offices and waiting room. We hired an investment counselor and established retirement accounts and insurance programs. Most of all we became more serious about getting our clients to meet their financial obligations.

Since then private practice has proved to be a happy experience for both of us. The establishment has changed somewhat over the years as our educations increased and interests changed. Our location remains the same, but we both see fewer clients than before, since Derek is doing more psychoanalysis and I have become a faculty member at Catholic University. But we still have time to participate in many conferences and professional workshops. At such meetings we are frequently asked about what it's like in private practice. It appears that almost everyone who is or plans to become a provider of mental health care is considering private practice these days. People want to know how to get started, how to get referrals, how to become qualified, and how to avoid all the problems of private practitioners. They have the same questions we had when we started, and we seem to be giving the same kind of advice as we were given. Provide quality service, we stress, but don't forget to use sound business practices too. We realize that many will not heed our advice, not at first anyway. They will see us as people with distorted priorities. If we advocate using business practices in private psychotherapy, it might appear that we are less devoted to clients' well-being than to our own. Having shared this viewpoint, we can easily appreciate such feelings now. But we also recognize that we can provide for our clients' well-being only if we remain in practice. In any event, we are sure the time will come when the doubters will have to dust off their own notes.

Meanwhile, there are many others who want to know as much as possible about the business of psychotherapy before they commit themselves to it. They are the people to whom this book is addressed: it is a framework within which to consider the nature of private practice management. It is for those practitioners now employed in institutions who are considering moving into independent practice. It is for students who are considering career alternatives and want to understand the procedures, problems, and techniques of the private practitioner. It is for use in classrooms and professional conferences concerned with management, administration, mental health policy, and service delivery. It looks at the questions of values facing private mental health care providers as well as the conceptual principles and practical factors to be considered in private practice management. It considers the advantages and disadvantages, benefits and liabilities of private practice, to society and to clients as well as to the practitioners. Private practice is not for everyone; it is not the major solution to the ills of society. It is only one of many approaches to the total mental health care delivery system. But as one of those approaches, and as an activity that occupies a major portion of society's resources, it deserves systematic analysis and balanced scrutiny.

Many people have made important contributions to the production of this book and deserve more appreciation than my words can adequately convey. Of course, my partner and friend, Derek Hawver, must rank high on this list. We discussed every idea contained herein, and he reviewed the manuscript at all stages of development, never complaining when I borrowed freely from his library and frequently monopolized the use of our common office facilities for work on the manuscript. I am also deeply indebted to Professor Thomas L. Briggs of Syracuse University. Tom and I wrote several books together, and writing this one without his help made me recognize more than ever how valuable his advice and friendship have been. To this book he still contributed major input from his wealth of knowledge about private practice issues. He too criticized, reviewed, and helped in the development of this work.

I am also grateful to my colleagues at Catholic University. Particularly helpful were Dr. Richard Bateman, Dr. Martha Chescheir, and Dr. Elizabeth Timberlake, who provided information, ideas, conceptual frameworks, and editorial assistance. Dean Joan Mullaney of the National Catholic School of Social Service gently cajoled me into resuming my interest in writing, the culmination of which is this book. The manuscript was patiently typed and retyped by Janet Young. The editors at Columbia University Press also proved to be most helpful, competent, and devoted to the development of a quality product. Dr. Charles Webel provided many challenging ideas and directions which led to a major refocusing of the book. Joan Schwartz and Karen Mitchell helped to give coherence and clarity to the text.

But no one deserves more thanks and gratitude than does the love of my life, Maggie York, who provided me with a quiet, comfortable environment as well as moral support and encouragement during these long months of writing and researching. Finally, I must thank the many practitioners in private and institutional settings who allowed me to interview them, examine their offices and procedures, and describe their methods. I have described some of them, pseudonymously, without any other important changes. But whether they were analyzed in detail or only as a group they were all cooperative and eager to assist me in passing on the extensive knowledge which they had to offer.

ROBERT L. BARKER

Washington, D.C.

THE BUSINESS OF PSYCHOTHERAPY

ONE

WHAT IS THE PRIVATE PRACTICE OF PSYCHOTHERAPY?

PSYCHOTHERAPY is undoubtedly the world's oldest profession. It has existed in one form or another since the human organism first became a social creature. Members of our species have always needed, and therefore have always sought, the kinds of responses and behaviors from other human beings which are the essence of the psychotherapeutic relationship. We have always looked for encouragement, acceptance, and advice. We have always needed the opportunity to give vent to our emotions and our ideas. And we've always seemed to need people in our lives who could give us feedback and help us understand ourselves and our places in the world. We can infer, since it is still true, that throughout humanity's time on earth some kinds of people have been better than others at developing and maintaining this kind of relationship. Some people are naturally more easy to talk with, and some are more able to be objective, nonjudgmental, and helpful in enhancing one's understanding and self-awareness. We also infer that some people who were in greater demand for this type of relationship were rewarded for their efforts. Their rewards were sometimes only feelings of satisfaction, but sometimes there were also material rewards. The provider of the service might have been given money or property or might simply have felt better for having provided it, or believed that giving of himself in this way would advance him in the afterlife or in the eyes of his fellow man. But whatever the reward, it seems inevitable that both the provider and the recipient of the psychotherapy service have always been beneficiaries of the interaction.

It is not possible to know that psychotherapy relationships with institutionalized reward systems existed before recorded history. But with the advent of the written word we can be certain that there were such relationships. The methods presently used by psychotherapists were described in detail in some of the oldest documents and transcripts known to exist. For example, many records from ancient Mesopotamia, the cradle of human civilization, show that a major activity of highly influential physician-priests had psychotherapy at its core (Zilboorg and Henry 1941). These religious healers spent much of their time counseling people and providing what would now be called individual and group psychotherapy. Their well-documented methods were clearly designed to relieve anxieties and help their clients understand their feelings. They used such devices as drug therapy, catharsis, free association, dream interpretation, advice giving, hypnosis, behavioral modification, and many others which are still in the psychotherapist's repertoire. The techniques utilized by the physician-priests of Mesopotamia were eventually emulated or duplicated in other cultures throughout the world to the extent that virtually every society developed an institutional role for the provision of such services.

Even the word *therapist,* as applied to the practitioners of these techniques, is of ancient vintage. Homer, in the *Iliad,* uses the term to describe the central character Patroclus and his relationship with Achilles. Patroclus would spend days listening to Achilles' incessant complaints and vituperation. Achilles was, of course, the hero of the Trojan War, but as described by Homer he probably could also be diagnosed as suffering from manic-depressive illness. He was encouraged by Patroclus to lie down and to ventilate, to shout out his anxieties, to cry and to talk and to reflect aloud upon his unhappy situation. Granted, Patroclus might not have been a very *good* therapist by current standards. He slept with his client, wore his clothes, and literally fought his battles for him even to the death. Such behavior might be looked upon as incompetent practice, or at least an extreme misuse of the transference phenomenon, but there are probably some psychotherapy schools of thought today which condone and even advocate such techniques. The methods used in psychotherapy have always been highly diverse, wide ranging, and flexible. There seems to be room for many kinds of behaviors under the psychotherapy rubric. In any case, when Achilles mourned the death of his helper he cried out that he had lost his *therapon* or therapist, and that his life thereafter would be changed as a result (Thomas 1981).

THE FIRST THERAPIST IN PRIVATE PRACTICE

Just as the *practice* of psychotherapy and its *title* are part of antiquity, so too is its private practice. Most psychotherapy has always been and still is institution based, with the great majority of it occurring in religious temples, educational academies, or public health care facilities. But even in ancient times there have been isolated and atypical instances in which the private practice of psychotherapy took place. Perhaps the world's first psychotherapist to enter full-time private practice was the Greek physician named Asclepiades. He began his work in 100 B.C. after he had completed his formal training at the Lyceum in Athens and after he had spent several years engaged in research and travel. A brilliant but nonconforming young man, Asclepiades often found himself in conflict with his colleagues and employers. He kept challenging and ridiculing the prevailing theories that physical and emotional illness was caused by the displeasure of the gods and by imbalances in bodily humors. He was, accordingly, not held in high regard by the medical establishment of his day, and he was often forced to conduct research on his own. One of his many interests was in the understanding and care of the mentally ill, and he eventually discovered and developed important treatment methods which are valid to this day. He learned to treat depression with catharsis and physical exercise. He treated anxiety neurosis with wine and hot baths. He was the first to use music in the treatment of psychosis. But the traits which made Asclepiades an innovative and unconventional physician also led to his passionate wanderlust, his desire to explore the world and experience life styles and cultures which were different from anything encountered in Greek intellectual society. Physicians of that era were usually employed in the academies, royal courts, and houses of worship that had proliferated in the socially close-knit city-states. They were obliged to limit their travels so that they wouldn't be too far from their sponsors. But for Asclepiades, such restriction was more than he could long endure. He craved mobility and independence and the opportunity to go wherever in the world his curiosity led him. To travel and to support himself by doing the work for which he was trained, he would have to practice his profession in a very unconventional way. He would have to treat people and collect fees directly for his services.

Eventually Asclepiades made his way to the rapidly growing, rough-hewn boom town of Rome. He immediately felt at home with the energy and social vitality of his new environment, and his intended short visit turned into a lifetime residence. At first the Romans distrusted this foreigner with the strange ideas and odd techniques of medical practice. But his methods seemed to work, and soon more and more Romans began to seek his services and pay him for his help. Eventually Asclepiades had a thriving private practice. He was becoming wealthy and was treating the city's leaders and social elite. Cicero and Marc Antony were two of his many clients, and he ministered as much to their emotional distresses as to their physical ones. But despite his successes, Asclepiades remained a virtual pariah in the medical establishment of Rome. Most Roman physicians had been educated in Greece and they followed the Greek model of institution-based practice. They envied Asclepiades but despised him for rejecting their practice theories. They were especially angry because he accepted direct compensation for treating the sick (Bromberg 1975). It simply wasn't done by reputable physicians. They were salaried workers, employed by their nation's institutions, and they came to believe that it was somehow unethical, selfish, opportunistic, or beneath the dignity of professionals to ask for money to perform what was supposed to be a noble duty. The only ones to ask for money directly were beggars, street peddlers, jesters, magicians, barbers, and other disreputable types who sometimes practiced the healing arts as a sideline. Most people who deviated from this behavior were exposed to rejection by colleagues and sometimes even to societal sanctions.

At all times through history those who have served the needy, the ill, and the handicapped have been inclined to look upon private practice as suspect and disreputable. Since psychotherapy itself has not always been looked upon favorably by many cultures, the combination of the two—psychotherapy and private practice—has rarely been considered meritorious. Thus, those who have engaged in the private practice of psychotherapy or counseling have sometimes been exposed to the same sanctions and disapproval by their professional colleagues as Asclepiades experienced 2,000 years ago.

THE ATYPICALITY OF PRIVATE PRACTICE

American psychotherapists now live in a time and place which is uniquely favorable to the private practice model. We inevitably become immersed in the mores of our culture and tend to think that what we currently experience or perceive is natural and best, and that anything else is abnormal and inferior. Thus, it is easy for us to think of private psychotherapy practice as the standard, the "normal" way of delivering therapy services. It becomes all too easy to think of the institution-based model of delivering psychotherapy services as a somewhat deviant, atypical, or less desirable economic expedient. This impression is, of course, highly inaccurate. In every other nation and culture on earth, besides the United States, private practice has little significance as a means of providing psychotherapy services. It certainly exists in other countries, but the proportion of private compared to institutional psychotherapy practice is miniscule. American psychotherapists, especially the younger ones, also tend to think that the private practice model has been the predominant one here for a long time. Actually, it has been an important part of this nation's total psychotherapy delivering system for only about the past thirty years. Prior to 1950 only a very small proportion of psychotherapy was taking place in the offices of private practitioners. Since then, the utilization of private psychotherapy has greatly increased, mostly because of the trend toward insurance and other forms of third-party payment. But even with these increases, private therapy still provides less than an estimated 20 percent of all the psychotherapy that occurs in the United States. The other 80 percent is still done by salaried employees of institutions or agencies whose income comes from general tax revenues or voluntary contributions (HEW 1980).

The United States has a vast network of these organizations and publicly funded institutions. For example, there are over 1,800 psychiatric outpatient facilities and an additional 650 federally funded community mental health centers nationwide. This does not count the thousands of university guidance and counseling centers, the 200 suicide prevention centers, the 400 family service agencies, or any of the health and social service agencies, nursing homes, settlement houses, institutions for the handicapped and disadvantaged, and other organizations which provide selected client groups with psychotherapy and counseling. The numbers of personnel who deliver these psychotherapy services are many times greater than the numbers of psychotherapists in private practice (NCHS 1979).

Why, therefore, does the impression persist in this country that most psychotherapy takes place in private offices? No doubt the perception has come from two related circumstances. One is that the most influential psychotherapist, Sigmund Freud, was a private practitioner. The other is that the most influential of all the psychotherapy professions, psychiatry, delivers most of its services through private practice. Since Freud and psychiatry are well known to the other professions and to the public, this perception results. Before Freud and his disciples there were few psychiatrists in the world who were not institution based, working in universities and hospitals for the insane. Almost all members of the other psychotherapy delivering professions, all the psychologists, social workers, clergymen, nurses, and educators, were also institution based. Freud himself initially preferred this trend and, indeed, he sought employment in the hospitals and health care organizations of Vienna. But his ideas and practice methods were too unusual for the medical establishment to enthusiastically embrace. They were uncomfortable about his practicing his strange blend of philosophical, metaphysical, and medical techniques under their authority. So, like Asclepiades before him, Freud found that private practice was the best opportunity he had to support himself and his family and remain within his chosen profession. His followers and succeeding generations of psychiatrists have tended to look upon private practice as the standard for their profession, partly in emulation of Freud and partly because the other medical specialties were beginning to move toward the private practice model. Psychiatrists understandably identify with their fellow physicians and the treatment delivery methods of the medical profession. In the United States, most physicians have always favored providing their services through private practice. Thus, more than 90 percent of all psychiatrists have, at some time in their careers, engaged in private practice, and 75 percent of them are in full-time private practice at any given time (NCHS 1979). Even though psychiatrists comprise only a small proportion of all those engaged in psychotherapy, the other professions and practitioners often look to psychiatry for leadership and role modeling. Some of the other psychotherapy delivering professions defer to psychiatrists, accord them greater authority, and often subordinate their own methodologies to them. Members of the other therapy professions often study the writings of psychiatrists but seldom read the works of other professions. Society, too, has endorsed the preeminence of psychiatry in delivering psychotherapy services and has provided the profession with legal and economic sanction for its leadership position. Since most of the members of the preeminent psychotherapy profession are private practitioners, as was the most influential psychotherapist, it is understandable that the private practice model would seem to be more prominent than it really is.

THE EXTENT OF PRIVATE PRACTICE IN PSYCHOTHERAPY

Despite the fact that it is a minority activity within psychotherapy, private practice is still very extensive. Psychotherapy itself is a huge business, and its private practice sector represents a significant part of it. Psychotherapy has grown as fast as almost any other industry in America since 1960. Well over 7 million people now receive psychotherapy services every year in the United States, and more than $2 billion is spent for those services (Gross 1978). The number of psychotherapists and professional groups providing psychotherapy services has increased by the thousands since 1960 and is now one of the nation's largest occupational groups, with at least half a million practitioners in full- or part-time independent or institutional practice. These figures may be very conservative estimates because they do not encompass the clients, providers, and monies spent on any activities which are not generally acknowledged as psychotherapy. For example, the $2 billion figure is for expenditures only for members of certain psychotherapy professions in specified mental health settings. It excludes funds spent in public schools for guidance counselors, or in family service agencies for marriage counselors. It does not cover the money spent by businesses or large organizations such as the military services on counselors or personnel guidance workers. And it does not cover the money emotionally distraught people sometimes spend on their lawyers and bartenders telling them their troubles. The 7 million people receiving psychotherapy each year do not include the other millions who receive counseling, advice, or therapy in their churches, schools, or personnel departments. It is even more difficult to be precise about the number of people who are providing and receiving private practice based psychotherapy. This is because private practice is basically a cottage industry, taking place in settings and circumstances which elude census counts. Many therapists are not licensed or subject to any public regulation whatsoever, and much of the money spent for their services comes directly from the client rather than public or insurance funds.

Specifying the extent of psychotherapy and its private practice depends on what one means by psychotherapy. Defining the term is a complex task, and many disparate, rather inconsistent, definitions of it are now commonly utilized. Wolberg (1974) found at least forty different, widely used definitions, and other writers have been adding to the list every year. The definitions seem to be of two major types. One type indicates that it is a process that exists between the therapist and client and includes a range of activities or behaviors between them. Anything that falls within the range of these behaviors is considered psychotherapy and anything outside the behaviors is not. The trouble with such definitions, of course, is that there is no universal consensus on the appropriate range of behaviors. There are more than 200 different schools of psychotherapy, each with its unique behaviors and each with an implicit view that all rival schools use rather inappropriate behaviors (Lesse 1979). Furthermore, however one defines the appropriate range of psychotherapy behavior, it is difficult to say that such behavior is the exclusive province of a particular therapist, profession, or theory base. Almost anyone who has any compassion at all sometimes engages in the same behaviors as psychotherapists. What is to say, therefore, that one behavior is psychotherapy and the other is not? The question is often answered by resorting to the second type of definition of psychotherapy. These definitions indicate that the practice behaviors aren't so much the crucial variable as is the therapy provider. If he belongs to one of the specified professions, or is employed in one of the designated institutions, his behavior is seen as psychotherapy. But if another person does exactly the same thing but is not a member of one of these professions or not employed by these institutions, his behavior is not considered psychotherapy. Thus, if a psychiatrist or social worker behaves with clients in the prescribed therapeutic way, the activity might be called psychotherapy, but if an astrologer or phrenologist did the same thing, it would have to be called something else. This type of definition also implies that everything the member of the specified profession did would be psychotherapy. If a psychologist spent half his time providing therapy and half in administration, national figures showing psychotherapy expenditures would include his whole salary, though only half would have actually been spent on psychotherapy. The purpose here is not to dwell on definitions of psychotherapy, but rather to illustrate the complexity of psychotherapy and its private practice sector. This book will view psychotherapy and its private practice segment in the broadest, most inclusive terms possible. The term *psychotherapy* will hereafter be taken to include all counseling activities, all the traditional and newer psychotherapy techniques, all the professions which claim to be doing psychotherapy, and all the settings where people get help with their emotional problems. *Private practice* will be taken to include all transactions in which payments for psychotherapy services are made directly to the therapist.

WHO ARE THE PRIVATE PRACTICE PSYCHOTHERAPISTS?

Using this inclusive view of psychotherapy and private practice, it is possible to develop a somewhat clearer picture of its extent. Figures do exist which show how many members of psychotherapy delivering professions there are and how many are engaged in private practice (NCHS 1979). Psychotherapy seems to be done by six major occupational groups. These are (1) the four traditional "mental health team" professions, (2) the guidance and counseling professions, (3) the non-mental health professionals who do psychotherapy as a component of their practice, (4) providers of "alternative therapies," (5) lay therapists and indigenous workers, and (6) parapsychology-oriented practitioners.

Mental Health Team Professionals. This group consists of four professions: psychiatry, psychology, social work, and nursing. They were originally charged with the responsibility of caring for the mentally ill in institutions but subsequently expanded their range of professional interests to include outpatient psychotherapy and work with clients who are not mentally ill. Often called "the helping professions," though they certainly do not have a monopoly on helping, these groups are the oldest, most traditional, and probably the dominant segment of the psychotherapy providing industry. Psychiatry is the smallest but most influential of this group and of the entire psychotherapy field. It is, of course, a medical specialty and makes up about 9 percent of all direct practice physicians. There has been a decline in this proportion in the past few years with fewer student physicians opting to become psychiatrists. In 1970, 10.3 percent of all medical residents were in psychiatry but that number decreased to only 5.6 percent by 1976. This is attributed in part to the fact that psychiatry is among the lowest paid of all medical specialties, even though it is the highest paid psychotherapy profession (Sharfstein and Clark 1980). There are 25,000 psychiatrists nationwide, with 19,000 of them in private practice. Almost all psychoanalysts are also psychiatrists, and almost all of their practice is in the private sector. In recent years, nonphysician lay analysts have been entering the psychoanalytic ranks. But the relative numbers of people in psychoanalysis are very small, because of the labor and time intensity of the method. The typical analyst might treat only eight to twelve people each week and continue with virtually the same people for years. However, psychiatry works with a relatively small proportion of those in therapy, too. Of all the physician visits in the nation, only about 2.6 percent are made to psychiatrists. They also directly treat only about 15 percent of the total number of clients seen by the mental health team professions (HHS 1980).

Psychologists make up the second profession within the mental health team and their numbers and relative influence seem to be growing the most rapidly of all the psychotherapy delivering professions. There are about 75,000 psychologists in the nation, of whom one-third, or 25,000, are engaged in direct practice (NCHS 1979). Most psychologists are employed in research, academic, or industrial settings. But direct psychology practice, more than any other psychotherapy profession, has been successful in achieving its long-term goal to acquire professional independence from the dominance and supervision of psychiatry. Clinical psychologists are now licensed to practice psychotherapy independently, without medical supervision, in all fifty states. Unlike most of the other nonmedical psychotherapy occupations they are reimbursed directly by third-party payers such as insurance companies, with no medical supervision (Mendelsohn 1976). Psychologists have lately been turning their efforts to another kind of conflict, within their profession. They have been working to achieve autonomy from the nonclinical, academically oriented psychologists who dominate their profession. One product of this effort is their current movement to develop professional rather than academic schools of clinical psychology ("Development" 1981). There are now thirty schools of professional psychology established since 1973 which emphasize experiential training over academic work ("Five Year Report" 1981). Another conflict within psychology is the rivalry between clinical and counseling specialties (Goldschmitt et al. 1981). There are 15,000 members of the American Psychological Association who belong to the clinical specialty and 5,000 who are counseling psychologists. The clinical psychologists are, for the most part, working in private practice settings, while the counseling psychologists tend to work, in addition to private practice, in schools and other institutions.

The third of the four mental health team professions does more psychotherapy than the other three. It is social work, which has over 100,000 members who have professional degrees. Most social workers have traditionally been employed in social agencies and government supported institutions, but now almost 10,000 of them are engaged in part-time private practice and another 5,000 are in full-time private work (NCHS 1979). While institution-based social workers have been the major deliverers of psychotherapy, much of their work has been under the supervision or bureaucratic authority of psychiatrists. For example, in the nation's 1,800 outpatient psychiatric facilities, 24 percent of the direct psychotherapy is done by social workers, compared to 11 percent by psychiatrists and 18 percent by psychologists (NCHS 1979). But for the most part, such facilities are supervised by the psychiatrists. Social workers have not obtained, or even sought with the fervor of psychologists, complete autonomy. They are also experiencing difficulties in private practice because they are confronted with three serious obstacles. One is internal conflicts the profession has about its values. Coming from their heritage of helping the poor and disadvantaged has made it difficult for social work to support with much enthusiasm any movement into private practice. Some social workers see private practice as "elitism" and as abandoning the tradition of serving the disadvantaged. The second obstacle is licensing for private practice. The profession has not been very successful in attempts to obtain licensing laws to regulate social work practice

(Hardcastle 1977). This seems to be because social work has had so much difficulty defining what its practice is, what it does that is unique, and what qualifications are necessary to do it. The third obstacle social work has faced is the difficulty of developing suitable tests of its members' professional competence. Most of the competency examinations developed so far do not seem to test what is uniquely social work knowledge. Unless these obstacles are overcome, social work may continue to find private practice difficult.

Nursing is by far the largest of the mental health professions with over a million members, and every state licenses its practice (Jackson 1981). The number of nurses who practice psychotherapy is of course much smaller, and the number of private practitioners is smaller yet. Nurses who enter the private practice of psychotherapy are usually psychiatric nurse specialists at first. Most of them in private practice have additional auspices in addition to nursing. For example, many become licensed both as nurses and as marital and family therapists, after acquiring additional training. Others work as members of private practice psychotherapy teams, often with physicians, and often in the capacity of cotherapists. For example, many of the male-female sex therapy teams, which are growing in numbers, are made up of physicians and nurses. Mental health nurses, even more than social workers, have had a tradition of practicing psychotherapy in institutional settings under psychiatrists' supervision, but now nurses are beginning to demand more autonomy and increased responsibility. One manifestation of this is in the numbers of nurses who are now practicing outside hospitals and outside physician supervision. At the vanguard of this movement are nurse-practitioners (Manley 1981). Among the duties of this relatively recent branch of nursing is counseling to individuals, families, and groups in mental and physical health subjects. Their numbers are growing rapidly. There are now 200 professional schools to train nurse-practitioners at the masters and doctorate levels, and they are expected to graduate 40,000 practitioners by 1985 and 55,000 by 1990. Already about 15,000 of them are employed in private practice and most of them include psychotherapy in their range of activities (*New York Times* 1979). Undoubtedly this profession will become increasingly important and influential in the near future.

Guidance and Counseling Professions. This second group of providers of psychotherapy is much larger than the first, even though it is often not accorded the recognition that its numbers would seem to warrant. Among the professions which make up this group are pastoral counselors or clergymen, school guidance counselors, vocational and rehabilitation specialists, marriage counselors and therapists, and counselors for special problem areas. One reason this group seems less influential than other psychotherapy delivering professions is an implicit pecking order or elitism in the professions. The view seems to prevail that somehow counseling is inferior to therapy and that guidance and rehabilitation are specialties that do not require as much expertise. This seems to spring from the notion that therapy is a more complex activity which deals with more seriously disturbed people. This view holds that counseling or guidance is for normal people who don't really need much help with "deep" psychological conflicts. It is seen as a method of simply telling clients what they should do rather than enhancing their abilities to learn for themselves how to be effective. Because of this connotation, many of the members of these groups have been expressing displeasure at being called "counselors" rather than therapists. Members of the counseling psychology specialization are frequently suggesting that they have lower status or prestige than clinical psychologists (Goldschmitt et al. 1981). Many professions which had once been happy with the counseling appellation are changing their names for this reason. For example, the largest organization of professionals who help people with marital and family problems recently changed its name to the American Association for Marital and Family *Therapy,* from *Counseling.* But such titular chauvinism is quite unfounded and invalid. Since *therapy* is so ill defined, as we have seen, and since there is so little consensus as to what its behaviors actually are, it is unfair to claim that its methods are better than the methods used in counseling. Furthermore, there are no empirically based findings to justify the view that what counselors do takes less skill or training or leads to less important results than therapy (U.S. Congress 1980). And there *is* ample evidence that the "mental health team" professions are now treating more healthy people than are other professional groups (Torrey 1975).

Pastoral counselors (or are they calling themselves "pastoral therapists"?) have been delivering these services longer than any other professional group. They are the direct descendents of the physician-priests of Mesopotamia and have been, throughout history, the largest and most important professional group in helping individuals come to grips with their emotional conflicts. Clergymen provided counseling and therapy, particularly for marital and family problems, mostly within the auspices of their churches and synagogues for most of their histories. But the seminaries and theological schools in recent years have vastly increased their offerings in subjects concerned with the human psyche and social relationships. As a result, clergymen have become even more interested in providing this kind of service (Crabb 1978). Their movement into private practice, then, was inevitable. Before the 1960s, few clergymen provided psychotherapy services outside their church auspices, and when they entered private psychotherapy practice it was usually after resigning from their ministries. But it is now becoming commonplace for clergymen to retain their church roles and in addition to set up private practice offices. The pastoral counseling centers, or similarly named organizations, have been proliferating throughout the nation, so that nearly every large and middle-sized city, and even many small towns, now have at least one such organization. They are usually staffed by one or several clergymen, not always even of the same denomination. The offices are mostly located in some setting off the church premises, though more churches are allowing their pastors to see clients for their own direct renumeration in the church office. This makes it possible for the minister to supplement his typically meager church income and relieves his parishioners from increased pressures for higher tithes or contributions. The clergymen sometimes have value conflicts about this role, and thus far have found it difficult to get third parties such as insurance companies to help their clients pay for the services.

A second professional entity within the counseling group consists of the 60,000 counselors and guidance specialists employed in the nation's public and private schools (Stickney 1968). These professionals usually have master's degrees or higher in education, with heavy emphasis on psychology. They often were promoted from classroom teaching to this role, in which they consult with students about careers, studies, and personal problems. Often they "treat" the students and sometimes their family members. Many of these professionals eventually leave the educational system and enter private practice, particularly when they achieve retirement eligibility from the schools. Many of them also work in mental health facilities or outpatient psychiatric clinics during their summer vacations.

Personnel, vocational guidance, and rehabilitation counselors are another large group of psychotherapy deliverers, with over 18,000 employed nationwide. Their settings are mostly in Veteran's Administration Hospitals, penal institutions, state mental hospitals, schools, and industrial and business personnel offices. Their counseling orientation often starts out heavily focused on such practical matters as career guidance, but almost invariably these counselors expand the interviews to discussions about personality conflicts and social relationship difficulties (Brammer 1968). Most of these professionals have bachelor's or master's degrees in specialized training programs in personnel and guidance, with a heavy emphasis on psychology and sociology. About half of them have now been professionally certified or licensed to practice, and all new members must pass certification examinations. This group comprises a majority of the membership of the American Personnel and Guidance Association (NCHS 1979).

Another segment in this category of psychotherapy providers are the nation's marriage counselors and family therapists. The public generally perceives this to be a very large, distinct professional entity, though it is anything but. Most of the people engaged in this type of work are members of other professions and owe their primary allegiance and identification to those professions. The aforementioned American Association of Marital and Family Therapists is the nation's largest of several organizations of this type and has approximately 15,000 members. Almost all of them are involved in part- or full-time private practice. However, all but 2,000 of them are also members of other professional groups. Most of the AAMFT members are, in order of group size, clergymen, social workers, psychologists, and psychiatrists. Special and unique education for marriage and family counselors has never really caught on. Only since 1975 have separate professional educational facilities been developed with much success, and now there are twenty professional schools of marital and family therapy at the master's degree level and four at the doctoral level. The schools are often affiliated with university departments of sociology, home economics, and anthropology, but the graduates are often members of the other professions as well (Nichols 1979).

Non-mental Health Professions in Psychotherapy. This third group of psychotherapy deliverers are members of professions whose primary function is to help with some specific types of problems faced by their clients and who use psychotherapy as an integral but only supplemental part of this process. Basically they help clients through physical, social, legal, or relationship problems. Included among these professions are speech and hearing pathologists (30,000 members), occupational therapists (16,000 members), physical therapists (25,000 members), and the 14,000 specialized rehabilitation professionals who are employed as corrective therapists, manual arts therapists, music therapists, and therapeutic recreation specialists. All of these professions are employed in institutions such as mental hospitals, prisons, institutions for the handicapped, and physical care hospitals. Their techniques are highly specialized and their training emphasizes not only the specialty but also engaging clients in psychotherapeutic aspects of relationships. Almost all of these specialists are publicly regulated and licensed. Currently less than 5 percent of them are in private work (NCHS 1979).

Providers of Alternative Therapies. This fourth group of psychotherapy providers is a disparate collection of professionals, semiprofessionals, and people with no special education at all. What brings them together is their common interest in and enthusiasm for a particular ideology or philosophy. These ideologies have often originated in oriental cultures or are based on religious, philosophical, or folk wisdom. The philosophy behind them often suggests methods and techniques for helping people overcome emotional conflicts or helps them understand themselves better. Their goal is frequently to enhance individual feelings of well-being and inner harmony and to develop "oneness" with the environment. They are frequently called "alternative therapies" because their methods and theory bases are not developed from the traditional ideologies of the established mental health professions (Magaro et al. 1978). Included among these ideologies are transcendental meditation, bioenergetics, Silva mind control, Scientology, biofeedback, Rolfing, human potential encounters, Zen, yoga, gestalt, acupuncture, psychic healing exercises, shiatsu massage, kirlian photography, macrobiotic dieting, and many others. Obviously practitioners of the traditional and the alternative therapies are not mutually exclusive. Many of the traditional mental health professionals use some of these methods as part of their own therapy methodologies. However, there does seem to be some alienation between the alternative and traditional therapists groups in general. It seems to occur because of the missionary zeal that is sometimes associated with the ideologies of both groups. It is unfortunate that this happens because it reduces the cross fertilization that would otherwise occur. There are undoubtedly considerable skills and knowledge which each group possesses which could be of great value to other groups.

The training for the alternative therapists can range from very rigorous, demanding, and lengthy, to nothing more than having experienced the therapy. Many who have partaken of the therapy and benefitted therefrom have become so interested in it that they have become therapists themselves. Much of the therapy that occurs in the alternative ideologies is based on the private practice model. The traditional mental health care institutions have not seemed eager to embrace many of the alternative methodologies, so the practice has had to be private. Funding for such treatment, unless it is done as part of an institution's research projects, comes from the recipient of the therapy. Occasionally private benefactors contribute for the therapy of others, but this is not typical. However, the fee for this service tends to be much lower than that charged by traditional private practitioners. Third-party payments are very rare, and public regulation is infrequent. Much of the therapy is too experimental and innovative to meet the standards of public regulation. The numbers of practitioners of these methods, and the numbers of clients served are impossible to determine. Many alternative therapies are rather faddish, enjoying great interest and enthusiasm for awhile and then being suddenly ignored in favor of another therapy. Both clients and practitioners move from one methodology to another with great ease and frequency. It is not likely that accurate figures about the costs of these services will be available until some of these methods establish themselves as part of the traditional segment of the psychotherapy providing industry.

Lay Therapists. This fifth group of psychotherapy providers has always been a very important part of the mental health care industry, and its numbers of practitioners have been the largest of all the groups. These people are usually volunteers, and their training is usually short, rather informal, and obtained for the most part on the job. They don't claim to be professionals or autonomous therapists. Included in this group are personnel in hospitals, community organizations, and drug treatment centers; and members of Alcoholics Anonymous, Al-Anon, Neurotics Anonymous, Gamblers Anonymous, TOPS (Take Off Pounds Sensibly), and a variety of other discussion-oriented self-help groups. Millions of people are involved in these groups, and various studies suggest that their results are comparable in success to those of professional therapists (Torrey 1969). The costs for these therapies are usually nominal, with the "practitioners" not being paid at all. Naturally, there is little movement by members of these groups to engage in private practice. Some weight-loss organizations have used the private practice model with considerable success, but volunteerism has been the norm for most of the other providers.

Exceptions to the no-pay, voluntarism standard among lay therapists are the self-help groups which provide intensive workshops to large numbers of individuals. Lifesprings and "est" (Erhart Seminar Training), are the major examples. They typically gather hundreds together for weekends of intensive encounter therapy sessions. They foster group experiences and self-awareness in social situations. The clients of these workshops pay several hundred dollars, and the providers of the direct contact are usually volunteers or laymen who have themselves experienced the programs. The costs are certainly no more than the same amount of time with a professional person would cost, and the clients who have experienced these programs tend to be enthusiastic about the benefits received. Lifesprings and est are now located in major centers throughout the nation. They are becoming very large businesses and beginning to serve a considerable part of the population (Durlak 1976).

Parapsychology Oriented Practitioners. The last group to be discussed is made up of astrologers, phrenologists, fortune-tellers, mediums, tarot card and tea leaf readers, and various others associated with occult phenomena. They have a long history of delivering their special service, going back to ancient times. Their methods and ideologies grew out of unenlightened man's attempt to explain his feelings and understand his personality. Their current appeal is still to those groups of people who are not exposed to scientific explanations of human personality. Most professional psychotherapists deny having anything in common with this group and would object to being included in any categorization with them. These practitioners are seen as being disreputable, not adhering to any professional standards or values, and placing their own pecuniary interests over the interests of the client. Their ethics are questionable and they seem subject to very little public scrutiny or regulation. Nevertheless, because they appeal to a great many people and use verbal interaction to help ease their clients' anxieties, they see themselves as providing a valuable and important psychotherapy service. It seems obvious that if they were to suddenly disappear and if all their clients then sought the services of professional psychotherapists, the professionals would have a very difficult time coping with the increased demand.

Members of these groups justify their roles and suggest that their methods are just as valid and successful as are the traditional ones. They say they use traditional methods, including advice giving, suggestion and persuasion, and insight development. They develop an expertise in getting their clients to reveal personality characteristics to the provider and then to themselves. They claim their goals are similar to the goals of the traditional therapists. They attempt to make the client feel at ease, more secure, and more certain of how to handle future obstacles. They do not acknowledge that their methods are not scientifically replicable and they deny that their results are not efficacious. But they do claim that such charges are just as appropriate for the traditional psychotherapies. They point out that the traditional therapies have an unprovable theory base, that *their* methods are not replicable, and that the effectiveness of *their* methods is still unvalidated (Gelwin 1981).

Almost all the practitioners in this group are in private practice. Their practices are built on providing satisfactory answers to their clients and making them feel they have benefitted as a result of the transaction. They do not have licenses to practice, and are rarely subject to public regulation. Their payments are invariably through direct fee for service from the client, and their charges are usually based on what they think the traffic will bear. The amount of money spent for these services is highly conjectural, but it is undoubtedly very great. Many practitioners do not record their proceeds even to the Internal Revenue Service, and the clients do not usually reveal the amounts they have spent for such services. The purveyors of these services are highly mobile, so estimates about their numbers and their costs are unreliable.

These six groups do not by any means encompass all the psychotherapy or counseling services that take place. There are many individuals and members of other occupational groups which also engage in such behavior. For example there are 400,000 people who work in mental health and social service related fields who do some counseling and therapy as part of their work (NCHS 1979). Many professional people in other disciplines, such as law, medicine, social sciences, and business also provide some counseling. Those who are in private practice come from a wide variety of backgrounds, training, and experiences. In some ways, the public, especially consumers of private practice psychotherapy, is faced with a difficult choice when it comes to seeking these services. Caveat emptor might well have to be their motto.

THE NEED FOR UNIFORM STANDARDS: DIFFERENCES
BETWEEN PRIVATE AND INSTITUTIONAL PRACTICE

The psychotherapy deliverers and their allied fields are so disparate that it is impossible to encompass them all in any systematic analysis. They have no common training, experiences, goals, methods, interests, or results. There is relatively little cooperation among the various groups, and a great deal of internecine conflict. It has often been suggested that there is need for a "fifth profession," one called "professional psychotherapy," which is distinct from all the aforementioned disciplines and groups, but which encompasses some of the best elements of each (Henry et al. 1971). The fifth profession (the other four being psychiatry, psychology, social work, and nursing) would have its own training methods and standards, and the methods utilized would encompass most of those now used in a compartmentalized fashion by the various disciplines. There would be one competency examination, one standard for testing, and a single certification and public regulation system. Achievement of this unity, especially after considering all the groups which might become involved, seems a long way off.

The problems which come from this disparity are much more serious and dangerous in the private practice sector than in the institution-based model of service delivery. Private practitioners have fewer controls on their behaviors, and their relative autonomy makes it possible for them to avoid being scrutinized for competence by their colleagues (Langsley 1978). In the institution-based model, there are controls, peer group pressures, and bureaucratic standards which provide some protection to the consumer. The incompetent practitioner would be less likely employed and if hired he could be fired more easily than happens in private practice. This is not to suggest, however, that psychotherapy practiced in institutions is unequivocally superior to that practiced in private settings. Nor is the converse true. Both models have their positive and negative features. In both, there is a great need for clearly defined and enforced standards of practice in order to protect clients. The client is more at risk with the private practitioner who does not have public regulation or bureaucratic supervision to contend with, unless the private practitioner is willing and able to adhere to the standards professionally prescribed in his practice. When the practitioner lives up to this ideal, the service which he has to offer may be equal or superior to the service offered in institution-based practice.

Five major standards of conduct and professional behavior distinguish the private practitioner from the agency-based therapist. First, private practice is professionally rather than bureaucratically controlled. Second, the private practitioner determines his own treatment methodology and clientele rather than having it prescribed for him by his employers. Third, his practice income comes from fees for direct services rendered. Fourth, his education and experience must be sufficient to enable him to work autonomously. And finally, the private practitioner must be publicly as well as professionally regulated or licensed. Each of these merits attention.

Professional versus Bureaucratic Controls. The first characteristic which distinguishes private practice from its institution-based counterpart concerns the auspices under which the practice is sanctioned. All organizations and social agencies use bureaucratic principles in their methods of operation. Divisions of labor, specialization, delegation of responsibility, and definition of roles to prevent worker's overlap are among the essential components of bureaucracies, including all therapy providing institutions. The therapists who work in these facilities are bureaucrats. As such they are required to negotiate the stresses, opportunities, and constraints that permeate organizational life, regardless of their position in the organization. It is the nature of any organization to predetermine the behaviors of its members, which thereafter must be prescribed and enforced by the organization. Otherwise it would be a disorganization. In social agencies, clinics, and institutions which employ therapists, many behaviors are predetermined for the therapist. His own range of possible decisions is circumscribed within these limits (Hess 1980). His range of behaviors is limited to the needs and requirements of the organization. This does not imply that the institutional therapist is nonprofessional or that professionalism and bureaucracy are mutually exclusive. There is ample opportunity for professional judgments and decision making in institutions, as long as they fall within the prescribed limits. The private practitioner is essentially nonorganizational. He doesn't spend a large proportion of his time in administrative activities, and his range of decisions and behaviors is limited only by his own professional requirements and personal judgments. His limitations of practice are primarily prescribed by his professional association, and he is only personally bound to honor his profession's mores.

The most important element in the professional versus bureaucratic system of controls has to do with the obligation to the client served. It is inherent in the value systems of all psychotherapy professions that the practitioner's first and foremost obligation is to the client. This principle is commendable in the abstract but leads to difficulties in the implementation. An employee of any organization is obligated to fulfill the conditions of his employment above all other considerations while on the job. It is unreasonable to expect most employees, whatever the standards of their profession, to place something else above this obligation. The employee therefore tends to conform to the policies and requirements of the organization rather than to the needs of a given client if there is any conflict. The issue is rarely tested, fortunately, since the organization's requirements and those of the clients are in fact generally quite compatible. Most organizations which employ therapists are very strongly influenced by their professional employees and the values and methods of those employees. They usually develop their rules in order to conform to employee wishes. This is why it is not readily apparent that the organization's values take precedence over the therapists'. But when specific events rather than theoretical ones are considered, it becomes more apparent. One agency policy, for example, might be to maintain a waiting list for potential clients. But suppose an individual needs treatment before his turn comes up. If the therapist knows treatment is needed, but also knows that the agency policy is firm, what is he likely to do? For another example, a client may begin receiving treatment from an organization which has a policy of providing treatment only for short amounts of time in order to be available to as many clients as possible. When the deadline is reached and the client still requires the service but meeting the need is contrary to the organization's policy, what is the therapist likely to do? Certainly in these examples there would be some flexibility in agency policy, but if the flexibility results in a virtual elimination of that policy, the efficient organization would have to begin a tightening-up process. If the therapist took advantage of the flexibility and continued to make exceptions, he would not be likely to remain in favor with his employer for long. Eventually there would be enough pressure on him to assure his subsequent conformity to agency policy above all other considerations, or he would not long remain an employee. In sum, whenever the professional person is employed by an organization, that institution's needs will almost invariably supersede those of the client (Noll 1976). The private practice model does not encounter this dilemma, and the principle of client precedence is unquestionable. The major distinguishing characteristic of the private practitioner is that he is an employee of the client. He may be "fired" or replaced at any time if his work is not satisfactory to the client. The organization's employees may be fired only if their work is unsatisfactory to the organization. The client has the same authority over the private practitioner as would any other employer, so the therapist is not faced with divided loyalties or obligations. The client-therapist relationship is implemented, or the therapist is "hired," when both reach an agreement. This agreement, or contract, may be implicit or explicit, but both parties come to it without manifest influences from other auspices. Without these influences, the primacy of the client interest is more secure. The major threat to this primacy would be the therapist's personal motivation to exploit, or otherwise let his own interests predominate over, the client's. In institution-based practice there are peer and supervisory controls against this sort of event. Nevertheless, the primacy of client interests is inherent in private practice, even though some practitioners might attempt to deviate from it.

Determining Treatment Methodology and Clientele. The second characteristic which distinguishes the private psychotherapy practitioner from the therapist employed in institutional settings concerns the ways clientele and treatment methods are selected. In the private practice setting, the practitioner chooses which people he will see and what method he will use in their treatment. Such decisions are often outside the control of the institution-based therapist. It is the organization's policy or criteria in these settings which determines what therapist will see what client, and what method will be used. The organization might have an intake worker or supervisor who determines which staff member would be most appropriate to work with the client, or the decision might be made at random, depending on which therapist is next on the list. In smaller organizations there may be only one or two therapists, but it is still agency policy and not the therapist's own decision which determines whether or not he is permitted to see a given client. Many clinics and organizations, but certainly not most, have recognized the importance of effective matching and have learned that therapist-client interactions are significantly improved when care is taken. Matching refers to the preferential assignment of certain types of clients to specific types of therapists. But in organizations the client selection or matching process is generally not made by the therapist who will provide the therapy. In private practice such decisions are always made by the therapist himself. He decides what type of client he is best suited to work with and targets his practice to this type of clientele. He may pursue more knowledge about a given type of client or a given type of technique, but the decision to do so is his alone. Obviously, however, there are risks in this process too. Therapists are not always able to judge their own competence. Most private practitioners cannot always be objective about their limitations. In the organization this potential problem is reduced by having other, more objective people make the decision.

The same potential benefits and liabilities also exist with respect to choice of treatment methods. The organization's policy often predetermines the methods which are to be employed in providing the therapy. Supervisors often require that the therapist use a specific technique or provide only a specific type of therapy because of the agency's requirements. Many organizations which employ therapists focus on or provide only one kind of particular service or treatment method. For example, there are organizations which specialize in such things as group therapy, transactional analysis, behavioral training programs, psychoanalytic methods, to name only a few. If a therapist worked in a probation office and wanted to use intensive psychoanalytically oriented methods with his charges, he would probably feel negative pressures from his employer, who wished to move cases through faster. Or conversely, if he was employed in a psychoanalytic institute and wanted to see one hundred clients weekly, he might have some difficulties. Such problems do not occur to the same extent in private practice. As a professional person who has the education, experience, skill, and knowledge to make his own decisions about what is the best available treatment approach for any given problem, the private psychotherapy practitioner makes this determination with his client. Neither makes this decision with reference to the requirements of an organization's standards. If, for example, the therapist ascertained that the client's problem would be best treated by involving the entire family in a Bowen Family Therapy approach, it would be within the private practice therapist's province to recommend and possibly provide such treatment if he had the background to do so. If the therapist were employed by an organization which subscribes to a Family Network Therapy approach however, the therapist would not be able to utilize the Bowen method even if he felt it would be better for the family. Again, there are risks in the private practice model about determining one's own method of treatment. The private practice therapist might be more inclined to prescribe treatments which are within his own realm of expertise even though that technique might not be the best method available for the particular client. The agency-employed therapist, on the other hand, is subject to more controls. He is exposed to the techniques of other therapists and might be inclined to borrow ideas or techniques from them.

The Method of Reimbursement. The third characteristic which distinguishes the private practitioner from the agency-based therapist is manner of payment. The client directly pays the private psychotherapist to perform a specific service. The payment is directly related to that service and only that service and is not made for any activities that do not directly benefit the client. For example, when the therapist takes a special course to improve his abilities, the client is not obliged to pay for that training. The therapist's income is entirely dependent upon the actual units of service which he has delivered to his client. Usually these units of service are hours of psychotherapy administered. This is in contrast to the organization-based therapist who is paid a salary for conforming to the employers' expectations. The organization might require the therapist to maintain regular hours, provide therapy to all assigned clients, attend workshops, and engage in administrative duties. The therapist is entitled to his salary regardless of how much direct work with his clients he provides. The only exception is the atypical case in which organizations pay their employees on a contractual basis, so many dollars for seeing so many clients. In such instances, the therapist is actually receiving fee for service payments, but the amount of the fee and the conditions of payment are still determined by the employer rather than the therapist himself. The contractual therapist is not engaged in private practice, despite fee for service, because the organization pays him.

Education and Experience Requirements. The fourth characteristic which distinguishes private practitioners from organization therapists is the amount of education and experience required of each. Private practice is a very demanding activity. The therapist must have a great deal of knowledge, and his practice skills must be thoroughly integrated into his professional being. He must be able to call upon those skills and knowledge in order to make the independent judgments and immediate and correct decisions about how best to serve his client. There are no supervisors nearby to add ideas to his decision-making process. There are no agency or clinic policies to predetermine what kind of clients to serve or what methods to use. He usually has no peers readily available to listen to his ideas or provide feedback. Furthermore, the private practitioner is more visible to the public than is the therapist who is employed in an institution. The private therapist's misjudgments are more apparent since there is no organization to obfuscate the errors or conceal their perpetrator. With all these considerations, it is crucial that the private practitioner have an extensive, solid, formal, professional education and sufficient practice experience to integrate this education into practice. Most private practitioners are subject to public regulation, professional certification, and a variety of quality assurance programs; it is clear that these sanctions cannot substitute for the therapist's own education and experience. Public regulation cannot test all that one acquires through professional education or obtains experientially.

Professional education is fundamental, the foundation upon which all other quality assurances rests. Professional education, as opposed to academic education, is practice based. It entails considerable classroom and academic work but it also includes a considerable amount of experiential training. The student-therapist works with clients, under supervision, and thus is able to integrate what he is learning in the classroom with actual practice skills. Professional education can take many forms depending upon which profession is doing the educating. Whether the student is in residency, internship, or field placement, the practical-theoretical balance is the essence of the professional education model. Engaging in practice with only a theoretical and conceptual base would be hazardous to the client as well as to the therapist. It would be like playing on a professional basketball team after having only read books on how the game should be played. It takes practice, trial and error, and considerable coaching before one can do it well. Without this coaching, which begins in the professional school, the therapist would do well to avoid private practice.

After the therapist obtains sufficient formal education, it is still worthwhile for him to maintain close relationships with his colleagues and other professionals until he has enough time to refine his practice skills. Regardless of the quality and length of one's education, and regardless of how much of that training is experiential, the therapist still needs more time and exposure in practice settings to consolidate and integrate the training with the practice. It is one thing to work with clients as an intern or resident and quite another to be faced with professional decisions without the guidance and support of supervisors or colleagues. Most psychotherapists, consequently, take their first jobs in clinics, social agencies, hospitals, or other organizations where they have this supervision. In such settings, consultation opportunities and peer relationships are more accessible. It would be risky for the new professional to enter private practice without this opportunity. Many of the helping professions require that their members work in organizational settings for a specified amount of time prior to independent practice because of this fact. Entering private practice immediately upon completion of professional education is considered highly dangerous and unethical for the therapist in these professions. Other professional groups are not so strict about this, possibly because they feel their formal education and residency requirements are so stringent and lengthy that additional observation is unnecessary. Still other professions simply do not have well-enforced sanctions to control the practices of their members. These professions are essentially powerless to prevent their members from entering into private practice immediately after formal education is complete.

The specific amount of time one needs in order to acquire sufficient education or experience has not been dealt with here. Professional organizations and state laws have prescribed what are considered minimum standards, and responsible therapists will adhere to these standards. The minimum standards vary from profession to profession, as we have seen, and they vary from state to state, as we shall see. These standards keep changing as the knowledge base keeps expanding. What are now considered to be minimum standards for education and experience may not be appropriate in a few years, as new findings and techniques are utilized.

Professional and Public Regulation.   The fifth and final characteristic distinguishing private from institutional psychotherapists concerns licensing, certification, and public and professional controls on the practitioner's behaviors. The employee of an organization may belong to a professional association and adhere to the norms of the association, but he also must conform to the norms of the organization. As long as he works within the auspices of the organization, his behavior and practice may be subject to more intense scrutiny and control by the organization than by the public or by his profession. But the private practitioner derives all his auspices from the public regulation and the professional certification of his practice. Most of the professionals in private practice require licenses from their state in order to practice their profession outside of organizational auspices. Licensing is important as a means of protecting the public from incompetent or unethical practitioners. The client has no other way of distinguishing between who is and who is not competent and ethical, since he cannot hold any agency accountable. There is no one license or professional certification for the practice of psychotherapy, just as there is no single profession of psychotherapy. Therefore legal sanction is conferred on the practitioner by the state through licensing, and the license is granted to him, not as a psychotherapist but as a member of his primary profession. The organization psychotherapist usually seeks to be regulated publicly and professionally too, but since he has the auspices of his organization, it is not nearly as crucial for him to have such regulation as it is for the private practitioner. This issue will be discussed at length in chapter 9.

In conclusion, it must be clear that psychotherapy, and its private practice component, has a long history, a variegated group of adherents and practitioners, and a set of norms which distinguish it from other professional practices. This is a testament to the fact that psychotherapy appeals to many different kinds of people, both as consumers and practitioners. It is a complex art and a business which requires expertise not only in the type of service delivered but also in simply managing and maintaining the practice. Those who have entered into the private practice of psychotherapy have encountered considerable obstacles and problems. These are things which each practitioner must over-come to successfully achieve his goal. The rewards of private practice in psychotherapy are considerable, both materially and in personal satisfaction, if it is done well. But doing it well does not come automatically. It comes from preparation and knowl-edge. It comes from the ability to overcome whatever reserva-tions one might have about the value and ethics of private prac-tice. The first obstacle the private practitioner usually has to face is the value dilemma of being in a business where his living is directly dependent on the misfortunes of others. Once he gets be-yond that hurdle he can look to the practical, actual obstacles which must be addressed if he is to engage in the business of psychotherapy.

TWO

PRIVATE PRACTICE
AS A BUSINESS

PRIVATE psychotherapy practice is a business. Its purveyors are selling something, a service, to customers or service consumers. It is a capitalistic and money-oriented activity whose very essence is the pursuit of profit. Private practice contains much of the malevolences or benevolences inherent in any business. Whatever one's prejudice about business, whether it is viewed as a major cause or a major solution for the woes that plague mankind, one is likely to similarly feel about the private practice of psychotherapy or counseling. If someone tends to view business as leading to the maldistribution of the earth's resources or to a greater production of these resources he is likely to view private practice in the same way. If he sees the businessman as a predacious, manipulative, greedy, self-serving oppressor of the poor he probably will see the psychotherapy business person similarly. If the business person is seen as an enterprising free spirit who creates better and more efficient ways of providing for the needs of mankind, the psychotherapy independent practitioner is likely to be viewed that way too. Whatever the perception is about business, whatever the value judgments attached to it, one conclusion cannot be logically avoided: private psychotherapy practice is no better or no worse than business, because it *is* business.

A NEGATIVE VIEW OF BUSINESS IN THE HELPING
PROFESSIONS

Many people in the helping professions are ambivalent about business if not overtly antipathetic to it. They sometimes talk about business pejoratively and use terms like *profit motive, capitalism, free enterprise* in rather derisive tones. Concepts associated with business too are viewed with similar disapprobation. *Competition, individual initiative, survival of the fittest,* are seen as virulent remnants of the pseudophilosophy known as Social Darwinism (Hofstader 1944). When a psychotherapist utters such words, they are often seen as shibboleths which seem to reveal that he is indifferent to the needs of the less affluent or that he has a proclivity to exploit the disadvantaged.

It is understandable that many in the helping professions view business in this fashion. They did not enter their professions simply because of an interest in money. They wanted to help, to use themselves in assisting others to experience more productive lives. They usually began their careers in hospitals or social agencies where they see, often for the first time in their lives, the myriad tragedies that befall human beings. They see ubiquitous mental illness that accompanies those who have been exploited in the economic system. Coming from such experiences, it is little wonder that many helping professionals are not enthusiastic about business. Many of them come to see business as a villain, a perpetrator of miseries and injustices. It follows for them that anyone who enters business, especially anyone who enters the business of psychotherapy, is not a helper but a contributor to human injustice. The private practitioner becomes a stereotype. In one popular impression he is envisioned as a wealthy psychiatrist being chauffered in his Rolls Royce to his lavish Fifth Avenue office, where he charges exorbitant fees for listening to the trivial complaints of rich dowagers. It is fun for some people to view all psychotherapists as being in similar circumstances and sharing such values. It is fun but inaccurate. Obviously not all members of the helping professions who enter private practice are seen this way. But the view is prevalent that there is something unwholesome, something mercenary and lacking in virtue in the psychotherapist who sees clients and then asks to be paid for it rather than seeing them under the auspices of a publicly supported organization or agency.

ALTERNATIVES TO THE BUSINESS MODEL

If the capitalist business system were replaced by the publicly owned and operated alternative, then there would be no role for psychotherapy in private practice. But if all mental health care needs were met through public resources and administered by public institutions, one wonders if the mental health of the populace would be noticeably improved. There is ample reason to raise the question. During the forty years from 1935 to 1975 in which the government and insurance funded and administered health and welfare sector expanded geometrically, the incidence of mental illness, social problems, and injustices did not decline (Piven and Cloward 1971). It is therefore doubtful that even more funding would at last lead to the desired improvements. It *might* lead to the improvements but it is difficult to project from recent history. This is not to imply that social programs should not exist, or that they have been failures. It is not to suggest that the provision of mental health care services and psychotherapy should not continue to be supported under public auspices. Clearly there are an infinite number of relevant intervening variables which explain why increased public expenditures have not led to a decrease in the rate of emotional dysfunction. It *is* to say that statistics can be deceiving and that impressions can be wrong. It is valid to question the premise that the public model of delivering psychotherapy services is the only one and that the private model is contrary to the values of the helping professional. It is valid to question the charge that the private practitioner is in league with the enemy, the business enterprise system.

The view of this book is that the principles of business practice and psychotherapy are not antithetical, nor are the values underlying the business system and the helping professions at odds.

They are both simply components of our society with which we must learn to deal. The psychotherapy business should be seen as but one element in an entire panoply of interrelated social forces. It will not and cannot be a major change agent for bringing about seriously needed improvements in the social structure. Its basic role is to help individuals and sometimes small groups of people in their efforts to more successfully cope with the social environment. Psychotherapy is thus a "residual" rather than an "institutional" means of bringing about changes and improvements. Institutional means are those programs and social structures designed to enhance human well-being, to anticipate social problems, and to prevent their occurrence (Wilensky and Lebeaux 1958). For example, the justice and the law enforcement systems are institutional programs, as are the public health and preventative medicine systems. The parks and recreation programs of any community probably have more to do with institutionally preserving the mental health of residents than does the entire mental health industry. Mental health workers are more inclined to treat people who have already been harmed, so their efforts are residual. Their practices have little or nothing to do with prevention. They are usually called upon after normal social patterns break down. They basically seek only to restore something to what was considered normal before the dysfunction occurred. A primary goal is to help people cope with, or perhaps adjust to, an environment which itself might be sick. Psychotherapy, and particularly the private practice of psychotherapy, is only a residual activity and nothing more should be be expected of it. Psychotherapists, of course, can and should be involved in working toward institutional improvements in their society, but such efforts take place not through their roles as therapists but through their roles as citizens.

Of course, there will always be a need for both institutional and residual programs in any functioning society. Without institutional means of enhancing the human spirit, without preventing preventable problems, jobs which simply treat or restore would be impossible (Kahn 1969). It would be analogous to physicians trying to treat everyone during a typhoid epidemic, using only symptom relieving medication and giving no thought to vaccines or to cleaning up the environment. But by the same token, there will always be individual breakdown and individual problems. No society can ever become so utopian, so perfect, and so just that some of its members will not have problems. No two people will ever agree on what is perfect anyway. There will always be some who are unhappy, disadvantaged, at the bottom of the economic spectrum. There will always be people in any society, no matter how noble that society is or how many institutional and preventative resources it has, who will need individualized treatment programs. This is where the role of the psychotherapist is appropriate. It is frankly not such a grandiose calling or a particularly influential endeavor, and the social impact it can have, at best, will be minimal. The impact it will have will be with individuals, and in an open and free society individuals will make their own choices about how and with whom they will meet their needs. Some will choose psychotherapy in public organizations. Some will choose it in private settings. But most will avoid psychotherapists and counselors altogether.

ECONOMIC JUSTIFICATIONS FOR PRIVATE PRACTICE

Even if all helping professionals believed that business is not necessarily bad and that private practice has a place, albeit a minor one in the social system, therapists may still not believe that the business-oriented private practice model can be beneficial in the delivery of psychotherapy services. Yet there are economic and social advantages which should be considered. Five economic and social reasons justify the private practice of psychotherapy as a supplement, not a replacement, for the mental health care delivery system.

First, it costs society as much to provide services through agencies and public facilities as through private practice. For example, several studies conducted in family service agencies have indicated that interview costs in those facilities have exceeded the current rates charged by therapists in private practice in the same area (Briar 1966). Other analyses show that the cost per service or session is at least no more in private practice than in institutional mental health settings (Gruber 1973). In one large but typ-ical social agency overhead costs were such that it took twelve dollars of income for the agency to provide one dollar's worth of direct service to the client. This is not uncommon, because social agencies, hospitals, clinics, and so forth are heavily staffed by bu-reaucratic personnel who spend little if any time in actual service delivery. The larger the organization, the more likely this is to occur. The costs in private practice are considerably less because of smaller overhead. In agencies only about 29.5 percent of total staff time is spent seeing clients or providing collateral services. If a psychotherapist in full-time private practice spent only 29.5 percent of her working time in direct service, then less than one-third of her working time would be generating income and she would be in serious financial difficulty. To stay in business, she must devote a larger proportion of her time to direct and collat-eral services.

Those who debate whether private or public services are more economical have recently shifted the focus of their attention. There is much available data demonstrating that institutions and agencies cost society just as much for the same amount and qual-ity of care as the private psychotherapists. The argument now is whether the two models can or even should be compared (Sharf-stein et al. 1977). But those defending the economics of the in-stitutional care system are saying it is unfair to make the com-parison. Private and public services are not comparable economically, they say, because of differences in population served, differences in treatment modalities employed, and differ-ent economic incentives operating in each. The overhead is lower in private practice because there is more incentive to keep the hours filled, while in social agencies, mental health clinics, hos-pitals, or other organizations more time is presumably spent on improving the social conditions which lead to the problems. Costs alone are not a good measure of comparison anyway. Cost-effectiveness would be better. But to compare cost-effective-ness it is necessary to be able to compare the effectiveness of dif-ferent kinds of psychotherapies. So far the tools made for such comparisons are woefully inadequate. Until they improve, cost-effectiveness analyses will be highly conjectural (U.S. Congress 1980).

The second economic factor to be considered is that clients often appear to do better in therapy when they pay for services received than when they do not (Shireman 1975). When the client has a financial as well as an emotional investment in the process of working through his difficulties he seems to have greater incentive and motivation. Studies frequently show a positive correlation between fee-paying and therapy outcome (GAP 1975). Studies also show that clients feel the service is worthwhile only when they pay. They are more willing to pay if they feel the service provided was worthwhile (Ayers 1981). Of course, it is always argued that the client who is able to contribute to the costs of psychotherapy does better because he is not as disadvantaged to start with. It isn't the fee that causes motivation, says this view, but rather the better circumstances of the client. This argument is another one which is impossible to resolve because of the difficulty in comparing outcomes. It is not possible to know why fee charging makes a difference because improvement is still so ill defined.

The third economic consideration has to do with consumerism. The private practice model of service delivery is more compatible with the increasingly influential consumer movement. This movement rightly seeks to enhance the opportunity for informed choice in the marketplace. In the private practice model there is a choice of many different types of practitioners. Their costs are specified in advance and their credentials are available for consumer scrutiny. This doesn't happen in the agency or publicly supported service institution to the same extent. The consumer doesn't have much choice about who is to deliver the service. There is no shopping around or comparing costs or credentials, and the consumer has little say in the methodology to be used in his behalf.

The fourth consideration is that the services of private psychotherapy practitioners are available to a much wider portion of the economic spectrum than is generally realized, and organization-based service is available to a more narrower range than is generally acknowledged (Cloward and Epstein 1965). The more affluent clients in subsidized agencies pay fees which are as high as they would have to pay to see a private practitioner. The less affluent clients seen in institutional settings are often covered under various insurance programs or government reimbursable systems. Because of such coverage, agencies charge them about as much as they charge their more affluent clients. Many private practitioners, on the other hand, see more economically disadvantaged clients who can get private help because of insurance or subsidization, and who have sought private care from a belief that such services are more effective or less stigmatized than services in an agency or public organization (Turner 1978). Third-party financing has made the clientele in private and public settings almost interchangeable. In 1960 the consumers of medical care paid almost half the total costs, while government paid little more than 20 percent. But in the last few years direct payments by clients have accounted for only about a quarter of the total health expenditures, while government's share has gone up to 40 percent (Schwartz 1980). This trend isn't likely to continue, however, and is possibly going to move back to less government funding. But it seems unlikely that there will be a return to the "two class" system of providing for mental and physical health care needs that existed before third-party financing became so prevalent.

Another factor suggesting that the availability gap between private and public services is not so wide has to do with the relative accessibility of the two groups. Public organizations are often less accessible than private practitioners. They keep hours which are less convenient for many clients, are often located far from their natural clientele, and their waiting lists are often very long. Greater accessibility and economy are also evidenced by the fact that many private therapists are being contracted by social agencies and public institutions on a fee for service basis to carry a segment of the agency's services. Not only does this provide services for clients who might otherwise have to be placed on waiting lists but "agencies have found that the productivity of private practitioners has been high and indeed an economical way of providing services" (Turner 1978).

The final economic consideration is that private psychotherapy can reduce rather than foster economic discrimination. Only when all people have equal access to a service will that service be nondiscriminatory. The less affluent are stigmatized by any program which serves them exclusively. It will be seen as being inferior, whether it is or not. The less affluent will seek the same treatment available to the rich. Any other system is certainly discriminatory. The alternative would be some means to permit everyone in need of therapy to make his or her own choice about the provider. To have such a choice, those who are at economic disadvantage need financial help. They would then be able to purchase it like anyone else. It could be done through a voucher system of reimbursable credits or through some form of universal insurance program (Garfinkel 1975). This would be analogous to the food stamp system in which the needy make purchases in the same grocery stores that the affluent frequent. Such a system would be similar, though with marked improvements, to the present Medicaid system.

These five considerations are presented to give some balance to the sometimes one-sided argument that private practice is deleterious and costly to society, and that its practitioners are less concerned with the well-being of society than with lining their own pockets. The private practitioner is often subjected to such claims, and her values and priorities are often in question. If she is to be able to succeed in the business which she has chosen, she must reconcile these points of view and come to feel certain that private practice is not only consistent with her values, but also economically justifiable to society. If she cannot reconcile this dilemma, if she continues to believe that private practice is a business which is antithetical to her values, then she and her potential clients would be better off if she practiced psychotherapy under institutional auspices. There are too many other concerns that she will have to face to be distracted by this issue. She will have to overcome too many obstacles in private practice to be further weighted down by guilt feelings or misplaced conscience. The challenge to any businessman or woman and the obstacles to be overcome are a full-time preoccupation.

WHAT KIND OF BUSINESS SHOULD IT BE?

Once it is decided that private practice is consistent with psychotherapy's values, the next question to face is the type of business one wishes to establish. Just as there are many different types of business whose proprietors use different types of practices and techniques, so too are there many possible business models to emulate for the private psychotherapy practitioner. There are businesses which border on the unethical and there are those which find honesty and stability to be more important than anything else. This wide spectrum is particularly found in businesses which provide services. Nearly everyone has had unpleasant dealings with service personnel who overcharge, improperly fix things, don't honor their guarantees, and have a going-out-of-business sale every month. Those businesses in which the purveyor is a professional person are by no means exempt from complaints, though perhaps the professional identity puts some constraint on excesses and unscrupulous practices. Most professionals depend on word-of-mouth to build up their clientele. Consumer satisfaction and conviction that the professional is both personally honorable and belongs to an honorable profession are important to most private practitioners. Yet some professional practitioners inevitably engage in business activities which are unethical by the standards of their profession and contrary to ethical business practices. Encouraging a client to remain in therapy longer than is necessary simply because he is particularly interesting or remunerative is one example of such practice. Using the sessions for purposes other than those in the best interest of the client is another. Criticizing the work of another professional to ingratiate oneself with the potential client is still another. Charging excessive fees, using the information one reveals in the therapy situation for personal enrichment, discontinuing a client's therapy because of financial reverses, all these are also examples of dubious practices in which professionals sometime engage.

It should go without saying that it is contrary to the practitioner's long-term interests to deviate from the value-norms of her profession or from a high standard of ethical business conduct. There are ample opportunities, through ethical means, for the private practitioner to provide an adequate living for herself while providing a valuable service for her clients. It is highly recommended that one who enters private practice adhere to the highest professional and business standards. The emotional as well as the financial rewards will be more than adequate.

COMPETITION AMONG PRIVATE PRACTITIONERS

Competing with one's fellow businessmen is an accepted and encouraged business practice. It is consistent with the "rugged individualism" and "survival of the fittest" concepts so cherished by many in the business community. It is certainly considered to be an ethical and sound business practice to compete for the limited number of customers and customer's dollars. It is the sort of adversary position among businessmen that they feel instills in them the industriousness and creativity needed to provide increasingly improved service.

Fee-for-service professionals rarely think of themselves as being in an adversary position with their colleagues. Instead they think of themselves and their colleagues, as well as their kindred spirits in the other helping professions, as comprising a fraternity of mutually cooperative professionals. No psychotherapist in private practice would be considered ethical in her profession or by her colleagues if she spoke like car salesmen: "Well I guess Dr. Jones is an adequate therapist but remember, her rates are higher than mine and my training is a lot better. I've got a lot more clients than she has, you see, so my rates can be lower because of greater traffic and volume." Or: "I have a 75 percent cure rate among my clients and Dr. Jones only has a 60 percent rate, so you can see my service is really the best buy." Not only would such a practice be frowned on by colleagues and other professionals, but most clients would also tend to be skeptical about entering into a working relationship with such a practitioner. There is an implicit, though incorrect, view among private practitioners that there is no limit to the number of customers because human need for such services is inexhaustible. The need may be there, but the ability or willingness of people to avail themselves of psychotherapy is limited.

Rather than being overtly competitive, most practitioners find it to their advantage to develop a very cooperative relationship with their fellow private practitioners. Many practitioners establish regular meeting times to discuss cases and problems common to their practices, and to be mutually supportive and thus end some of the sense of isolation that is often the bane of the independent practitioner. The practitioner who overtly acknowledges that she is competing with her peers for the finite number of potential clients would soon be subtly excluded from the professional community. The consequences of this exclusion would not be immediately apparent but it would gradually dawn on her that things have changed. There would be a little less cooperation from other private practitioners, certainly a lack of referrals from them, and if not outright disparagement of her practice ethics, then at least a lack of discussion about her when people ask who are the best practitioners in the area to consult.

This is not to say that private practitioners do not engage in various forms of low-keyed competition. The most acceptable and frequently practiced form of this type of competition is one-upmanship. This is seen and heard in typical dialogues between any two private practitioners and almost becomes a humorous diversion rather than any serious effort to beat the other person. The dialogue might sound like this:

> JOE: I've been treating a movie star for the last six months. I can't reveal her name, of course, but everyone would know her at a glance.
> SAM: Well, I don't like working with movie stars. I've seen a lot of them and everyone I've seen has been a hysteric anyway and everyone knows how boring working with hysterics can be. Be-

sides I've been getting so busy with all my therapy groups that I am looking for a bigger office in a really spiffy location.

JOE: Oh yeah? Where are you going to locate? I'd recommend my area but there are already a lot of very expensive therapists there.

SAM: No, I wouldn't like that area at all. I want a more scholarly community because of my research into the psychosocial characteristics of anorexia.

JOE: Oh really? Well, I just read Minuchin's new work on anorexia and you'll be fascinated with his findings when you get the book. He sent me an advance copy so not many people have seen it yet.

And so on. One-upmanship is competition but not for the clientele. It is competition for prestige. It tries to enhance one's view of oneself when it is taken seriously. It is simple self-aggrandizement, sometimes at the expense of the other professional person, but it is accepted and smiled upon in the professional community.

The more serious form of competition that is not only tolerated but accepted by the professional community is some form of self-promotion. This is universally practiced and it is encouraged in the professional community, though for reasons other than to enhance one's competitive position. It takes many forms, such as getting media recognition, publishing, making contacts with groups from whom referrals are made, and generally being more visible than the others. This is acceptable because such practitioners are simply establishing their credentials and brightening their image, and not at the direct expense of their colleagues. The psychotherapy professions encourage it because it is a good reflection on their group as a whole when one of their members achieves something noteworthy. Such behavior is ultimately beneficial to all because the practitioner must have the skills if she is going public, and public scrutiny will motivate her to enhance and refine those skills.

Beyond these relatively mild forms of competition it is inadvisable, unnecessary, and impractical for the private practitioner to engage in aggressively competitive practices. Her time is better spent improving her skills and increasing her knowledge. As this is accomplished she should get her share of the available business.

HOW LUCRATIVE IS PRIVATE PRACTICE?

While it is true that competitive behavior improves the income potential in many businesses there is no indication that it does so in private psychotherapy practice. The amount of remuneration one derives from private practice varies according to many circumstances, but competitive practices don't seem to be among them. It is true that the private practitioner receives more income for each hour of direct service to clients than does his agency-based counterpart, but the differences aren't nearly as great as many might imagine. Institution and agency therapists, especially those who are not psychiatrists, tend to be terribly underpaid considering the amount of education and experience they have acquired. This is particularly true of nurses, social workers, and counselors. To these people especially, the private therapist's income seems to be a great amount. The agency-based worker asks how much the private practitioner charges per hour and concludes from the answer that the private therapist is vastly wealthy. There is a tendency to think that the hourly fee charged can be multiplied by forty hours to determine the weekly income and that this amount can be multiplied by fifty weeks to determine the annual income. This type of calculation is simplistic and deceiving. It must be looked at more carefully to obtain a more accurate picture.

Rare is the competent therapist who could or should continue indefinitely practicing fifty weeks a year. Seldom seen is the practitioner who maintains a weekly caseload of forty clients or more. Unheard of is the therapist who collects 100 percent of her billings. And inconceivable is the private practice whose overhead expenses are not a considerable portion of the gross income. When the actual amount of time in direct service and the overhead expenses are averaged into the hourly *net* receipt from each client, the picture appears a little less lucrative.

There are two types of overhead for which the private practitioner must pay. The direct overhead expenses of the solo full-time private practitioner range between 20 percent and 30 percent of gross income. Direct expenses include such items as office rent, business telephone and answering expenses, secretarial salaries, furnishings, stationery, postage, and filing and storage fees. They also include such expenditures as insurance premiums, payments for consultation, and costs for attending courses and improving one's professional expertise. The indirect overhead expenses are more difficult to measure and, in fact, are not even taken into consideration by accountants and tax collectors. If the practitioner becomes ill and needs to cancel her cases for the day, or if she doesn't schedule her clients for the following week in order to attend a professional conference, she is paying indirect overhead. The agency-based therapist takes for granted that her paycheck will be the same no matter how many clients she saw this week, or how long she attended the professional conference. She takes for granted that if she is ill or takes a vacation, her income will remain the same. If she takes classes or attends professional conferences, it is typical for the employer not only to maintain her salary during her absence but also to pay for the costs of attending the conference. When the private therapist does anything else but provide direct service, the income is commensurately reduced.

In addition to direct and indirect overhead costs, the practitioner is faced with other realities of the business world. For one thing, not all the clients she has served will pay all they agreed to pay. The average private practitioner receives about 85–90 percent of her billings. It rarely exceeds this amount even after the therapist employs collection agencies and uses other costly means to enforce the agreement she made with the client. Other income loss comes from clients' cancelling their appointments after it is too late to fill the slot. Still another loss comes from the important and necessary practice of seeing some of her clients at reduced rates or rates which vary according to the client's economic circumstance.

Very often the psychotherapist, if her clients are to be covered by health insurance for her services, must reduce her fee to the amount the insurance company deems the "reasonable and customary charges" in her area. This amount is usually less than the amount most therapists in the area are actually charging for these services. The psychotherapist then has the choice of accepting the lower amount or not enabling her client to be eligible for the coverage. To achieve client eligibility she must agree to the insurance company's terms. Another cost to some therapists also results from insurance company rationale. Since the insurance coverage is explicitly for health costs, most government agencies and private insurance companies require that a physician be involved somewhere in each covered case. Because of this many private practitioners who are not insurance eligible contract to work with a physician, often a psychiatrist. The typical format is for the therapist to visit the physician's office on a regularly scheduled basis to discuss each of the cases which are eligible for insurance coverage. While most nonmedical psychotherapists are understandably sensitive to supervision by members of other professions, it is an expediency with which many private practitioners have learned to live. They do not consider it supervision, but rather consultation, and most physicians usually consider it to be the same. But whether it is consultation or supervision, when insurance reimbursement is involved, the therapist must pay the physician for his time at his usual rate. This becomes an additional cost for the practitioner.

The private practitioner must spend a significant portion of her work day engaged in activities other than fee for service. She certainly is obligated to communicate with former clients and other helping professionals who are engaged in service to the client. To remain in private practice and continue obtaining referrals, the therapist must spend some of her time communicating with referral sources, engaging in public relations activities, and participating in professional activities. If the psychotherapy practitioner is cognizant of the social and environmental impact on her clients, and if she cares anything about that impact, she is also likely to spend some of her working time in the community or in helping to change the conditions which lead to so much discomfort for the clientele she sees. Again, these activities are often built into the job of the agency-based therapist. When the agency therapist meets with her fellow staff members, writes or delivers a paper, spends time with her peers to discuss cases or new ideas in her profession, it is all part of her job. When the private practitioner does the same thing it is at her own expense. The private practitioner must pay for her own retirement benefits and insurance, usually at higher individual rates, while agency workers usually are eligible for lower group rates. If the private practitioner wishes to reduce such overhead expenses as billing and secretarial tasks or performing her own custodial and maintenance chores, she pays a different type of cost. These activities come at the expense of time away from her family, or time away from enhancing her professional skills, doing what a person with considerably less education could be doing. The list of costs and income losses for the private practitioner can go on and on. When it is subtracted from the alleged amount the practitioner is earning in the practice, the profitability is obviously much less than originally believed.

The following illustration of a practitioner's income situation shows how this can be so. Suppose a private psychotherapist's hourly fee for service is $50. At that rate it might be deduced that the therapist earns $2,000 per week if she sees an average of forty clients weekly. Then if she works an average of fifty weeks per year her annual income would be $100,000. It would be more if she saw more clients weekly or charged more per session. But then the debits are considered. If the therapist takes off one week per year to attend a professional conference or training seminar her annual income is reduced by $2,000, to $98,000. If she takes three weeks instead of two for vacations a further $2,000 reduction is made, to $96,000. Then suppose an average of ten clients per week are less affluent and are seen at half the regular rate. This reduces the workers annual income by $12,000 ($25 times 10 clients times 48 weeks equals $12,000), down to $84,000. A further deduction must be made to account for the supposedly full-fee clients who are covered by insurance companies which won't pay $50 for psychotherapy. Suppose companies pay $35 for psychotherapy services in the area, and then only if the therapist gives assurances that she won't require the clients to make up the difference. If ten weekly clients have this type of coverage the annual income is reduced by another $7,200 ($15 less for 10 clients equals a weekly reduction of $150, times 48 weeks equals $7,200). This reduces the income base from the $84,000 to $76,800. It is likely that an average of five clients per week might cancel their appointments with sufficient notice that they cannot be charged, but it is not likely that the vacant hours can then be filled by other clients. This reduces the annual income by another $12,000 (5 times $50 equals $250, times 48 weeks equals $12,000), down from $76,800 to $64,800. The therapist could easily spend one hour per week in consultation and another hour in travel to and from the consultant's office, plus three hours weekly in administrative work. The resulting five-hour weekly loss would result in an annual reduction of another $12,000 down, from $64,800 to $52,800. The administrative activity is unavoidable because it includes necessary telephone conferences with potential clients and communications with colleagues about clients. Then if the therapist spends any time in indirect service in behalf of clients or in community work it necessitates further reductions. If only five hours per week were thus spent, the annual income would be reduced another $12,000, down from $52,800 to $40,800.

The annual $100,000 gross is already sounding considerably smaller, and the overhead and other inevitable costs haven't yet been considered. About 25 percent of the average full-time private practitioner's gross income goes for overhead expenses. If the gross income is considered to be $41,000 the overhead is likely to amount to $10,000 annually. If 10 percent of the practitioner's charges never get paid, it costs another $4,000 per year. This has now reduced the practitioner's net or spendable income to $27,000 ($41,000 minus $14,000). Any other time taken away from the work schedule, such as for more intensive case recording, worker illness or unavoidable times when she can't meet with the clients all are additional debits. And this is all based on an hourly charge of $50. If the worker charged less or had less than a full schedule there will be proportionately less income.

The factors which were considered to reduce the therapist's income were all realistic and in most instances necessary for each practitioner. Many therapists, in fact, find it necessary to take more vacation or training time away from their offices than was here indicated, and many spend more time in indirect or community work. Most therapists who want to build their practices find they must spend considerably more time in professional promotion and administrative work than just a few hours weekly. Still, private practitioners do find ways of keeping these factors from greatly reducing their incomes. Mostly they do it by working longer hours, and by not even considering the many hours they spend in additional training, administration, consultation, and indirect services to be part of their work activity. These things are done on their own "free" time. If the considerable time the private practitioner spends in all phases of her work which is necessary to the maintenance and development of her practice is calculated into the hourly income rate it isn't likely to be that much greater than the amounts received by many agency workers with commensurate training and experience. When private practice is financially rewarding, it is basically because of hard work and ample devotion to the job.

SUCCESSFUL BUSINESS PRACTICES

At this point it is necessary to stress that the private practitioner has no assurance of earning even the smaller amount described above if she doesn't adhere to established business principles in conducting her practice. She may find that she is very successful in getting more clients than she can see, but unsuccessful in managing her money in such a way as to maintain a viable enterprise. Or she may not have the foggiest notion of how to build her clientele, but she knows where each of her dollars is spent. Once she had decided that private practice is a business and that business principles are not contrary to her values, then her next step is to consider her business objectives as well as her professional ones. She wants to determine ways to maximize her gross income. She wants to find ways to keep as much of the gross for herself as possible. She wants to limit her overhead expenses and invest her proceeds wisely. She needs to establish a retirement fund, and maintain standards of expertise and professional competence to validate her attempts to add to her clientele.

It must be recognized that success in private practice as in any business is contingent on two ingredients: the ability to satisfactorily provide service by adhering to high professional standards and the ability to remain solvent or economically viable by using sound business practices. Of these two, the first is infinitely and unquestionably more important for the private practitioner in psychotherapy or counseling. Without the ability or knowledge to skillfully provide services which are useful and satisfactory to the client any other considerations are irrelevant. Nevertheless, the second ingredient is also important. The private practitioner may be highly knowledgeable and skillful in delivering psychotherapy, but if she is a poor business person she is not likely to remain long in private work. Because the first is so much more important than the second, almost all the attention in professional education and literature has been rightly concerned with it. Virtually nothing is said about the business practices that one must utilize in order to maintain a private practice. The psychotherapist has an opportunity to feast on the vast amount of knowledge to which she is exposed, but she might as well fast when it comes to business knowledge. Because of this imbalance, the focus of the remainder of this book will be on business aspects of private practice.

In the following eight chapters these and a variety of other business matters will be discussed. Chapter 3 deals with the reasons psychotherapists and counselors enter into private practice and the many different types of practices they might have. In chapter 4 the business issues involved in establishing the practice setting are of concern. The focus in chapter 5 is on the administrative aspects of the private practitioner's setting. Chapter 6 covers the ways private therapists build and maintain their clientele. Money matters are the focus of chapter 7, with particular attention paid to such concerns as bookkeeping, income taxes, and retirement planning. Chapter 8 deals with problem areas encountered by private practitioners, such as malpractice risks and legal issues. Chapter 9 focuses on the therapist's need to maintain professional standards, particularly in the independent practice setting, and it deals with such matters as continuing education, accountability, licensing, and competency examinations. Chapter 10 offers a discussion about the future of private practice and recommendations for its enhancement.

THREE

MODELS AND MOTIVATION IN PRIVATE PRACTICE

Marcia Brown, Ph.D.
Clinical Psychologist
Emotional Disorders of Children
By Appointment

THE fresh, newly installed sign had been placed immediately beneath another, slightly older one which read, "Karen Wilson, M.D./Thomas Burton, M.D./Practices Limited to Psychiatry/ By Appointment." Marcia Brown contemplated the names for a moment, suppressed a twinge of anxiety, and entered her new office.

The crisp autumn morning sunlight poured through the large picture windows which dominated the brightly decorated room. She squinted momentarily before her eyes adjusted to the light. She stood in a combination waiting-office–group-therapy room containing two couches, chairs, assorted tables, lamps, and decorations arranged in a semicircle. Near the entry door was an L-shaped secretary's desk and chair. The desk had a typewriter, adding machine, and lamp on it but otherwise was bare. Behind the desk was a wooden credenza and matching filing cabinets. Marcia scanned the room before her eyes moved toward the three doors opposite the secretary's desk. Each door had a small brass sign at eye level saying respectively, "Dr. Burton," "Dr. Wilson," and finally "Dr. Brown." She tensed as she moved toward her door. It was Saturday morning and the doctors wouldn't be in today. She would be here alone with her clients.

If they showed up, that is. But why wouldn't they? They had no way of knowing they would be Marcia Brown's first private practice clients.

She opened the door and quickly surveyed her consultation room. She had furnished it with extra pieces from her home in order to save some money. It looked pretty good, she thought. In one corner was a small desk and chair. Next to it was a large walnut cabinet. Over her desk were three filled bookshelves. There were a loveseat and two overstuffed chairs at right angles to each other. They were in earth-toned fabrics that matched the drapes and carpet. She felt pleased but anxious. The clients would be here in a few minutes.

As her tension mounted, she found herself tidying up the immaculate, perhaps even sterile room, needing something to do. She straightened her desk equipment but was mostly unaware of her surroundings by now as she reminisced about how she got in her present position. She had spent her entire psychology career, the past eight years, at the university hospital's pediatric department. She loved her work, felt she was doing a good job treating the kids and their parents, and couldn't imagine ever wanting to do anything else. She met many people on the staff at the hospital, young doctors, other psychologists, social workers, and she found she worked well with them. Many of them worked briefly at the hospital, just for a year or two before leaving to hang out their shingles. She listened to many of them extolling the virtues of private work. "There are no hassles, Marcia. It's great. You can do what you know is the best for your clients, not what that old coot in administration says you have to do. And if you're good enough you'll make a lot more money than you will at the hospital. Of course, if you're not good, you'd be better off staying."

Marcia knew she was good. Parents kept asking to work with her. She had a fine reputation. The hospital knew she was good too. They tried to promote her to administration or chief of psychological services several times. But she wanted to work directly with her clients, and didn't consider the offer to leave them a promotion. She had thought more seriously about private practice when two of her closest friends, Tom Burton and Karen Wil-

son, established their own office several months ago. Now they
were doing less hospital work. Marcia knew it would be just a
matter of time before they left the hospital for good. They kept
telling her about their extra office. They wanted her to join them.
All three would be independent of each other. All expenses
would be split evenly, three ways.

Marcia decided to take the plunge. What would she have to
lose anyway? she thought. She wasn't married and had no children, so her personal responsibilities weren't heavy. She had
saved some money out of her hospital salary, so if the clients
didn't come to her at first she could survive. She would keep her
job at the hospital and just work part time in the new office.
Maybe she would ease out of the hospital job, or out of the private practice, depending on which seemed to work out best. She
would start out slowly, just seeing her clients on Saturdays, and
then maybe one or two evenings a week. Her only risk would be
the overhead of the office. The rent was high, but manageable
since she only had to pay a third of it. Tom and Karen had been
renting furniture for the reception/secretarial room, and the cost
of that was modest. She had furniture at home that would be
perfect for her own office. She regretted not having a separate
playroom for the children, but knew she could improvise. Anyway, she had an attractive large cabinet which would fit perfectly
in her office and it would store a multitude of toys and games,
which she could use for the children's play therapy. She calculated that her monthly expenses, counting telephone, rent, supplies, answering service, and promotion expenses would equal
about one week's pay from her hospital job. She felt confident
she could manage that even if she saw no private clients at all.

But the clients did come. The first one arrived as scheduled and
Marcia's anxiety immediately gave way to focus and concern for
the problem that was presented. She saw five families in her first
week of private practice and the number each week thereafter
slowly grew. It was now three years since Marcia had seen her
first private client. During this time she maintained a schedule of
around fifteen hours per week. She decided not to give up her
employment at the hospital, however, even though it now meant
limiting the number of new clients she could take. To give up the

hospital job would mean giving up many advantages which she had taken for granted. Her private practice experience revealed much isolation, little peer relationship even in a shared office, a paucity of feedback from other professional people, and the unrelenting pressure of sole responsibility for her work. The hospital also provided her with some financial fringe benefits which she couldn't duplicate as a private practitioner, such as insurance and pension. She found, by remaining at the hospital and continuing the part-time practice, that she could have the best of both worlds. She wished she had done it several years earlier.

DIVERSITY IN PRIVATE PRACTICE

Marcia Brown is very representative of private psychotherapy practitioners, so much so she is almost stereotypical. A majority of them begin their private psychotherapy careers sharing office space with other professionals and engage in private work on a part-time basis. When they first enter private practice they tend to feel apprehension and doubt, and after they have become established they become more conscious of the sense of isolation and lack of peer relationships that usually exist. Many have entered private practice to increase their incomes, but other motivations seem more important for most. They do so because of the challenge, the opportunity to be master of one's own professionalism, the need for respite from bureaucratic entanglements, and especially, the opportunity to continue in direct practice. Direct practice, working face-to-face with clients to help them resolve their problems, becomes more difficult for the experienced and capable therapist to continue because of agency pressures and organizational inevitabilities. There is a bureaucratic principle, supposedly humorous, called Boyle's Law, which says, "Talent in staff work will recurringly be interpreted as managerial ability" (Dickson 1978). This law works in the psychotherapy professions, in that the most capable and knowledgeable direct practitioners are the first ones to be promoted to administrative and supervisory roles. They find they must leave the work for which they were trained and motivated, to move into work for which they have no particular interest, ability, or training. But accepting such positions is often their only way to achieve peer recognition, increased income, and more control over their own professionalism. Many are drawn to private practice solely because it is the only option available to them if they wish to stay in direct practice rather than become administrators. Others are in private practice because it allows them the freedom and flexibility to use new and innovative approaches in providing their services. Remaining in an organization often means that they must employ the methods and techniques which are standardized by it. Pressures to conform are implicit but omnipresent.

SOME MODELS OF PRIVATE PRACTICE

To illustrate the diversity and methods used by some representative members of the psychotherapy professions, several examples follow. They show how people get into private practice and reveal something of the feelings and pressures which they encounter along the way.

A Psychiatric Nurse. The first example concerns a psychiatric nurse who now has no hospital affiliation but who devotes all her professional energies to her part-time private practice in counseling. Joyce Wilson is thirty-eight, married, with two preadolescent children. She earned her R.N. and eventually her master's degree by the time she was twenty-five and she had courses toward her doctorate. She worked in a community-supported psychiatric clinic for four years but then ended her employment after she married and began her family. For the next ten years, Joyce devoted most of her energies to her family, even though she remained active in professional nursing associations. She also maintained her friendships with her colleagues at the psychiatric clinic and occasionally participated with them in staff conferences.

As her responsibilities at home diminished with her children growing older and becoming more independent, she decided to return to her profession. Her husband's work as a lawyer provided sufficient income for the family, so her decision wasn't based on economics. It was based on the fact that she needed the stimulation of a variety of people, the challenge of helping them overcome problems, and the opportunity to contribute to society's needs.

She went back to the psychiatric clinic to discuss with her old friends the possibility of a job with them. The response wasn't encouraging. Yes, they would be delighted to have her return, but they just didn't have the money or space to employ her right now. Hadn't she heard about all the changes in the past few years? All the public agencies were cutting back. Their public and private sources of funds were drying up. More and more clients were being covered by insurance programs and those people were going to private practitioners. Besides that, they told her, there was a long list of people who wanted to work at the clinic, people who were well qualified and capable. The clinic responded that when openings occurred they would inform one of the applicants, but implied that it probably would be a long wait.

Joyce was disappointed. She had really felt a part of the clinic staff and regretted that she wouldn't be able to work with them. What, then, would her alternatives be? She could contact other agencies, but the same story would be likely. She would have less of a chance at other agencies, where she wasn't known, than at the psychiatric clinic. That meant she would have to give up her idea of resuming her clinical work, go into hospital nursing, or establish a private practice.

As she contemplated the last possibility, her enthusiasm grew. But where would she locate her office? What kind of clients would she see? Who would refer clients to her? Her previous experience and her special interests seemed to gravitate toward working with depressed women and housewives who had marital and sexual problems. She had earned a favorable reputation in work with such difficulties and had published an article on the subject in a professional nursing journal.

The neighborhood in which she lived would be an ideal location for the kind of clientele she hoped to reach. Her home was in an affluent suburb of a large midwestern city. Her house had a rarely used basement apartment with an outside entry. With a little work it would be very suitable for a solo practice. Minor carpentry, painting, and decorating made the apartment into an attractive office and waiting room which was well separated from the rest of the home. A sidewalk leading from the street directly to the basement entrance was installed. She and her family did much of the work themselves, and as they worked they discussed her next task, that of building up a clientele.

Promoting her newly established office was not difficult. She was gregarious and felt comfortable meeting people. She notified all her former colleagues at the psychiatric clinic of her plans and requested that they keep her in mind for referrals. She also discussed this with her family doctor and with another neighbor who was a physician. She had announcement cards printed, declaring herself to be an independent nurse-practitioner specializing in work with depressed women. The cards were sent out to everyone she could think of, to former clients, to other professional persons she knew through her ANA contacts, and to people she met through her work at the psychiatric clinic. Her husband helped by spreading the word among his lawyer colleagues. She began to feel more confident of her success and knew that if she could just get started the practice would become self-perpetuating as clients referred other people.

Her confidence proved to be well founded. Since the opening, she has been gradually increasing the size of her practice. Her original goal of about twenty hours a week was reached by the beginning of last year. Many of her referrals are now coming, as predicted, from former clients who reported satisfactory results to their acquaintances. She has experienced some unattractive features of her practice which she hadn't anticipated but has already learned to accept. For one thing, though she originally attempted to work with her clients only during weekday hours, enabling her to have the evening and weekend time with her family, the plan didn't work out that way. She has found that many of her clients and potential clients were working and found it difficult or impossible to meet with her during weekdays. Consequently, despite her wishes to the contrary, she sees clients two evenings a week and occasionally on Saturday mornings. This hasn't proved to be of great inconvenience or sacrifice to her family, however, as they have indicated that just knowing she is

in the home gives them a feeling of closeness. Another unanticipated consequence, however, does take her away from her family
more than she would like. She finds that it is necessary to spend
considerable time attending conferences, taking courses to enhance her knowledge and skills, and going to a consultant to ob-
jectify her work. She had not anticipated this because in her hospital and agency experience her training and consultation usually
took place as part of her job. In private practice, where it has
proved to be even more crucial, she finds she must do it around
her practice and at the sacrifice of her client and family contacts.
These disadvantages are more than outweighed by her general
satisfaction with the whole experience. She finds it rewarding, financially as well as emotionally, and derives considerable satisfaction from knowing that she is providing a unique service to
those who would not avail themselves of the opportunity if they
could only go to a social agency.

Joyce Wilson's experience in private practice is representative
of a large proportion of those who enter clinical practice without
agency affiliations. Having a low overhead by virtue of a home
office, and not being economically dependent on the proceeds
from the practice is comfortable and not an uncommon situation
for many private practitioners. The experience is somewhat more
difficult for those who enter private practice with a commitment
to full-time work and a dependency on practice income.

A Full-Time Private Practitioner.   Such a person is Bill Brenner, who has been in full-time private work since 1969. Bill entered the U.S. Air Force immediately after receiving his master's
degree in social work. His first practice experience, accordingly,
was in a large military hospital psychiatric unit, where he worked
primarily with military families. As an Air Force social worker,
Lieutenant Brenner provided the hospital with assessments of
hospitalized airmen and developed his skills in group therapy.
After his three-year military obligation was over, the Air Force
offered him a commitment scholarship, which would enable him
to return to graduate school and obtain his doctorate. After receiving the doctorate he returned to active military service to repay his obligation. This experience was at the peak of the Viet-

nam War, and his military duties involved him in work with wounded airmen and their families as well as Vietnamese refugees. Eventually, as the war subsided and he kept getting promoted into more administrative responsibilities and less direct work with clients, Bill needed to decide the course of his career. The Vietnam experience convinced him he didn't want a career in the military. An academic career was a possibility, but he still would regret giving up his clinical work. The demand for members of his profession in the late 1960s was great, with the establishment of the Great Society and War on Poverty programs. Still he craved independence and autonomy, having had so little of it in the highly structured military life. But full-time private practice for him would be very risky. He had a wife and young son to support. His economic resources were meager, after several years of rather low-paying military jobs and considerable financial obligations that came from his doctoral education.

Bill borrowed money to rent and furnish an office and plunged into private practice. The office was located in a medical suite in a high rise residential apartment complex, not far from the Air Force base where he had just served. The office was arranged in such a way that he was able to share a waiting room, storage space, and secretarial services with a psychiatrist/psychoanalyst who had an adjoining office. He invested heavily in equipping his office with paneled walls, plush carpeting, leather chairs, and brass accessories. He engaged a twenty-four-hour answering service and employed a part-time secretary. His overhead was substantial and his resources were few, so in the early years of his practice he was not certain that it would survive.

He had few clients at first, and most of them came from his contacts at the military hospital and from friends of the military clients he had seen while at the facility. Because of financial difficulties, he was several times on the verge of discontinuing his practice and obtaining employment as an instructor in a school of social work or as a practitioner in a social agency. But he persisted, using his ample free time to enhance his contacts and build his clientele. He wrote volumes of letters to potential referring persons and made countless telephone and personal calls on physicians, lawyers, other social workers, social agencies, schools, and hospitals in the area.

This activity paid off. His practice developed substantially, and within three years he was spending over forty hours weekly with his clients. Most of his referrals have come from former clients since then, but a large number also come from physicians with whom he has established a relationship of confidence and mutual respect.

Bill realized that his practice would have developed faster and more successfully except for a serious false start. His eagerness meant that he was willing to provide services for anyone who asked. He was not identified with any area of special skill, interest, or competence. Identifying himself solely as a social worker often resulted in questioning glances and considerable confusion among those to whom he was introduced. He needed more focus, more specialization, more identification with an area of competence. He objectively evaluated his own skills and practice weaknesses as well as special interests and disinterests. He had discussions about his possible areas of specialization with his colleagues and professional friends. The focus of his education and most of the subsequent training he had obtained, as well as his most satisfying moments, were in the areas of family therapy, marital counseling, and group work with dysfunctioning families.

"It was like I was starting all over again," he reported. "I went back to all my referral sources and told them I could only handle family breakdown problems from now on. I suppose they assumed I was so busy I only had time for certain kinds of people and I'm afraid I didn't try to set the record straight!"

Bill has built a solid, full practice in his community, where he has established a reputation for competence and success with his clients. He feels in retrospect that the key was to have a focus, a specialty which is observable and identifiable to others. The focus permits him to concentrate on relevant knowledge from among the vast amount of facts that the generalist would have to know. He is able to develop an expertise in a narrower realm, rather than diffusing his energies and concerns to all possible areas. He regrets that his specializing has excluded him somewhat from looking at the broader aspects of his profession and has even kept him from looking at models of intervention that are different from family therapy. "But you can't really have it both ways, I don't think," he says. "I had to choose and I think everyone has to do likewise. You can't be really good in one thing if you are expected to or expect yourself to master everything."

Bill represents a growing trend in social work. He is among the substantial group of full-time private social work practitioners whose numbers are probably now in the thousands (NASW 1982). He typifies the fact that a significant number of this group provides a specific service for a limited clientele. This model is analogous to the specialized social agency which serves only a select type of client, or a limited range of problems, or uses a specific treatment technique. It is also analogous to the specialization that occurs in many other fee-for-service professions, such as law, medicine, nursing, and education. This is a departure from general private practice, and portends the development in the near future of subspecialties within the field (Buttrick 1972).

A Pastoral Counselor.   Reverend Ronald Stewart had taken all the courses his theological school offered in psychology, human growth and development, and counseling. He had always known he would be a minister whose forte would be therapy and counseling, and he wanted to be well prepared. As an undergraduate Ron had majored in psychology as well as preministerial studies. In theological school he thought he would specialize in pastoral counseling and possibly get his first job as an assistant minister in a large church, where he could spend most of his time counseling. However, he was assigned as the only minister of a small, young church fellowship in a newly developing suburb. The fellowship had not yet been able to afford a church building and was meeting in the chapel of a funeral home. Ron's first professional years were devoted to developing and expanding the church and giving it a solid foundation in the community. He was also newly married and had his own young family, which needed his attention. This left him little time for counseling.

Ron not only was a good counselor but he proved to be a dynamic speaker in his pulpit. It wasn't long before the church had its own building and a growing congregation. Most of the new church's members were young families who were just getting established. Naturally many couples were undergoing considerable strain and having numerous marital and personal problems. The church had grown and was becoming more stable, and the demands of getting it established were no longer so great, so Ron was finally able to spend more time counseling his parishioners. His reputation as a competent, caring pastoral counselor grew within and beyond the community. Some people started attending his church because of his skill in the pulpit, while others became members because of the way he had helped them with their emotional and relationship problems.

As his reputation grew, and as people he had helped told their friends about him, he found that he was becoming very busy in his therapy and counseling work. But many people who came to him for help were not and would never be part of his congregation. They were either not interested in church affiliation or were already members elsewhere. Ron certainly had no aversion to helping anyone he could, whether they were his parishioners or not, but the more people he worked with the less time he had for his ministerial responsibilities and for counseling his church members. He had to draw a line somewhere, or his church would suffer. It was still not large enough or affluent enough to support an additional minister.

He had discussed his dilemma with several of his colleagues in weekly meetings with local clergymen. He found that two other ministers were sharing his experience. None of the three felt they could charge counseling fees to people who attended their churches, but they had to get some compensation for work with nonchurch people. Otherwise their parishioners would, in effect, be supporting the therapy and counseling of others. However, the ministers questioned the ethics of counseling nonchurch people in their church studies and then charging them fees for the service. They decided there was but one solution. They would open a fee-for-service pastoral counseling center staffed by the three ministers.

The office they established was in a nearby house which was

already being rented by a small law firm. The house had an un-occupied two-room wing with a private entrance. The three min-isters decided that they would fix up the outer room as a recep-tion area where they could keep their files, telephone, and other accoutrements. The inner office would be the consultation room. They would each occupy the facilities on specified days and times, so that all would have equal time there but would not be in each other's way. This pastoral counseling center became an immediate success, with each minister keeping his allotted time filled almost from the beginning. Ron had been tempted at first to expand the number of hours he would have available at the center, but decided that the demands of his church would make this impossible. He still sees his parishioners without charge in his church study, but those who are seen in the center's office are charged his standard hourly rate. The office reception area has posted the fee schedule, since all three minister's rates are iden-tical. They find that such posting clarifies the nature of the con-sultation and avoids issues about clients not understanding that the consultation would be accompanied by a bill. Ron is thus supplementing his rather meager church salary by seeing clients for fees, and his congregation is happy with the arrangement since they know that his income from the church is being supplemented.

A Psychotherapy Entrepreneur. Pat Miller worked for five years in a university affiliated counseling and guidance clinic after she had obtained her master's degree in marital and family therapy. By then she decided she would enter private practice. The decision to change settings was the result of considerable disruptions in her personal life. She and her husband decided to divorce. They had been married eight years, and most of the time together was spent struggling to put themselves through their re-spective schools. Her husband had just finished law school and was now about to join a law firm in another city. The effort they put into their educations took its toll on their marriage, despite the fact that both were sincere and caring people.

Despite ample warnings that the divorce was imminent, Pat was devastated when it finally took place. For months she found it impossible to skillfully serve her clients in the guidance clinic, especially those who were having problems similar to her own. She cared too much about her clients to give them less than optimal service, so she took a leave of absence from the clinic and sought professional help.

First she went to a psychiatrist whose approach was to help her understand the nature of her unresolved inner conflicts and feelings of inadequacy. She found this helpful and much needed, but the approach didn't address her confusion about her marriage and her feelings about its loss. Eventually, she went to a social worker in a family service agency in a neighboring community and felt this too was helpful. The focus here was on eliminating her fears about relating to men and her conflicts about being acceptable in her community as a divorcee. She returned to work in the guidance clinic soon after her treatment ended, but the experience of her divorce and her subsequent therapies resulted in a profound change in her thinking. Her views about therapy, about what was needed by many clients, and about what she now had to offer as a result of these experiences had been altered irrevocably.

Several months after she had returned to the clinic she decided to enter private practice. She wanted to work with people, particularly women, who were involved in divorce. She wanted to specialize in working with such people, and she wanted to develop her own methods of helping them. The guidance clinic, of course, had other requirements and a wider variety of clients to serve than Pat wanted to work with. Her departure was amicable and accompanied by the agreement that Pat and the clinic would provide future assistance to one another.

She was ambitious and confident, so she rented a suite of offices in a modern high rise office complex near a subway line. She incorporated as the "Divorce and Marital Counseling Center, Patricia Miller, M.A., Director." An attractive logo was designed for the stationery and office door. It was also placed on the cover of an attractive brochure which Pat had printed to describe her services. "DMC Center uses professionals to help people overcome the crises they experience when their marriages are dissolving" said the brochure. It described Pat's credentials and listed the names and credentials of several consultants whom she had employed. The consultants came from several different disciplines, including medicine, psychiatry, religion, law, social work, and psychology.

She gave wide distribution to the brochure and promoted her organization with many talks at civic groups, women's organizations, PTA meetings, and wherever an interested audience would gather. She appeared on radio and television talk shows. Soon, newspaper reporters sought her out for interviews when they did stories on divorce and separation in the community. Her clientele was increasing dramatically within a few months of the start. The brochure, the media, the speeches, the contacts were resulting in a full caseload. It was fortunate that she had had the prescience to lease a suite containing many offices, because she began to enlarge the range of services she offered. She was able to employ two additional part-time psychotherapists for salary rather than fee for service, and she employed a psychiatrist to come to the office one afternoon weekly for consultations with them.

In the course of her speeches and presentations to civic and women's groups, Pat discovered a significant unmet need in the community among those who had no particular marital or family problems. There were many people who were untrained but had a strong desire and commitment to help others. Pat organized a volunteer group of such people to assist her clients. She established a program through this resource to work with battered wives. It was a network of volunteer women who would provide emergency refuge until Pat's service could help resolve the conflict. The temporary refuges were, for some, places to stay for longer periods while the clients regrouped and began their lives anew as single women.

Pat Miller's Divorce and Marital Counseling Center has continued to grow. The services are paid for directly by the client, even though the organization uses a sliding fee system and provides gratis services to people in particular need. Pat, recognizing the aversion many of her clients had to gratis service, developed a system of benefit in kind for them. As part of the contract for services, these clients agreed to repay by providing several hours weekly of secretarial or maintenance services for her offices or the homes of the volunteers. She finds that some of the clients who made such agreements fail to repay, but most are happy and eager to participate. Pat envisions the future of her service in ambitious terms. She believes that she will be employing more and more counselors and psychotherapists in forthcoming years. She hopes to establish a similar facility in another part of the city soon and eventually to establish such centers in other cities as well. She even thinks about franchising agencies nationwide.

Such programs have been proliferating in recent years, and if there is a clientele for them there must be a need. Yet existing social agencies, which have a tradition of meeting public needs through the community mandate, view such programs with a mixture of concern and anger. The traditional agency exists to meet the needs of all the people in the community and gets its support from the community as a whole. If private entrepreneurs encroach on this turf, drawing many clients away from the traditional social agency, important public support for the agency begins to dry up. If only those at the lower end of the economic spectrum are served in the traditional agency because the more affluent go to facilities like Pat Miller's, it would result in a two-class system of providing services. Private practitioners who encounter this argument point out that many of the traditional social agencies are also gradually seeing a larger proportion of their clients from the upper end of the economic spectrum. Besides, they say, if the fees are as high in the agency, which is subsidized by additional public funds, then the traditional agencies need to work toward greater efficiency rather than encouraging monopolies and discouraging diversity in the provision of services.

The Rugged Individualist. Dick Larson, M.D., has been in private practice for twenty-two years. Most of that time he worked autonomously. He completed college with a premed major and was about to enter medical school in 1950 when the Korean War interrupted his plans. He had been in ROTC in college and was a reservist with considerable flying experience. Thus, his call to active duty was inevitable. After training he spent the next year piloting F-86 Sabres in dogfights around Mig Alley. Twenty-two missions later, as he was just coming out of a successful encounter with a Russian fighter, enemy ground fire brought his Sabre jet crashing down in a remote North Korean village. Wounded, near death, he was captured and imprisoned. He spent what he called the worst year in his or anyone's life in a POW camp, experiencing brainwashing, constant unrelenting psychological torture, isolation, and interrogations. His wounds, especially the broken arm and the shrapnel-filled leg, were barely looked at by his captors. The wounds managed to heal by themselves, though improperly, so that he had only partial use of his arm and leg from then on. Finally the ceasefire occurred and Dick was returned stateside, where he spent the next several months recuperating in a Veteran's Administration hospital. The hospital provided him with a considerable amount of physical therapy to partially rehabilitate his arm and leg. Dick also underwent psychotherapy and group treatment with staff psychiatrists and social workers. A psychiatrist helped him to reintegrate his bruised psyche, which was the result of the Korean incarceration. The V.A. staff helped him to work toward his return to his community, restore his fragmented relationship with his family, and develop his posthospitalization plans to return to civilian life.

These treatment experiences reawakened Dick's interest in medicine. Soon, with the help of the G.I. bill, he went to medical school. He knew from the beginning that his specialty would be psychiatry, and he soon decided he would become an analyst as well. After his formal training, he worked as a staff psychiatrist at the state mental hospital where he had residency training.

During his employment at the hospital he established his predisposition toward the psychoanalytic method and began seeing a few patients daily in intensive therapy. Naturally the hospital, which was already understaffed with psychiatrists, took a dim view of this activity. Dick was told that the hospital could not afford to give such intense attention to only a few people when there were so many others who were receiving scant psychiatric attention. The board of directors and hospital professional staff would soon be demanding that he increase the total number of clients he served. Dick decided it was time to relocate.

He had been able to save some money while at the hospital, so he took a year off. He went to Europe, where he took some courses and contemplated. When he returned to America he decided he would enter private psychiatric practice and study part time at the psychoanalytic institute. He opened his office with a colleague who also planned to become an analyst. The two men worked together for three years, building their practices rather quickly, before Dick felt he was well-enough established for a solo practice. He established his consulting and waiting rooms in space adjoining his apartment. He completed his psychoanalytic training and his own analysis in five years and now has a full-time analytic practice. His caseload now rarely exceeds ten patients, though he sees them daily. He feels fulfilled and purposeful in his chosen career.

PRIVATE PRACTICE FAILURES

Thus far all the examples have presented private practitioners who have found success and satisfaction in their work. It is not difficult to locate these and many other psychotherapists like them to obtain information about how they were able to do well in private practice. A greater amount of effort went into locating psychotherapists who would describe their unsuccessful experiences in private practice. The information that could be obtained from these people would be valuable in helping others avoid the same fate. But locating such people proved an impossibility.

Hasn't anyone failed to make it in private practice? Is it so easy that anyone who tries it is assured of success? If not, where are those who did not succeed? It is suspected that they exist, possibly in large numbers, but that they do not see themselves as "failures" or they rarely admit failure to their fellow professionals.

They attribute their return to institutional practice to a combination of circumstances: they didn't like the isolation; they missed all the old gang at the agency; they had guilty consciences asking for money for helping and making a profit from the misfortunes of others; taxes took all their income anyway; the clients were not as interesting as those in the agency; filling out insurance forms and making out bills was a bore; never having enough time for the family wasn't worth it. The list goes on and on. They are excuses but most of them are valid.

Most private psychotherapists who return to institutional employment don't have a sense of failure. Many enter private practice because of the notion that the grass is greener on the other side, and once there they see it isn't so green after all. Most who leave private practice do so because they don't want to endure the long hours, the haggling over money, the necessity for self-promotion, and the incessant pressure to maintain levels of professional competence that are required of the private practitioner. The only overt failures are probably those whose practice skills are so lacking that their referral base dries up, or those who are lacking in the managerial and financial skills which anyone in any business must have. This is speculative, however, because again, it is very difficult to locate therapists who would acknowledge such experiences.

One can determine some other causes of private social work practice failures by inference, by looking at the common factors that seem to exist among those who have been able to achieve their goals in private practice. One can conclude that the presence of these qualities enhances the chances of success and the absence of them is the invitation to failure.

QUALITIES FOR SUCCESS

There are seven qualities the therapist needs for success: motivation, competence, ability to self-start, assertiveness, adequate financing, business sense, and a service motivation rather than a self-interest one. Above all else, to be successful in private practice, the therapist must be *motivated*. He must want to build his service into a viable entity which is self-perpetuating and rewarding. He needs motivation particularly at first, when he must spend considerable amount of time and money in such activities as personal promotion, office design, and making sure that his practice skills are beyond reproach.

Second, and also very important, the therapist must possess demonstrable and visible *competence* in the service he is "selling." There is no one to hide behind in private practice, and if skills and knowledge are lacking, one must work rapidly and intensely to make the needed improvements. Otherwise, the word will quickly get around that the psychotherapist has serious limitations.

Third, the therapist must be a *self-starter*. Many capable people with superior skills cannot do well in private practice or any solitary activity because they require the stimulation and pressure that comes from working in organizations. In private practice, such external pushes do not exist. It is terribly easy to put off reading that dull text, or writing those letters to the referring physician, or to sleep in in the morning instead of calling on the civic association and becoming known to a group of community leaders.

Fourth, the therapist needs to be somewhat *assertive,* at ease with people in new encounters, not too proud or reserved to make himself known to possible referral sources. Many psychotherapists are excellent when their duties are limited to helping people with therapy, but less adequate when it comes to presenting themselves to community leaders.

Fifth, the practitioner who succeeds is usually in a *financial position* which permits him or her to nurse the practice along in its initial stages. In the beginning, most practices are not even able to carry their own overheads, much less support the practitioner. This is, no doubt, the major reason most therapists opt to enter private work on a part-time basis. It also accounts for the predisposition of many to operate out of their homes or use offices established by others. The disadvantage of part-time work is that the practitioner does not have enough time to do the things that are required to build up his private practice. Many part-time therapists are not seeing their practices grow because they are holding back, not pulling out all the stops to build a clientele, not devoting the time it takes to achieve their alleged goals.

The sixth quality private psychotherapy practitioners must have to assure their success is a *business sense,* including management skills and the willingness to think of their practices as businesses. Psychotherapists have had little training in this aspect of their work and often rely on trial and error. The business sense includes a willingness to ask clients for payment, an ability to maintain complicated financial and tax records, knowledge about pension plans, investment opportunities, management systems for overhead reduction, and a plethora of other data. Finally, he must be interested in *service*. The successful private practitioner dare not have self-interest as his sole motive for entering independent work. He must not succumb to the picture he often projects to his agency-based counterpart, that he is narrow-minded, money-hungry, and socially irresponsible. If he were any of these things, he would not last long in private practice, and during his short stay therein he would be a very frustrated, unsatisfied, noncontributing psychotherapist.

MOTIVATING FACTORS

If the first and foremost quality necessary for success is motivation, each private practitioner must have good reasons for entering the field. Why should anyone have motivation for an endeavor so full of risks and problems? Motivation is a very individualized, unique quality, and each person defines his reasons for wanting something in his own terms. However, when private practice therapists are asked what motivates them, regardless of the diversity of their respective fields, their answers are remarkably uniform. The major motivating factor is not, as one might expect, the opportunity to make more money. In fact, money is rather low on the list. Many different private practitioners have described their own motivations and those of their colleagues, and the following is a composite of their revelations. What emerges are nine factors which are incentives for therapists to enter private practice. They are listed in their apparent order of importance.

The Opportunity to Practice Autonomously. Any person who studies for years to develop a complex set of skills to bring about needed changes in individuals and society wants, needs, and deserves the opportunity to use these skills as he sees fit. Working under the auspices of supervisors or agencies largely precludes the opportunity to think of oneself as a professional person. Making one's own decision on how to help the client is a compelling need for many who enter private practice. Their concern is not so much with professional recognition, but the opportunity to fulfill their professional roles as professional people.

Desire for More Work Flexibility. The opportunity to define one's own hours, determine which clients will be seen and when they will be scheduled, to determine for oneself when and what professional meetings to attend, and soon comprises the second most important motivation for private practice. All agency-based activity, as well as any social organization which must utilize personnel in a coordinated, organized way, will put constraints on one's behavior. However, many psychotherapists feel these constraints exist only in organizations and not in private practice. This, of course, is a great misperception, as most veteran private practitioners easily recognize. In private practice there is no respite from the schedule one makes in advance. One finds it very difficult to pick his own hours to work. Vacations are set at times which aren't too inconvenient for clients. The private practitioner is on call constantly and is often called at all hours for emergencies. The flexibility of private work is in some ways illusory.

Opportunity to Remain in Direct Service. The third major motivating force for entering private practice is related to agency and organizational pressures to move into roles of nondirect work with clients. The psychotherapist is "promoted" to supervisor, administrator, instructor, or liaison person, and thereafter rarely has an opportunity to perform the roles for which he was trained. Yet if he remains in direct practice, he will soon find that his income is not keeping up with inflation and that his peers are now considered to be his superiors. The ego, the pocketbook, and the peer pressure make remaining in direct practice a very difficult thing to do. One option for many in this position is to enter private practice. Many do so while remaining in the agency as administrators. Others enter full-time practice, feeling that it is the only way to work directly with clients.

Desire for Economic Improvement.   Money is only the fourth most important motivating factor in one's decision to enter private practice, but obviously it is of considerable interest. Agency-based therapy pays less than does successful private practice, and funding cutbacks and less interest by the public in funding agency programs make it seem inevitable that therapists' salaries will remain lower for some time to come. The promise of improving this situation is what leads many into private practice. Many in institutional employment see their part-time practices as providing supplementary income to that of their agency salaries. Many in full-time independent practice feel that their incomes would be considerably less in an agency. Again, for some this proves to be illusory, especially when one considers some of the inescapable financial liabilities of private practice.

Avoidance of Bureaucratic Conflicts.   This fifth most important motivator is a negative one, based not so much on any perceived attractiveness of private practice but rather on discontent with unattractive parts of institutional employment. Many therapists become frustrated and disillusioned with the problems they encounter in working in large organizations (Billingsley 1969). Such organizations have to serve many masters and are obliged to adhere to many norms, regulations, and patterns of behavior which become almost intolerable for many therapists. They decide to leave such circumstances because of discontent with the jobs, not because of an intense desire to become private practitioners. They enter independent work because it becomes their only alternative to the institutional setting.

Challenge.   Some therapists want to find out what their abilities and limitations are. The challenge of providing services independently and making a living while doing so seems very attractive. The constraints of working in organizations often limit one's sense of being challenged, and it is perceived that such is not the case in private work. The notion of being one's own boss, making one's own decisions, risking the consequences of one's actions, and reaping the rewards for making the correct decisions are all compelling reasons to enter independent practice.

Opportunity for Higher Status, More Recognition. Many psychotherapists are sensitive to the fact that they do a job which is not held in high esteem by the general public. They frequently bemoan this fact and seek ways to upgrade the image of their profession. Often they perceive that working in agencies reenforces this image, by implying to the public that they are not quite professional enough to work autonomously, without supervision and considerable direction. It is often believed that private practice in psychotherapy has higher public esteem than institutional employment. If it is seen as the top of the pecking order, it follows that many are motivated to enhance their prestige by this route. Again, this may be illusory. Prestige essentially emanates from the recognition that one is doing a good job and is competent. In private practice there may be more prestige, but only for those who have proved to be skilled in their diagnostic and service delivery methods.

Opportunity to Provide Better Service. Many have argued that the private practice model affords the opportunity to provide more efficient, more effective, more client centered services than the agency or organizational model. Many psychotherapists who are motivated to do the best job possible are convinced that they must enter private work if they are going to be able to provide the services which are up to their own levels of expertise and skill.

Opportunity to Work with Better-Motivated Clients. Least in the order of motivators for private practice, but still a consideration for some, is the perception that private clients have more incentive and interest in working to resolve their problems. Many studies, in fact, have demonstrated that this is indeed the case. When a client pays for the service he receives, his incentive to work at it is greater than when his fees are subsidized. Some who work in agencies feel that they can't do all they would like

to be able to do with their clients because of the client's unwillingness or lack of motivation. This is particularly true in agencies
and organizations where the clients do not seek psychotherapy of
their own volition, such as in probation centers, penal organizations, and similar places. Many therapists, then, feel that private
work will afford them opportunities to be more successful in
providing services because they have clients who really want to
work on resolving problems.

FOUR

THE PRACTICE SETTING

ONE of the most positive aspects of being in private practice is the opportunity to make one's own decisions about the location, style, and contents of the practice setting. If the right decisions are made, the practitioner can have a work environment which complements his unique style and the needs of his particular clientele. Of course, some find it tedious to search for the right location and obtain the right equipment, but the end result usually makes it worthwhile. The great amount of time necessarily spent exploring various neighborhoods and potential office buildings, negotiating with realtors, haggling with furniture salesmen, shopping in office machine centers, working out formats with printers about stationery, going to banks or affluent relatives for money to finance these expenses, is not wasted. When the office has been found, furnished according to the therapist's tastes and needs, when the business becomes operational, the resulting satisfaction endures as long as the practice continues. Some of the satisfaction is enhanced by remembering the frustrations of working for others and not having such choices. Employees don't have to go through all these complications. But their offices may be arranged differently than they might like, with furniture that doesn't at all reflect their taste or that of the majority of their clientele. The building could be decorated in institutional drab or impersonal coldness. The office might be located a long commute from one's home, and might contain rooms that are too large or small to accommodate the therapist or clients comfortably. The type of furniture and the availability of equipment and supplies, the arrangement of the office and waiting room, all can be rather unpleasant for the therapist whose tastes and individuality are compromised by the needs of the organization. The employees in such circumstances have little choice but to make do, and their acceptance of the physical setting often sets the tone for the way they will conduct their work thereafter.

The opportunity exists for the therapist upon entering private practice to avoid these problems and create an environment which makes his operation much better than it otherwise would be. But all too often many therapists do not avail themselves of this opportunity. Some merely fall into a location because someone they knew was located there. Some merely put together the furnishings of their office in the fastest and least expensive way. Some enter into arrangements with other practitioners and are influenced by the others so that their own tastes and needs are subordinated. Many who enter private practice simply acquire equipment on an ad hoc basis. They make their decisions through trial and error. But doing otherwise is difficult for many because they have had no experience or information about the many factors that need to be considered before making the necessary choices. This chapter will discuss these factors and focus on the major elements that must be considered to establish and equip the private practice office.

THE RIGHT LOCATION

Careful planning about where to locate is the prerequisite of establishing the successful practice. Thoreau was wrong when he told Emerson that people would travel through the deepest woods, to the most inconvenient place to reach the person with a better mousetrap. An admirable person in many ways, Thoreau failed in three major business ventures in his lifetime and had to live off his friends (Krutch 1948). Successful businesses give care and thought to finding the right location for their specific purposes. No one would expect the operator of a McDonald's hamburger franchise to put up a building wherever he found an open space, and equip the place with whatever materials happened to be available. Businesses succeed because of the convenience of the location as much as the quality of the product or service.

The right location for the private practitioner is not dependent on heavy traffic patterns, but it is important to be in a location which is accessible to the type of clientele one hopes to reach (Williams 1975). Accessibility, however, isn't merely geographic. It is also a state of mind. The location should be where the therapist's natural clientele would feel comfortable. If the therapist specializes in treating children, for example, downtown office buildings aren't as conducive to the child's comfort as residential areas would be. If the clientele is largely going to come from the economically disadvantaged, a location in a posh neighborhood would be ill advised. If the therapy is going to be with the gay community or the swinging single set, the suburban areas might be out. There needs to be attitudinal as well as physical accessibility for the clients one hopes to reach. Furthermore, the type of office selected will eventually influence or determine the type of clientele served. A therapist may want to work with children, for example, but if his office is in the downtown business district he may find that his specialty begins to change, from fewer children to more business people.

Nevertheless, it often appears that many therapists in private practice decide about location on the basis of economics rather than on an understanding of a neighborhood or the effect of practice setting on the helping process (Turner 1978). It would be a serious mistake for the psychotherapist about to enter private practice to allow financial limitations to determine where his office will be. This would be a false economy because his potential clients and referral resources are likely to judge him and his capability largely on such external factors as his environment. Financing a lease on a suitable office can be very expensive, but if corners need to be cut this is not the ideal place to cut them.

SIX POSSIBLE SETTINGS

Psychotherapists in private practice have tended to choose one of six types of setting in which to conduct their work, each with distinct advantages and disadvantages. These are professional office buildings, office suites in residential apartment complexes, small detached buildings or converted homes, rented space in the office of another professional, the therapist's home, and facilities where the therapist has additional employment.

Office Buildings. Office buildings that cater to professional people such as lawyers, accountants, physicians, and consultants are popular among full-time independent practitioners, because of several important positive features. The building itself sets the tone for the businesslike nature of the therapy relationship. People feel they are going there to work. This no-nonsense ambience might repel some potential clients, but the ones who are attracted to it are more likely to be serious about confronting their problems, and more willing to pay for the service. Such buildings are easy for clients to get to, usually being located on major roads near public transportation or parking facilities. Locating in a building near public transportation is already important, and will probably become a necessity some day as the energy shortage changes people's transportation patterns and methods.

Another advantage of such buildings is that they can lead naturally to an important referral resource. Other professionals in the building, especially if the therapist cultivates an acquaintance with them, will refer clients. Many people who seek professional services will be passing through these buildings. They will see the therapist's name and specialty on the directory by the elevator, or on his office door, and it is not uncommon for some of these people to inquire about an appointment.

Locating in the building also avoids some of the problems of isolation faced by many private practitioners. If the therapist cultivates some friendships and possibly some consultation or collaboration contacts in the building there will be greater opportunities for him to occasionally visit a fellow professional. A practical advantage is that the maintenance of the office can be done by building personnel, freeing the therapist from this task. Finally, the office building choice avoids disadvantages encountered in some of the other settings. For example, there is no problem about proper zoning in such a location, and there is no difficulty convincing the Internal Revenue Service that the office is used entirely for one's professional activity.

However, on the other side of the coin there are several disadvantages. The major disadvantage is that it is the most expensive of the six choices, and if one is leasing the facilities, the rent keeps going up each year. Also, the setting is forbidding to some people, especially children. The buildings tend to be impersonal and rather cold and thus not an ideal environment for the trusting, warm relationship that one hopes to achieve with clients (Good et al. 1965). Sometimes such buildings have inadequate parking facilities, thus alienating those who prefer driving over public transportation. Some clients are not enamored with office buildings because they seek confidentiality and more privacy, and such buildings are often crowded with witnesses to the client's presence. The client wouldn't have this problem as much in the other choices.

Apartment Complexes. Office suites in apartment complexes are another choice but are among the least popular option with the majority of practitioners. This is surprising because this kind of location has a variety of features that are highly attractive. Many apartment buildings have office suites on the ground floor, often with private entrances. This affords clients opportunity for confidentiality about their presence.

If the complex has other professional suites, therapists won't be professionally isolated. The professionals in such a complex are likely to become closer with the psychotherapist than would be the case in the office building setting, and thus provide a more solid referral resource. The facilities generate some "drop in" clientele from residents who see the therapist's name and specialization listed.

Apartment complexes provide the practitioner's office with a more "homey" atmosphere, less forbidding to clients, and lends itself to a warmer relationship with the therapist. It is common to find these buildings with such amenities as swimming pools, tennis courts, and other recreational facilities. These facilities can offer an ideal short respite for the therapist to break up the rigors of his day, and usually the facilities are not crowded during a weekday.

Apartment suites are usually more spacious than suites in office buildings, and typically their costs are about one-third less for the same amount of space. Many of these suites are equipped with kitchens and have their own bathrooms, unlike office buildings. During weekdays at least the parking problem is not as severe as in the office setting.

The disadvantages are few, but they do exist. Sometimes residents in the complex feel uncomfortable with the behavior or appearance of the therapist's clientele and sometimes exert subtle pressures on them or the therapist which indicate their presence is unwelcome. There is typically less room for anything that appears to be deviant wherever people live, so it shouldn't be surprising that some residents would feel uncomfortable with the clients of the psychotherapist encroaching on their territory. Some therapists in this location say they miss not having many other professionals near them, and some sense of isolation does exist for them.

Houses or Small Buildings.   Detached buildings or converted houses are a third possibility in choosing the right location. Some therapists locate in houses or small buildings, usually in more commercial than residential areas. Often several professionals will occupy such facilities together after doing some renovating and equipping the facility for exclusive use as a professional office. Usually these buildings are owned by the therapist or the group of professionals who occupy the facility.

The positive features include a personalized, homey atmosphere and a considerable amount of convenience and accessibility for the therapist and client. Such settings are typically easy to get to by automobile, with no parking problems. Since they are used exclusively for the practice, they are modified to meet the needs of the therapist and his clientele with much more flexibility than would be the case in office or apartment buildings. If the therapist is sharing the facility with other professionals, the risk of feeling isolated is negligible. There is more possibility of working in teams, interprofessionally, or in models of intervention that are less like the clinical model (Barker 1969).

The costs to the therapist are high at first, because of conversion expenses and greater expense for utilities, but when these units are owned by the therapist, advantages on inflation and taxation tend to offset the higher start-up costs. With fixed mortgages that remain stable in inflationary times, after a few years the mortgage payments will seem much lower than rents for office or apartment. Income tax savings are considerable in using the building exclusively for the office. It may be depreciated rapidly for tax purposes, even though it is in reality likely to appreciate in value.

The disadvantages are that this type of setting usually requires more maintenance than the other choices, and the therapist must either do it himself or experience a rather difficult time getting service people to come to this out-of-the-way place. If the building is shared by several professionals, the sense of isolation is nil, but it is crucial that they are compatible. If they turn out not to be, the setting affords many unpleasant conflicts from which there is no escape short of the cumbersome process of extricating, selling, and relocating.

Subrenting Space. Rented space in the office of another professional is the fourth major option. Many psychotherapists just starting out in private practice make this choice, thinking of it as a temporary expedient, and as such it can be worthwhile. Often an established private practitioner has an office with an extra room which he rents to a newcomer. Or he rents the use of his own office during the hours when he is not there. This enables the new therapist to concentrate on establishing and building his own clientele without needing to worry, for the time being, about the physical setting. His start-up costs are very low, and he can learn firsthand what his requirements are. Then with this information, when he is able to start his own office, he is much better informed than he would have been without the experience.

However, as a long-term or permanent choice there are substantial problems with this type of setting. Unless the new professional is completely autonomous and recognized as such by the practitioner from whom he is subleasing space, he can feel that he is an employee or an extension of the other. But if he *is* completely autonomous, he is likely to feel very isolated in this setting. He might be using the office in the evenings and weekends during the owner's absence. The new therapist usually will not be able to equip the facility with much that is his own, and his own references and materials will have to be moved to the office every time he goes there. He will be concerned about the possibility of his client or himself damaging some of the property or otherwise disrupting the operations of the owner. The disadvantages of this method are so serious that it must be considered only a temporary choice from which the independent practitioner should extricate himself as soon as the factors that necessitated the choice are no longer present.

Home. An office in the therapist's residence is the fifth possibility and the most popular of the choices among private practice psychotherapists, both full and part time. The advantages are considerable. Heading the list are costs and convenience. If the home already has the space and the therapist is already occupying it, his expenses would be much less than those of renting or converting other facilities. Furthermore, he is able to deduct from his income taxes some of the costs of maintaining the home office. Of course, the IRS has greatly tightened its regulations concerning home offices since 1978, and the therapist is flirting with tax trouble unless he is scrupulous about the way the home office is utilized and reported (Lasser 1982). The home office is incomparably convenient for the worker. He has no commuting problems and is able to keep all needed material and equipment at hand. Many practitioners get double duty out of using the home office for their clients and then for their personal use, such as personal entertaining or recreation. Again, there may be serious income tax problems in doing so. These settings are usually warmer, and more homey, reflecting the worker's style better than the alternatives do.

Many therapists who have started out in their home offices indicate that they found it not to their liking. The home office is very isolated from the professional community. The therapist is deprived of the stimulation and opportunity for professional interaction. Furthermore, it is sometimes necessary for him to make substantial and expensive changes in the home, such as enlarging, building separate entrances, and soundproofing. Another disadvantage is that the therapist has little respite from his work when he does it at home. There is less separation and distinction between the two environments. Some therapists feel more comfortable when they can leave their work behind and recuperate from its demands in a different location. When clients come to what is obviously the therapist's home, it is harder for the therapist to maintain an aura of anonymity and therefore apparent objectivity. His clients know what kind of home he has, whether or not he mows his grass, what his economic circumstances are likely to be, whether he is married and has children or not, and many other personal things about his life style and values. This may or may not be an advantage for the therapist, depending on the type of clientele he has and the goals he is striving to achieve with them. One part-time home office practitioner told me: "I feel like I'm in a goldfish bowl sometimes. I'm always seeing my clients and former clients driving past my house on weekends or evenings. I guess they just want to check me out."

A serious consideration about the home office choice is potential zoning problems. Though the typical private practice is hardly disruptive to the neighborhood, in fact is barely noticeable to the neighbors, some legal complications can occur. Many state or local governments grant exemptions to allow private practice in residential areas, but this is by no means universal. The possibility of being unable to obtain this exemption should be thoroughly investigated before purchasing a house where one hopes to establish a private practice. There is no assurance that because the jurisdiction has allowed other professionals to operate out of their homes, it will continue to make such allowances. Some existing offices have been established long enough to be grandfathered in. Some jurisdictions have allowed only a limited number of home offices in an area because exceeding that number might alter the residential character of the neighborhood.

Another possible zoning problem concerns the nature of psychotherapy. Where the jurisdiction might allow home offices by members of one profession, there is no certainty that such allowances will be made for all psychotherapy professions.

A well-known case that occurred in suburban Washington, D.C., several years ago illustrates this point (NASW 1977). After a highly qualified, experienced, and well-trained social worker had begun her private practice in her home, which was in a neighborhood that had home offices for practitioners of several other disciplines, the county zoning board told her she could no longer continue her practice there, according to the zoning ordinance. The apparent idea behind the ordinance was to discourage use of home offices by such people as astrologers, palmists, plumbers, and maintenance people, but to allow physicians, attorneys, dentists, and accountants. Making this ruling about the social worker, however, was tantamount to a government agency declaring that social work was not a profession. The worker, backed by her local and national professional association, had to take the issue through expensive and time-consuming litigation in order to convince the jurisdiction that social work was a profession. The lack of public understanding about the nature of all the psychotherapy disciplines can easily lead to a recurrence of such problems in any neighborhood. The therapist wishing to set up practice in his home is thus wise to investigate these possibilities before committing any other time, energy, and money to the project.

Private Facilities at Place of Employment.   The sixth possibility is when the therapist is employed in an agency or institution and is able to use those facilities to maintain a part-time private practice. The therapist might be a college psychology professor, a clergyman, a social agency administrator, or a hospital based psychiatrist. Such a practitioner is often permitted the use of his office for private clients during hours when he is not on duty. This privilege is sometimes extended to institution-based psychotherapists as an employment fringe benefit and to enable them to supplement their incomes.

For the therapist there are significant economic advantages in this model, but serious other problems as well. The therapist is able to use his organization office at no cost to him. He is thereby freed of maintenance problems and doesn't have extra commuting inconveniences. He usually doesn't need to be concerned about zoning or income tax difficulties, and he has the propinquity of his fellow professionals.

But practitioners who utilize this approach sometimes experience role confusion, conflicts about priorities, and sometimes overlapping duties. Therapists in this situation sometimes have difficulty making it clear whether they are acting in the role of private person or institutional person. For example, a clergyman engaged in counseling might be uncertain as to whether fee for service is appropriate in the church office. Or a professor working with a student on an extended basis might find himself in a similar situation.

Since each of these six possibilities has distinct advantages and disadvantages, the therapist has to do some serious thinking before leaping into his practice. Impulsive decisions, or those based on only partial consideration of all the pros and cons, will have a major impact on the quality and nature of the practice. There is no one best place to locate for all private practice psychotherapists, but for each individual there is certainly an optimum setting, given his unique style, needs, and type of clientele.

AMBIENCE: THE "SOCIOPETAL" OFFICE

After the decision about office location has been made and implemented, the next important consideration is the physical layout, decor, and amenities of the practitioner's office. Psychotherapists are very sensitive to the emotional reactions of their clients and tuned in to every nuance of body language and speech, yet they often give little thought to the effect on clients of the physical space and ambience of the office (Turner 1978). Most therapists begin their work in institutions where they have little opportunity to make changes or influence decisions about the decor of the offices. It is understandable that the agency-based therapist would not have given much thought to this aspect of the helping transaction, but it is not understandable why the private practitioner should follow that example. He has complete authority to create the environment he wants.

Most therapists in private practice, who do give it some thought, attempt to create a setting which has *sociopetal* rather than *sociofugal* characteristics. Osmond first used these terms in his research in the design of psychiatric wards, but they are applicable in the settings of all helping and psychosocial therapy settings (Osmond 1957). Sociopetal arrangements are those in which the desks, chairs, tables, and other furniture are placed to bring people together and encourage interaction, while sociofugal arrangements inhibit interactions. For example, waiting rooms with benches or couches tend to be sociofugal while those with small clusters of chairs tend to be more sociopetal. Psychotherapists in private practice have been shown to have more sociopetal offices than do therapists who are institution based (Seabury 1971).

The typical private office arrangement, according to Seabury, has small waiting rooms with angular seating patterns that encourage the feeling of warmth and intimacy. The typical private practice interview room is about twice as long as it is wide (9 by 16 feet) and contains a couch, bookcase, desk, several soft chairs, small tables, and a large plant. Soft carpets, luxurious furnishings, tasteful wall hangings, and diplomas make the office feel more like one is sitting in a den or living room than an office. In these settings, the chairs where interviewing takes place are seldom more than six feet apart and many are two or three feet apart, with face-to-face or diagonal interviewing configurations.

Hall has done considerable research into optimum distances for people's communication and divided this space into four categories: intimate distance (within 18 inches apart), personal distance (18 inches to 4 feet), social distance (4 to 12 feet), and public distance (more than 12 feet) (Hall 1966). Of course, the distances vary according to cultural and psychological factors. Most private practitioners opt for close social distance or even personal distance in their interview settings. Sommer's work on the "geography" of physical settings demonstrated that interactions are enhanced when the people are sitting closely around a table, or somewhat diagonally to one another, rather than face to face or side by side (Sommer 1959). What is optimal depends on the purpose of the interaction and the nature of the therapeutic goal, but sociometric studies show that generally these patterns are fairly consistent in all types of social encounters (Sommer 1962). Close and diagonal seating arrangements tend to be sociopetal, and those that are side by side or farther than five feet apart are sociofugal. Agencies tend to have their offices and waiting rooms arranged more sociofugally than do private practitioner's offices.

Clearly the outcome of therapy is not dependent on the arrangement of the office, or on the amenities which it contains, but there is evidence that giving careful consideration to these things will result in an increased level of security, trust, and comfort a client and therapist experiences.

Office Amenities. The office must be suitable for the clientele of one's specialty and in keeping with the socioeconomic and cultural considerations of the client. For example, if the therapist is concentrating on work with the aged or handicapped, he would be ill advised to have his office at the top of a stairway, or if he works frequently with children, the office or playroom should be informal and not full of breakable, expensive objets d'art. If the clients are primarily adolescents, a Victorian overstuffed look would certainly be out of place. The facility dare not have a shoddy look if the therapist works with the middle class or an ostentatious look if he works with the underprivileged. But whatever the unique needs and specific characteristics of the clientele, a number of features are universally applicable for the conscientious private practitioner.

One necessity is *soundproofing*. Achieving it is rather challenging nowadays, especially in newer buildings with paper-thin walls, low ceilings, and clean, unbroken lines. But it is particularly important that clients' voices cannot be heard or that their words cannot be distinguished from the interview-consulting room to the waiting room. If the client in the waiting room hears what is said in the interview room, when it is his turn, he is often intimidated about expressing himself openly.

If it is not possible to soundproof the consultation room completely, a minimal requirement is to put sound barriers between the office and the waiting room. This can be done by adding a false wall, often merely out of reenforced paneling, in the interview room where it is exposed to the waiting room. Many practitioners also add an extra door between their office and that of the waiting room so that two doors must be opened between the two rooms. Carpeting, drapes, and numerous small pieces of soft furniture also help to absorb sound. Most private practitioners of all professions keep a radio or tape system playing innocuous music softly in the waiting room, which further reduces the opportunity to hear voices. Some practitioners who have some professional or personal aversion to playing music have installed inexpensive radio-like devices that produce "white noise." These instruments have a pleasant, almost subliminal humming sound which helps to conceal voices and also has a rather tranquilizing effect on some clients. Some offices are equipped with a tropical fish aquarium, which not only provides a pleasant visual diversion for the client, but produces a pleasant gurgling sound, which adds to the soundproofing of the office.

In the sociopetal office the interview room is set up so that the practitioner's desk is not the dominant feature. When clients see lawyers, accountants, or other consultants where there is considerable writing and calculation, the desk between the professional and client is appropriate and probably necessary. However, when warmth, trust, and closeness are the desired ingredients of the relationship, and when kinesics, or body motion communication, is a prominent feature of the method used, then it is not appropriate to have tables or desks between the interviewer or interviewee (Birdwhistell 1979). The desk will be needed, however, since one must make notes and write correspondence during the workday, but it is best located away from where the interview occurs. The interview room thus will include the desk and desk chair, the practitioner's interview chair, possibly two comfortable chairs or a couch for the client and any member of his family, and the usual bookcase, tables, and lamps arranged in such a way as to facilitate interaction.

The waiting room is arranged similarly. If the practitioner employs a secretary-receptionist, the waiting room will contain a reception desk with typewriter, telephone, and filing cabinets. In the solo practice without a receptionist, it is better to keep such equipment in the practitioner's office.

The therapist should always be alert to many little amenities which he might take for granted but without which the client may have considerable discomfort. Turner recommends such things as having the practitioner's name displayed so the new client won't be too uncomfortable to ask when he sometimes forgets, or having a mirror located near the door so the client can get himself more presentable before returning to the outside world (Turner 1978). Turner also argues for clocks visible to the client. "The increase in tension toward the end of an interview may be related to significant psychodynamic material but it may just as well be related to worry about missing a bus" (Turner 1978). Clients should know where the nearest available washroom is and should have easy access to it without having to ask. These amenities are not going to be make or break aspects of the therapeutic relationship, but nevertheless they facilitate the private practitioner's goals with his clients.

Office Equipment. Every private practitioner's office will need some bare essentials for properly equipping the operation. Beyond furniture, the office must have a lockable filing cabinet containing folders for each client, a telephone with a shut-off device, and the appropriate stationery and writing materials. Beyond that, as finances permit, the therapist will find it helpful to have dictation equipment, a desktop reproducing machine, equipment for audio tape recording sessions, possibly a postage meter, and a telephone answering machine.

Dictation equipment may be irrelevant without secretarial assistance, but when someone is employed, this becomes a valuable asset. The therapist is able to rapidly record his case records and notes after each interview. This is very important because there is limited time in which to record impressions, and it is crucial to do so in private psychotherapy. The dictation equipment permits the secretary to prepare the material at convenient times that do not interfere with the interview process. Some practitioners use secretarial services and report using their telephone to transmit such data, but this process raises questions about confidentiality. If there are no secretarial services available to the therapist, he is just as well off without this equipment because his notes will be in longhand anyway.

Telephones with shut-off capabilities are a necessity, unless the therapist has a full-time receptionist. Private practitioners don't always have that luxury, so most need to have their telephone in their interview rooms. It is distracting, inconsiderate, and unfair to the client to be interrupted during a session so that the interviewer can talk on the phone. It is also unfair to the telephone caller, who may not realize that the person to whom he is talking is being listened to by the client. The telephone company can easily adapt the telephone by adjusting the bell volume down to inaudible. Most practitioners now utilize answering machines or answering services which interrupt incoming calls and keep them from interfering with the interview. There are advantages and disadvantages in choosing either a machine or a service.

Answering machines enable the therapist to record his own voice instructing the caller to leave a message for a return call. The major advantages of the machine over the answering service are cost and convenience. Outright purchase of the machines is about the same cost as three to four months' use of an answering service. Since the caller gives his name and number on tape, there is no problem of inaccurate transmission of information, such as occasionally happens with answering services. For about twice the cost of the simple answering machine, one can buy an adapter which permits the therapist to call his own phone from wherever he is and pick up any messages. The adapter is a sound beeper which the therapist uses to activate the answering machine's playback when he calls his own number. The major disadvantage of answering machines is that they are very intimidating for many clients, particularly those who may be anxious, lacking in confidence, or who feel they are not articulate unless in a dialogue. The machines give the caller a minute or less in which to leave their messages and many callers simply hang up without saying anything.

Answering services don't often present this problem, but if it happens the therapist remains blissfully ignorant of the fact. In the answering service system the practitioner's public telephone number is located at a central switchboard, or there is a direct line from the office to the switchboard which the therapist may activate as he chooses. When the number is called, an operator answers according to the therapist's instructions. This is more personal than a machine and usually more comforting to the caller. The dialogue permits callers to collect their thoughts better at a less pressured pace.

This advantage is offset by several problems with answering services. Sometimes, when the operators are receiving many calls at once, the caller is put on hold for interminable lengths of time. When he does get through, the operator sometimes hurriedly writes down wrong numbers. Sometimes the operators are not highly skilled in dealing with clients and can alienate them. The greatest disadvantage is the relative cost. Answering services tend to charge a flat monthly fee, plus additional charges for the installation and a certain amount for each call they handle above a minimum amount. The monthly flat rate fee approximates what a therapist might charge for one- to two-hour-long interview sessions. This rate would be lower if the twelve-hour service were used instead of the twenty-four-hour answering capability, but most practitioners require the latter.

Copying machines are another valuable item to include in the well-equipped practitioner's office. The smaller, desktop models are becoming less expensive and are especially needed by therapists who give copies of case recordings to a client or client's doctor or lawyer when requested by the client to do so. Some practitioners use the copying machines in their billing procedures, enabling them to simply send the client a copy of the account sheet each month showing the amounts due. *Computers* are also becoming affordable for the small office and are extremely valuable in bookkeeping, billing, keeping records, and word processing. They are not used in very many practitioners' offices at present, but within a few years, no private practice psychotherapist's office will be complete without one.

Audio or video tape recorders are used with great effectiveness in many practitioners' offices. When the client consents to the interview being recorded, the resulting playback can be very useful for the client as well as the therapist. It enables the therapist to listen to and see more objectively various techniques he may be using, to hear new facets of what the client is communicating, or to focus on parts of the interview which seem particularly relevant. Clients find that they learn a great deal about themselves when permitted to listen or view the session over again. Some practitioners give or loan the cassettes to the client so he can review his efforts on his own. This often gives the client a fresh and different perspective about his manner of presentation of self. If the recording is audio only, the microphone should be plainly visible to the client but not obtrusive. The mike can be attached to the recording device, which can be in another room so that its noise or presence is not too intimidating. Most clients are happy to give consent to recording the session, and many indicate that they assumed it was being done even before being asked. Unless the microphone or camera is very conspicuous, the client's initial discomfiture, if any, is short lived and virtually forgotten as the session gets under way.

Stamp machines or postage meters are relatively unimportant options for the private practitioner's office, particularly if he is in solo practice. The volume of mail for correspondence and billings by one psychotherapist during the month will be small enough that personally stamping and sealing envelopes is no great inconvenience. If the office has a number of practitioners working together, a postage meter is a considerable convenience, and saves time rather than money. However, this can lead to conflicts between practitioners about which of them might be using the meter more than their share. The best alternative is the stamp dispenser, found in most office supply stores. It is a convenient, inexpensive, and very small machine which moistens one stamp, severs it from the roll of stamps, and firmly affixes it to the envelope with one motion. It holds the standard roll of 100 stamps which is available at any post office.

Office supplies and stationery are, of course, necessary in the office. Finding a good printer is essential because the practitioner will need personalized materials for the conduct of business. The necessities include plain and window envelopes, both short and long styles, matching letterhead stationery, face sheet forms for clients to provide basic information about themselves, and billing forms. These items all need to be printed with the practitioner's name, professional affiliation, license or certification when applicable, address, and telephone number. Another useful item is a receipt book to record cash payments and give clients a record of having paid. Most print shops provide such materials at afford-able rates and can do so in a short time. Many practitioners find it convenient to use the services of the large mail-order printing firms which specialize in printing for professionals. They provide professionals with complete catalogues of their products along with order forms and clear instructions for ordering customized printing and other office supplies and equipment. Orders made to them are promptly filled and returned to the practitioner with guarantees, by direct mail or parcel delivery. Among the large companies which send catalogues on request are Histacount Corp., Walt Whitman Drive, Melville, N.Y.; Professional Office Services, Inc., Box 450, Waterloo, Iowa; and Feld Printing Co., Box 44188, Cincinnati, Ohio.

Pamphlets, brochures, and referral resource lists are other es-sentials for the private practitioner. One of his major activities, like that of the institutional therapist, is channeling, or referring clients to those resources which can best meet the client's needs. It is therefore advisable to have an adequate supply of literature describing these referral resources to give to the client. Pamphlets describing these facilities are easy to acquire, and the facility is usually eager to have their pamphlets in the hands of potential referrers. So too are pamphlets produced by associations and foundations concerned with special disorders, handicaps, dis-eases, or programs. Organizations such as Alcoholics Anony-mous, American Nursing Home Association, The Epilepsy Foun-dation, American Youth Hostels, and hundreds more have attractive pamphlets and brochures for the worker to make avail-able to his clients.

THE ESSENTIAL REFERENCE LIBRARY

Many private practice offices are full of books, which are used primarily as props. The books are to demonstrate that the prac-titioner is a well-read, learned, scholarly individual who un-doubtedly is an expert. Whether the private practitioner has read the books or not does not determine his expertise. Still, some therapists find security in the mere presence of some books as potential reference sources. Reference materials are for helping to answer specific questions that come up during a typical day. Some have proved more valuable than others, and many private practitioner's office should have some of the following books. Most important, of course, are the definitive textbooks that are concerned with the therapist's specialty and profession. Others, described here, have universal applicability.

The DSM III. This is the latest edition of the *Diagnostic and Statistical Manual* of the American Psychiatric Association, published and distributed first in 1980 (APA 1980a). The book summarizes and categorizes every mental illness known to mankind, including the symptoms, genesis, and prognosis of each. Each illness or "diagnostic category" and the myriad of subsets under each category is given a number which is recognized and officially sanctioned in the psychiatric community of the United States and most of the Western world, and the numbers and categories are standardized internationally with the United Nations World Health Organization, ICD-9. It is important to have ready access to this code system, because it is often necessary to write the number rather than a description of the diagnostic category on insurance forms, or when confidentiality requires it. The book is the third and newest edition of the series that has become the standard way of looking at mental illness in America.

The Mini D. This is a companion volume to the *DSM III*, a small paperback condensation officially entitled *Quick Reference to Diagnostic Criteria from DSM III* (APA 1980b). The larger volume is essential by itself, while the *Mini D* is meaningless without the *DSM III*. It is like an index, a summary of a summary, and is useful for the practitioner when very little detail is needed. Its small size makes it especially helpful for keeping at one's desk to use while making case notes; the *DSM III*'s bulk often consigns it to the bookshelf.

The latest PDR. Another essential is the *Physician's Desk Reference*, which gives extensive and inclusive information on every prescription drug in the world (PDR 1982). The book is divided into four sections. One describes alphabetically all the drugs which are currently prescribed, how they are to be used, their chemical nature, the effects they have on the patients, the uses and contraindications, and the occasional side effects. The information is essentially everything a physician who prescribes the medication should know before doing so. Other sections of the book list the same information by manufacturer, by generic name of the drug, and by illnesses for which it is generally prescribed. There is also a section which pictures in full color virtually all prescription drugs commercially available. The reference can be a valuable tool for the private practitioner, helping him learn what drugs his client might be using and what the effects are likely to be. The client's behaviors or behavioral changes might be attributable to the medication, and the *PDR* provides this information. The pictures can be used by the client to help identify for the worker what drug he is taking if he cannot remember the name. Of course, only M.D. psychotherapists prescribe or recommend medication, but it is important that nonmedical psychotherapists be well aware of the kinds of medications being used and their effects.

The Merck Manual. Another book produced for and mainly used by physicians but invaluable for all psychotherapists is this compact summary of the major physical illnesses and diagnostic categories, their symptoms and choice of treatment, as well as a wealth of information about body functions and dysfunctions (Merck 1982). The *Merck Manual* was first published in 1899 and is periodically revised. It is only a summary and by no means gives the reader any more than clues as to possible causes and resolutions of illness. Physicians use the *Merck Manual* primarily to jog their memories, especially about medical aspects out of their own specialization. The psychotherapist can find such a reference useful in seeking a quick summary of the disease his client might have been experiencing and for which he is being treated.

American Handbook of Psychiatry (Arieti 1979), the classic seven-volume set of definitive articles on all phases of mental illness and treatment methodologies, is another worthy addition to the reference shelf. The books make it possible for the practitioner to read an in-depth encyclopedic entry on most subjects with which he is likely to come in contact if his clients have any emotional disturbance or social dysfunction or require treatment of any sort, from psychoanalysis to family group therapy to behavioral modification. No entry is exhaustive, and some of the material in volume 1 is somewhat dated by now, especially the entries on organic and nonfunctional causes of disorders.

Directories of agency resources. The private practitioner will find it essential to make up a book for himself listing all the referral resources and helping agencies in his community. Many communities produce such booklets, perhaps in conjunction with the United Fund appeals, listing all the agencies supported by the United Fund, describing their location, the services they provide, and their eligibility requirements. The best example of such publications is the *Directory of Social and Health Agencies of New York City, 1981–82 (Directory 1982)*. This book describes the myriad human service programs and organizations in New York and includes a section on referral sources outside the city as well as a bibliography of other useful directories, arranged by subject. Many jurisdictions have similar publications.

But where such books are published they are unlikely to contain all that the therapist needs. He would do well to produce his own personal guide, perhaps a loose-leaf notebook with dividers for each type of service. One section could list information about all the people who have made referrals to him, what their work is, and what information they might require in response to the referral. Another section would list information about all the psychiatrists, nurses, psychologists, and other helping professionals in the area whom one might refer to, consult or collaborate with about clients, or otherwise exchange information. Another page would contain lists of all the agencies in the area that provide services which might be useful to the practitioner's clients. This list could include private practice lawyers or special consultants on tenant rights, consumer grievances, adoption agencies, volunteer agencies, or nursing care facilities. This directory, made by and for the practitioner, would be constantly updated and would probably be his most popular and often used reference resource.

These materials are the indispensable reference resources and, of course, are by no means all the reference library a practitioner needs at his disposal. Depending on the area of special interest, he would do well to have a latest copy of the definitive or standard text in that area. It would also be useful for many practitioners to acquire the law book pertaining to his state's statutes regarding marriage, divorce, adoption, wills, custody, commitment, equal rights, and the myriad other issues which are often discussed in the practitioner's office. If such law books are unavailable or too expensive for their anticipated degree of usefulness, the practitioner can get copies of relevant laws through a good local library.

THE THERAPIST-CLIENT CONTRACT

The contract is an explicit agreement about the terms of exchange and responsibility between the therapist and client (Seabury 1976). It is devised by the therapist and the client together and specifies the goals of the relationship. The private practitioner's contract also includes information about the therapist's background, the charges and how they must be paid, and other information which the client needs about the transaction. It is necessary to provide the client with such information to prevent any subsequent misunderstandings and to give focus to the direction of the treatment. With recent legal decisions about confidentiality issues, it is necessary that the therapist define, in writing, what circumstances might force him to reveal information about the client (Bernstein 1977). It is necessary for each private practitioner to develop his own contract form to present to each potential client. The contract, in addition to providing information about the therapist and the nature of the subsequent exchange between therapist and client, usually contains space for outlining the goals of treatment. Two copies of the contract are signed by both therapist and client, and each keeps one copy. It can be later referred to by either party to give focus or understanding. The following is a typical contract used by a psychotherapist and her clients. It is not meant to be a model, as each therapist needs to develop his own according to the goals and methods with which he is most comfortable. This is presented as an illustration of the type of agreements that are typically made.

Margaret Scott, Ph.D.
Licensed Clinical Psychologist
Letter of Agreement

Hello. Welcome to my office. I hope you find your time here to be worthwhile. I'm giving you this letter in order to answer questions you may have. It will tell you how we should work together and what we both need to expect out of it. Please go over this carefully. Feel free to ask me any questions about it that you have, whenever you have them. At the end of this letter there is a place for both of us to sign our names. Signing means that we both agree with all the points in this letter. There is also space for us to write down the goals we hope to accomplish through our working together. We can review these goals as we go along. We can change them any time we want if it seems like a good idea to both you and me.

See Your Doctor. It is a good idea that your family doctor know you are going to be working with me. Please tell him/her as soon as possible. It is also important that I am informed about any work (s)he is doing with you. I especially need to know about any medication (s)he is prescribing for you and about any special health problems you may have. Please ask your doctor to give me this information as soon as possible. I think it is in your interests to include information in your medical record about your work with me. Therefore, unless you say otherwise, I will write to your doctor to report your progress. These letters can be included in your medical chart. You will be given a copy of these letters, before they are sent. That way, any corrections or things you feel should be left out or added can be done before it is sent. Please get a physical examination from your doctor as soon as possible. Have your doctor send me a summary of the results. This is to rule out the possibility of any health problems which might be causing the symptoms you are having.

Time. Each of our appointments is scheduled to last fifty minutes. I am usually able to begin promptly at the scheduled time. It is very rare that I am late for an appointment. If it ever happens, I'll try to let you know in advance, even if the delay is just a few minutes. If we must begin late, we will still be together for the full fifty minutes. If you arrive late for an appointment it will still be necessary for us to end the interview fifty minutes after it was scheduled to begin. The charge to you for these shortened sessions will be for the full amount. You will not be charged for a session if you cannot keep it and let me know at least twenty-four hours in advance. You will be charged if you fail to keep a scheduled appointment or do not notify me twenty-four hours ahead of time.

Costs. The charges for each of these fifty-minute sessions is $_____. This amount is the same if you attend the session alone or with other family members. The charge to you is the same if, with your consent, I see other members of your family in your behalf. If we agree to have interviews that are longer or shorter than fifty minutes, the charges will be based on the amount of time we are together. For example, if you have a twenty-five-minute session the charge will be half that of a fifty-minute session.

Method of Payment. You may pay by cash, credit card, check, or money order. You may pay me directly at the time of each visit or at the end of each month. If payment in full has not been received by the end of the month, my office will send you a bill. This statement will itemize the charges and show the total balance due. This amount must be paid within ten days after the month begins. Please discuss with me if you are having any financial problems which prevent you from paying in this way. We can make special arrangements if necessary.

Insurance. Your health insurance may help to pay these charges. You should find this out by contacting your insurance company or agent as soon as possible. If they will help you pay my fees, please obtain the proper forms from them and give them to me. I will complete them and promptly return them to you, not to your insurance company. After that it is your responsibility to submit the forms to your company. Ask them to send the money to you and not to me. It is necessary that you make full payment for the balance due to me by the end of each month, regardless of whether the insurance company delays in reimbursing you or not. The expenses of this office are great and they have to be paid each month. My landlord and the other creditors want to be paid on time and don't care that someone's insurance company is slow. You should note that health insurance companies generally do not reimburse expenses considered by them to be unrelated to one's health. Excluded by some companies are such things as marriage counseling, some forms of psychotherapy, family counseling, educational counseling, and some forms of social services. Some companies will only pay you for psychotherapy services when your physician has referred you to me and is involved in your treatment. It is important that you find out about these things from your insurance company if you plan on getting insurance reimbursement.

Confidentiality. My profession and my personal ethics require me to keep everything you discuss here in the strictest of confidence. I have no intention of ever giving out any information about you to anyone, unless you ask me to. I have no objection, however, to your revealing anything you want to anyone you want about our meetings. I will not tape record these sessions without your permission. If you permit me to record a session, you may have a copy of the tape. I keep a written record of our contacts. The reason our sessions last fifty minutes instead of one hour is because I use the extra ten minutes to write notes about our last interview. These notes help me stick to our goals. It also helps us get started where we left off last time. These notes are confidential but I believe they are your property as well as mine. I will give you a copy of them, to do with as you please, whenever you request them. I will have to charge you for the costs of copying them and for the cost of any blank tape cassette I give you. There is one possible exception to our principle of confidentiality. I don't anticipate that this would ever happen and I hope it won't, but you should be warned of the possibility. In this state, the statutes require that I may have to testify in court about you if I am subpoenaed to do so. This could happen if the jurisdiction believed I had information that might reveal any criminal wrongdoing. In such a case, my records about you would also be reviewed in the court. I do not support this statute or interpretation by judges because of my respect for your privacy, no matter what the circumstances. However, I must also obey the law. If this ever happened, I would attempt to discuss with you beforehand any testimony I might be compelled to present. Again, the likelihood of this happening is extremely remote, but you deserve to be informed of the possibility.

My Background. I have been in private practice in this office since 1974. Before that I was on the staff of the Community Psychiatric Clinic as a psychotherapist for three years. My profession is psychology. I received my bachelor of science degree in psychology from the Southern Methodist University in Texas in 1968. I received my master's degree in social work (M.S.W.) from the National Catholic School of Social Service, Catholic University of America, in 1970. I received my Ph.D. degree from the University of Southern California. I have published several articles on my specialty, marital and family therapy. I am a member of the American Psychological Association, the American Orthopsychiatric Association, the American Group Psychotherapy Association, and the American Association of Marital and Family Therapists. I have also been lecturing on family therapy at the community college since 1977.

Our Agreement. You are the boss. I am working for you in your interests. You determine what your goals are and my role is to help you reach them. I may help you to define your goals or show you what the consequences of reaching these goals might be, but you have the last word on this. On the next page of this paper we will list all the goals we think there should be. We both agree that they can be changed at any time

Signature. We the undersigned have read this statement, understand and agree with its terms. We will both comply with all the points in this on our personal and professional honor. It is understood that our relationship will discontinue whenever these terms are not fulfilled by either of us. Otherwise we will continue to work together until the goals are reached or until we decide together to discontinue.

_____   _____   _____
(signature)   (date signed)   (signature)

Obviously, this agreement is not appropriate for every private practitioner, but something similar to it is useful for most. Making the terms of the agreement explicit, spelling out simply and objectively the requirements for both the therapist and the client, it is an important foundation of the transaction. Any subsequent misunderstandings are allayed by referring back to the agreement or to the goals at the end. The agreement touches on several of the controversial issues which face the private practitioner, such as insurance coverage, confidentiality, and time and expense. Several points addressed in this contract will be discussed in further detail in chapter 8 when the risks involved in practice are discussed.

LEASING OR BUYING

The private practitioner also needs to give careful thought to determining the best available way of financing the opening of his office. The costs of establishing and equipping a private practice are going to be considerable, and the initial return is likely to be inconsiderable. If the practitioner puchased all the barely needed equipment and furnishings for his solo office at once the cost could easily reach five figures. Buying a building in which to locate one's office, or purchasing the services of carpenters and the supplies needed to remodel, would greatly increase the initial costs. This is a considerable investment, especially when there is no proven formula for estimating the probable or even hoped-for return. Borrowing money to get started might be more difficult for some psychotherapists just beginning because of the uncertainty inherent in their venture. The psychotherapist, if he can get a loan for this purpose, will have to pay very high interest rates or points on the loan because of current economic conditions.

Leasing the equipment is an attractive alternative for many therapists, until they are in a better financial position. Most practitioners think nothing of leasing the building in which their offices are to be located, but haven't even considered the same possibility for equipment and furniture. This is unfortunate because there are major advantages. The most important is that the initial outlay is considerably reduced. The monthly fee for the rental of the equipment is totally tax deductible, as well as deductible from the overhead of the operation. Often the amount spent on the rent can be applied to purchase at a later time if the therapist decides he wants to retain the equipment. Another advantage is that leasing permits the therapist to experiment with different types of equipment or different styles of furnishings, easily changing them. Then, when he finds that something he has leased is most suitable for his needs he is able to purchase it or one like it.

In the long run, the costs of leasing are far greater than for outright purchases and the selection is sometimes less than that available to the outright purchasers. After the practitioner is established, he is most likely going to want to own his furniture and equipment. The purchase price of the items will be tax deductible and come from office overhead, and it is possible to depreciate these items each year as they wear out, adding considerably to one's tax savings.

Once these decisions have been made, once the private practitioner has established an office suitable for the work he will be doing, and once the physical aspects of his office are determined, he must plan a system of administration. The way he sets up the financial and client records, the bookkeeping system, the insurance program, the tax and retirement accounts, and many other elements of practice management will largely determine the viability of his chosen career.

FIVE

PREPARING FOR BUSINESS

BEFORE the private practitioner sees her first client she must establish a system for properly administering her operation. Once the office has been located and equipped it would be tempting to simply hang out the shingle and open the door to welcome the multitude who will seek her services. But many inevitable problems will be avoided with advance planning. A system for office administration should include an accounting and bookkeeping plan as well as an organization for keeping case records. The practitioner needs to think about involving other people in her practice, people like a secretary/receptionist, a janitor, an accountant, a management consultant, some resource professionals, and possibly an assistant or a partner. She must get insurance for herself and whomever else works with her. Health, income, and office liability insurance may be optional but malpractice insurance is not. Before the first client pays her her first practice dollar, she must look to keeping peace with the Internal Revenue Service, which gives private practitioners very close scrutiny. If she does begin to earn money from the practice, and if she wants to keep as much of it as possible from the IRS, she needs to think about investments and tax shelters. Of course there is also the need for retirement planning. Only after she decides about these factors does she consider her shingle. What should go on it? It could be just her name, or her office could have an organizational title. In sum, considerable thought must go into the administrative aspects of the practice as well as the service components. Preparation and adequate administration are necessary ingredients for success.

ACCOUNTING AND BOOKKEEPING SYSTEMS

Some therapists who are just starting out in private practice with only a few clients, little income, and a relatively simple operation, establish their accounting procedures very informally. In some cases, to cite the worst possible examples, therapists simply put cash receipts in their pocketbooks and make a note of them on the client's chart or in the appointment book. Only slightly better is taking the cash receipts to the bank and depositing them in a personal checking or savings account. These procedures are unacceptable. As the operation grows and becomes more complicated many problems will emerge. For example, there might be no one place where receipts and disbursements are kept. Clients will want information about their previous payments. Tax auditors will want to know how much money in the checking account came from the practice and how much came from other sources. The practitioner will want to know if her practice is supporting her or she is supporting the practice. Clearly, there is a better approach. Before any income is received, or for that matter before any expenses are paid, a bookkeeping system has to be established. This system should include (a) a receipts ledger, (b) a disbursements ledger, (c) an annual file, (d) an office checking account, (e) financial record sheets for each client, (f) an appointment book, (g) an office credit card, and (h) shared receipts-disbursements ledgers when the practitioner has partners.

The heart of the accounting system in the well-organized office is the ledger, which contains information about all income, all expenses, and itemized financial data about each active client (Baumback and Lawyer 1979). The simplest and most effective ledger is a loose-leaf notebook. One page in it will be the *receipts sheet*. It should contain columns for date of entry, source of income (client's name), amount of payment and how paid, whether by cash, check, or whatever. All practice income is kept on this sheet. Every payment is entered on a separate line, in ink, and preferably by a secretary or someone other than the practitioner. Entries should be continuous, with no lines left blank. The entries should be made immediately upon receipt. The office should have a safe special place, such as a locked box or safe, where all the checks and cash are kept, until time for depositing them. At certain predetermined intervals (every Friday morning, every evening just before bank closing time, etc.) the deposits are made. The entries in the receipts ledger are totaled after every deposit. The total and the deposit should be identical and the total amount of the deposit should be recorded, in ink, in the ledger. This procedure has many advantages. It shows at a glance what the income picture is and it provides a cross-check to assure that all money deposited and all money received are the same. The IRS deems this procedure the proper way to assure that the practitioner is reporting all her income (IRS 1982a). Writing in ink makes it difficult to alter the books, and continuous itemization makes it impossible to leave out any entries.

The *disbursements sheet* is kept in the loose-leaf notebook on the second page. Entries here are also dated, itemized, continuous, and in ink. Every time an office expense is *paid* an entry is made. The entry should not be made at the time the purchase is made, but only when the bill for it is paid. This follows the IRS principle about *when* a deduction is to be declared. The entry should indicate how payment is made, whether by check, cash with receipt, or credit card. The items to be included in this record are office expenses only and should not include anything that is for the personal use of the therapist. The best rule of thumb about what to include and exclude is the income tax criteria about what items are considered personal and what are considered business expenses (IRS 1982b). The disbursements are totaled at regular intervals, perhaps weekly or monthly, and also recorded in ink.

When each sheet for the income and disbursements is filled, all should be totaled and thereafter kept in the *annual file* of all financial information. The annual file can be a folder or box or large envelope which is kept in a safe place in the office. In it, during the course of the year, are kept all financial records of the office other than those still active in the account book. Any receipts, bills, financial statements, canceled checks for office expenses, ledger sheets, credit card bill copies, and anything else pertaining to the office will be placed there. The annual file does not, however, contain the financial records of each individual client. This information is better kept with the client's chart. This file clearly defines the office expenses and receipts, separate from the therapist's personal expenses or other sources of income. It affords a clear year-by-year look at her practice and is of inestimable importance when it comes to figuring taxes. At the end of each year this file is retired and a new one immediately replaces it. The income and disbursements ledgers are also tallied at the end of the year and included in the annual file, and new sheets are installed in the account book.

An *office checking account,* completely separate from the therapist's personal bank accounts, is another essential. It is important to keep all practice income and expenses separate from any other income and expenses. This is the only way to determine the true financial situation of the practice without an extensive and time-consuming audit. Taxation for an office practice is based on different considerations from personal finances, so it is unnecessarily complicated and hazardous to mix the two. If the therapist receives any money from a client, either by check or by cash, all of this sum must be deposited. At first, it might seem tempting to withhold some of the payments from deposit, especially cash payments. One might think that it is inconvenient, when funds are needed, to take cash in hand to the bank and then withdraw cash from the same bank. If deposits are not made, the further temptation might be to avoid declaring as income some of these funds, and thus be subjected to lower income tax payments. This is illegal and needlessly risky as well as dishonorable. More will be said about this in the discussion about money matters in chapter 7.

The office checking account will be used for paying all the expenses related to the practice. No expenses except those of the practice should be paid from this account. The private practitioner will occasionally make office purchases by cash or credit card, so it is important to retain all receipts for these items and place them in the annual file. This should be an exception, however, as very few practice expenses should be paid other than through the office account.

Once the deposits have cleared in the bank and the practice

expenses are paid, the therapist may then write checks to herself for her personal needs and profits. This is equivalent to the office paying her a salary for her services to the practice. The amount her practice pays her is then easily understood by auditors, tax collectors, investment advisers, and by the therapist herself as her net practice income.

A *financial record sheet for each client* is another efficient part of the accounting system and affords a logical billing procedure. The loose-leaf account book, in addition to having one page for receipts and another for disbursements, should contain a single page for each active client.

If the psychotherapist has more than just a few active clients, it is, of course, helpful to keep the client sheets in alphabetical order in the book. The sheet for each client can be a complete record of that person's billings and payments. Some practitioners use this sheet as a master record which is reproduced and sent to the client as a bill.

The sheets can be somewhat complicated if all the relevant financial information about the client is to be included, containing such things as insurance payments, when bills were submitted to the client and to the insurance company, when receipts were sent in, and so forth. Printing firms which specialize in stationery and office supplies usually have well worked out billing systems available for purchase by psychotherapists. Some practitioners, however, devise their own client financial sheets to meet the unique requirements of their own practices.

A typical accounting sheet contains space at the top for the client's name, address, and other factual information. Beneath that is a series of columns labled for the following items: date client seen, type of service, charge, total amount due, amount due from insurance company, amount due from client, amount paid by client, amount paid by insurance company, and date paid. If this sheet is reproduced and used as a bill, a final column might say, "Please pay amount in the last column." This procedure provides a thorough and continuous record of all the financial transactions between the therapist, the client, and any third-party payers.

Practitioners find it more convenient and practical to keep such sheets in the loose-leaf accounting book with the receipts sheet as long as the case is active. It is always preferable to record receipts in two separate places. Having the client finance record in the same book as the receipts sheet helps prevent mistakes. It also saves the therapist or her secretary from having to go through the client's case records to get financial information whenever it is needed. Then, when the case is closed and no longer financially active, the sheet may be removed from the accounting book and placed in the client's case record.

An *appointment book,* in addition to providing the practitioner with information about her schedule, can also be a helpful addition to her accounting system. The therapist can make a notation in the book whenever a client has paid or whenever an expense has been paid. The book can be a backup for information about any financial transaction. Actually, the practitioner would do well to maintain two appointment books. The primary one is kept in the therapist's possession at all times, and it is here all appointments are scheduled and all financial transactions are recorded. A secondary one should be kept in the office or the receptionist's desk. At the beginning of each day it is filled out from the primary book. Then, if the primary book is misplaced the existence of the secondary one prevents office chaos. The second one also gives the secretary an opportunity to know what the therapist's schedule is likely to be.

An *office credit card* is not essential, but many therapists find it useful. The card is used only for office expenses and thus can be an important documentation for auditors or for the therapist's own records. It is particularly useful when the therapist attends professional luncheons or practice-related conventions. Using the card for all expenses related to these meetings is much handier than carrying the office checkbook around. It is practical, though not imperative, to keep the card only for the purposes of the practice and use another one for personal expenditures.

When the therapist has a solo practice, her bookkeeping is somewhat less complicated than when she is in partnership. If she has a partner, then additional records must be kept. The partners will have individual practice expenses for which they alone are responsible, as well as joint expenses which would be divided between them. It is useful in partnerships to maintain a disbursements sheet for the shared expenses. This sheet is kept in the office and is accessible to the partners at all times. Whenever the partners agree that a disbursement is considered a shared expense, whoever paid it makes the appropriate entry. Then, at the end of each month or week, the partners can settle with each other. At the end of the year, each partner gets a copy of the shared record for her individual records. Many practitioners who share office expenses find it expedient to have one of their number make all the joint payments and then be reimbursed by the other partners on a regular, perhaps monthly, basis. This eliminates confusion, forgotten bills, and duplications. It is important, however, that the partners have a high degree of trust and confidence in each other for the system to work.

SOLO PRACTICE OR PARTNERSHIP?

In part-time practice it seems that more therapists have their offices alone, but more full-time independent practitioners have partnerships. The part-time therapist often works alone because of the more casual nature of her practice. Often she is seeing clients in a home office on weekends or evenings, or renting after-hours space in someone else's office. The full-time private practitioner is more likely to have a partnership because it affords her considerable advantages, few disadvantages, and because it is a way of keeping up her own morale much more effectively than if she worked alone (Bruce 1962).

Partnerships may be formal or informal, consisting of everything from sharing all income, expenses, responsibilities, risks, and rewards to simply sharing an office and some expenses. Even the latter is important, however, because sharing expenses is a major attraction for partnerships. Overhead costs are reduced considerably when the partners use the same waiting rooms, office suite, secretary, telephone, and cleaning service. Sharing often makes it possible for the partners to employ a secretary/receptionist where one professional might not have the income or the needed work to justify employing someone.

If the therapist has a partner she also has a handy consultant, supervisor, or objectifier in the other person. No one can be so skillful that she can't benefit from discussing her cases with another professional person. Merely describing a situation can be a learning experience, and the impressions, advice, and other feedback that the partner provides are invaluable. Practitioners who work together often spend a small amount of time daily or weekly in mutual consultation, in order to enhance their practice skills. The partner is also a good source of moral support on those frequent occasions when the therapist is immersed in problems and worrisome clients.

Very often partners work out arrangements whereby they can cover for each other in emergency situations when one is unavailable. This permits the practitioner to go to meetings, take vacations, or get a peaceful night's rest knowing that her clients would be in good hands if the need arose.

Partnerships enable the individual practitioners to reach out further into the community too. If the partners constitute a clinic or private agency for work in some special area of concern or community interest, they usually can make a greater impact than could one therapist attempting the same thing alone. If the partnership is made up of mental health professionals, the treatment approaches can effectively utilize team approaches in work with the same clients. This provides great flexibility, efficiency, and effectiveness with some people (Barker and Briggs 1969). If the partners are from different disciplines there is an opportunity for stimulating exchanges of points of view and different ways of approaching similar problems that enhances the effectiveness of both (Kane 1974b). But the most important advantage of partnerships is the companionship they provide. The therapist in solo practice, seeing no one all day but clients, unable to let herself go or be herself with anyone, can burn out very rapidly (Maslach 1976). Those who don't burn out can become jaded, and often aren't stimulated to attempt new ideas or learn new techniques to the extent that one in partnership usually does. Even if the therapist is busy all day, with little time to confer with her partner, the mere presence of the other person in the office suite is a stimulus for thought and learning and a source of comfort and security.

Needless to say, partnerships aren't for everyone, and they can lead to problems between the therapists. It is difficult for many therapists to find someone compatible in work habits, values, goals, taste in office decor, and personality. It is especially difficult to find someone who is also willing to make the necessary financial agreements and working arrangements.

Some problems are inevitable. For example, if the partners have a single telephone or secretary they might wish to use at the same time there can be controversy. Or if one therapist specializes in working with clients who require more office expenditures than the other partner's clients there can be some uncomfortable moments. For example, if one therapist sees many children who tend to make noise and inflict more wear and tear on the waiting room furniture, the other therapist might resent having to share maintenance and furnishing costs equally. Some partners have some trouble establishing between them lines of responsibility or determining whose viewpoint will be respected more in case of disputes.

Bookkeeping can cause some problems too. If the arrangement is to share expenses only, it is necessary to keep a running log of expenditures that is always available to the partners. There must be clear guidelines between the partners about what expenses will be shared and what ones will not. There are some, but few, therapists who have partnerships in which income as well as costs is shared equally. Such a policy is fraught with danger unless very clear guidelines are established. This risk is that one therapist may feel the other is not sharing the burden equally but is reaping equal rewards, or not working as hard to increase the clientele. Most practitioners seem to feel that the best partnerships are those where some expenses and no income are shared.

It is worthwhile to put partnership agreements in writing, more for purposes of clarification than as binding contractual arrangements. If the partners need to rely on a written contract because they don't have trust and respect for each other, the partnerships won't survive long anyway. When roles are explicit and the partners are compatible, the arrangement has much more to commend it than solo practice.

OFFICE EMPLOYEES

If money were no object, the therapist might want to hire a staff to assist her with all the things that need doing in her office. Such a staff could include a secretary to transcribe all her case dictation into the client's charts and keep all the records in order; an office manager to oversee the running of the office, obtain supplies, hire and fire other employees, and maintain personnel insurance and tax records; a bookkeeper to record all receipts and disbursements, to pay the staff, to contact insurance companies about reimbursement, to contact clients about payment, and to contact former clients about paying overdue bills; a janitor to maintain cleanliness; a cotherapist to give the therapist a respite in her work with couples and groups; an assistant therapist to handle less complicated cases and to provide indirect services; a supervisor for the assistant and the cotherapist; and a regular consultant to give advice on dealing with certain cases. There are few if any private psychotherapy practitioners who would have such an operation. Even if it were affordable and efficacious, operating this way would seem too much like the bureaucracy-laden organization the therapist probably wants to avoid. In any event, there would not be work enough for such a staff.

Most private psychotherapy practitioners have one or no employees. When they have one it is usually a part-time secretary/ receptionist, an all-around person who assumes a variety of roles. Keeping track of the books, mailing out the bills, typing occasional letters and case records, greeting clients, and scheduling appointments can be done by one efficient person for two professionals in less than full time. While many therapists feel that such an expense is beyond their circumstances, employing such a person, even for a few hours weekly, is well worth the cost. It is a resource which pays for itself financially as well as in the therapist's efficiency. Other jobs can be done by the secretary, the therapist, the building maintenance people, or someone hired for a very few hours weekly. Cotherapists and assistants will not be hired unless the psychotherapist is well established and has a client caseload that is more than she can handle. When that happens and she has decided to employ another professional, the new person will be self-supporting and add to the organization.

MANAGEMENT CONSULTANTS AND INDEPENDENT ACCOUNTANTS

Before the therapist opens her office or after it is in full swing she may want to obtain the services of an accountant and/or a management consultant. A certified public accountant is as useful to the private practitioner as to any business person and the modest cost of employing one is worth the money in tax savings alone. CPAs charge roughly the same per hour as does the private psychotherapist. Even if the therapist relishes keeping her own books and preparing her own accounts and tax returns, it is still useful to employ an accountant. In preparing tax returns, for example, the accountant can be more objective, find greater deductions, and set up the forms for quarterly withholding of estimated taxes and for FICA withholding. The IRS is less likely to audit the practitioners whose forms are prepared by CPAs than those who do the forms themselves (Lasser 1982).

An independent management consultant might be another valuable resource for the therapist. The management consultant usually can prepare one's taxes and perform all the services that are provided by CPAs but also has other roles. Consultants deal with tax problems and show how to increase clientele, utilize income more efficiently, and improve work flow. They also provide advice about investments, retirement planning, and expenses. They can be consulted one time only or periodically. Many therapists employ management consultant firms, made up of CPAs, and have one one-hour meeting each quarter during the year, plus somewhat more time when income tax preparations are done.

TAXES

The private practitioner has a complicated procedure awaiting her in preparing federal and state income taxes, property taxes on the office equipment, and sometimes professional taxes. Her income is not simply reported on a W-2 form from an employer, but comes in numerous small checks and cash payments from her clients. Her deductible expenses are also extensive. At the beginning of each year she must estimate her anticipated net practice income and pay federal income taxes each quarter. The estimate must be fairly accurate because if the therapist's income is much higher than what she guesses, she might have to pay a penalty at the end of the year as well as to make up the difference. If she lives in a state which has income taxes then she must follow the same procedure for the state tax comptroller.

The therapist who is just starting out in practice may have a difficult time estimating her income in advance, so it is possible for her to revise the estimate each quarter and pay more or less accordingly. The therapist's income is likely to change dramatically in the first few years after entering private practice, either up or down. It is possible to use the federal tax approved procedure called income averaging in which, for tax purposes, any great increases in income can be spread over several years. This is also useful when the practice income is subject to great fluctuations from one year to the next. The federal tax system also has provisions for self-employed workers to contribute to their social security (OASDHI) insurance as part of their tax forms and payments.

There are many areas where the therapist can save on her taxes if she is aware of appropriate deductions. It is in her interest to get a good tax guide, which details these possibilities (*U.S. Master Tax* 1982). Whether or not she uses an accountant or management consultant, it is important to learn as much as possible about the tax system. Many psychotherapists are surprised to see how many legal opportunities there are for independent business people to minimize their tax contributions.

The federal government encourages business in the United States through a variety of tax incentives and deduction opportunities that are not available to the wage or salary earner. For example, it is possible to deduct the costs of traveling from one's home to the practice office, if the therapist has another job in addition to her private practice. The purchase of her furniture and equipment is completely deductible, but the therapist may be better off depreciating it. If she deducts it entirely during the year of purchase her tax rate might be lower that year but much higher in subsequent years when she doesn't make large purchases. In depreciation, the IRS allows the therapist to determine, within prescribed limits, how long the item is likely to last before needing replacement, and then considering that each year it depreciates in value by a proportion of that total amount. Thus, deductions are balanced out over the years.

If the therapist owns the building in which her office is located, she is permitted to depreciate the building, or that part of it which contains the office, at a more favorable rate than is the case for residences. This can add up to considerable tax savings. The building may be increasing in value but for tax purposes it is seen as declining in worth each year.

Some localities have property taxes or professional taxes on those who maintain businesses or professional offices. Local tax assessors may periodically visit the business or office, estimate the value of the furnishings and equipment, and send the therapist a tax bill. A small but growing number of municipalities are instituting a tax on professionals. This tax is above and beyond the professional's state and federal income tax. Sometimes, it is a flat annual rate determined by the practitioner's discipline, location, size of her office staff, or net income. Most professional taxes are based on a percentage of net practice income during the year. Many professional groups have contested the imposition of such taxes, and cases are being litigated in some communities now. It seems likely, however, that the tax will be levied in more states. Tax rates imposed by states are likely to increase also. They are usually simple to prepare since they almost invariably are modeled on the federal tax.

Private practitioners are approached from time to time by those who would help them shelter some of their income from taxation. Investment counselors and those who sell advice, programs, ideas, or shares in opportunities to make more money and keep what one has already earned are plentiful and highly competitive. They range from highly reputable and traditionally conservative "banker types" to rather sordid, scheming, high pressure "huckster types." The latter group often seems to be enticing practitioners to put their money into apartment complexes, cattle on the hoof, oil wells, whiskey that is still aging, and other commodities which presumably can be depreciated. The pitch is that the therapist's annual taxes are reduced because of the supposed depreciating value of the commodity; but then when the commodity is sold at a value higher than when purchased, it is taxed at the lower capital gains rate.

Some of these tax shelters have considerable merit and most people who have considerable income use various shelters of this type to lower their taxes. However, if the therapist seeks to reduce her taxes she is strongly advised to avoid any promoter who initiates the contact. She is likely to need reputable advice on tax shelter strategies, but her management consultant or banker can refer her to an established firm which specializes in these matters. She should consider strategies for investment at the same time she is considering tax shelter possibilities. Often the same advisors provide information about both. A sound investment program is important, but no more so than for the practitioner who is not in private practice.

RETIREMENT PLANNING

The best tax shelter currently available is the establishment of a retirement program. Not only does such a program enable the therapist to set aside income for use in her retirement days, but it also reduces the tax rate during her income-producing years. Private practitioners tend to work past traditional retirement ages, but even those most determined to remain active can be faced with senescence, obsolescence, reduced effectiveness, reduced clientele, changed interests, or burnout, and be obliged to pull down the shingle sooner than anticipated. Working for a social or government agency which has a retirement plan might reduce the importance of saving for retirement, but in private practice such planning is imperative.

Retirement planning rests on two cornerstones, the Keogh Plan and OASDHI insurance. Keogh is designed for self employed workers and thus is better for therapists than the IRA programs which were liberalized in 1982. The Keogh Plan enables psychotherapists in full- or part-time private practice, like all self-employed Americans, to formulate and control their own retirement plans, and benefit from federal tax incentives in the process. The plan, known as HR-10 or the Keogh Act of 1962, as amended in 1974, allows the private practitioner to set aside up to 15 percent of her annual *net* income earned in the practice, up to $15,000 per year as of 1982. The amount set aside is reduced from the practitioner's taxable income for the year, and any money earned from this account, whether it comes from interest or capital appreciation, is not taxed until retirement.

The practitioner cannot begin to withdraw from this account until she reaches age fifty-nine and one-half, and she must begin making withdrawals before reaching seventy and one-half. It is very difficult to withdraw funds prior to age fifty-nine and one-half, and when an exception is made after an exceedingly tedious process, it is penalized at the rate of 10 percent of the amount withdrawn. This penalty is levied through federal taxes. In addition, the amount withdrawn is also taxed as income for the year in which it is withdrawn. Penalties of up to 50 percent are levied on those who don't begin withdrawing by age seventy and one-half. This is to discourage people from using Keogh to build up an estate for inheritance rather than retirement purposes.

The retirement plan can be established at any age prior to retirement, and the annual contribution can vary from nothing up to the 15 percent (or $15,000) each year. Payment can be made in small installments or in a lump sum any time up to April 15 of the following year. When the account is started, contributions must be made in the calendar year for which it is applied, but thereafter the practitioner can have three and one-half extra months into the following year in which to make the contributions. It is possible, and relatively easy, to transfer the retirement account from one institution to another without penalty as long as the funds remain inaccessible to the practitioner ("Individual Retirement" 1982).

The most difficult decision about the establishment of a Keogh retirement plan concerns the type of institution or program to use to manage the account. It can be a very safe, conservative bank or insurance company, or a moderately adventurous mutual fund, or a highly speculative program dealing with securities, commodities, or real estate. The plan itself is relatively simple to establish if the practitioner chooses an institution which already has a model Keogh program. Most banks, mutual funds, insurance programs, and many other financial institutions have model plans. The practitioner can set up her own plan without going through any financial institution, but this is a cumbersome and time-consuming process and thereafter subject to very close and constant scrutiny from the IRS. As with all investments, the therapist should evaluate her own unique needs and interests and shop around for the vehicle that comes closest to matching them.

If the practitioner decides to start her Keogh account with an established institution she should look beyond the very competitive advertising campaigns that each of them seems to use to attract new customers. Most ads emphasize the same things anyway: annual income taxes will be lower through deferral to retirement when income is likely to be lower, and the institution is stable and venerable. Such assertions, while important and valid, do little to convince the discerning practitioner to put her money with one institution rather than another. This is because all the plans are virtually identical. The tax benefits are based on the federal program, not the institution's program. Federal regulation is extremely rigorous, so the stability and security of the institution may be virtually taken for granted.

The difficult decision has more to do with the degree of investment risk and potential return one is willing to accept. The practitioner may, for example, establish her account with a bank or insurance program which pays 5 percent or less a year in interest. If inflation continues at several times the rate of interest, the retirement fund is essentially losing money. Establishing the account in a more risky venture, say the stock market, mutual funds, money market funds, or commercial paper may possibly

lead to greater appreciation than through savings institution interest payments, but there is also a greater risk of losing one's
capital investment ("Savings" 1981). There is also risk of being
managed by a broker who buys and sells, each time reaping a
commission for his services. This unfortunate practice among
some brokers, called "churning," can decimate a retirement account that isn't carefully watched over by the practitioner.

Money market funds, certificates of deposit, and high yield
treasury bills have a high degree of security and pay rates of interest that approximate the current inflation rates, which at least
gives the practitioner the assurance that she isn't losing ground
in her retirement savings program, but they are not very liquid.
Most objective business consultants advise against using whole-
life insurance in retirement plans (Consumers Union 1978). They
provide a low yield on the investment and thus are not very effective for purposes of retirement. Most practitioners would do
better meeting their insurance needs with term insurance outside
the retirement program and using their Keogh contribution in a
more productive investment.

Many practitioners believe in a diversified program in which
the account has some investments in safe, low-yielding programs,
such as certificates of deposit and Treasury paper, and some
more liquid investments as well. A diversified investment program means that no more than 70 percent nor less than 25 percent of assets should be kept in any one type of holding. The retirement plan has no room for speculative low-yield stocks. The
practitioner would be better off keeping such investments in her
personal portfolio where capital loss becomes a tax deduction
and any realized profit is taxed at advantageous capital gains
rates (Harsham 1979). Regardless of how much trust and respect
the fund manager merits, the practitioner must always keep an
eye on the fund. She should know at all times what assets are in
it, and at what rate they are growing or declining. This nest egg
is too vital to trust its safety to someone else.

When retirement time comes, the practitioner has several options about the Keogh account. She can withdraw the entire
amount in one lump sum and pay income taxes on that entire

amount in one year. Or she can income average the taxes on this lump sum over the next several years. Or she can withdraw allocated amounts each year from the account and pay taxes only on the amount withdrawn. Or she can purchase an insurance-based annuity, which for one lump sum can give her a fixed guaranteed income for the rest of her or her spouse's life. She would pay taxes only on the annual amount received from the annuity. The advantage of the annuity is that she need never worry about outliving the amount of her retirement fund. The disadvantage is that when she or her spouse dies the payments stop even if they are far less than the amount paid into the annuity fund. Unlike OASDHI, commercial retirement programs, industrial retirements, and insurance annuities, the Keogh account holder's heirs are entitled to all the funds, after inheritance taxes, that remain in the account unless the fund was used to purchase the annuity.

The second cornerstone in retirement planning for the private practitioner is Old Age, Survivor's, Disability and Health Insurance, or social security. Private practitioners, like almost all other Americans except federal government employees, make regular contributions to the system based on their incomes. The contributions are filed and paid by the practitioner, and every other independent business person, as she pays her income tax using schedule C in form 1040. Social security tax and an annual report must also be made in behalf of any employees. The employer must match any social security deductions made for employees. The benefit amount from social security is based on earned income and contributions and is in no way contingent on other assets, including Keogh retirement monies. The amount of contributions one must pay to the OASDHI program has been increasing dramatically in recent years in order to keep the program solvent, and many people, especially younger professionals in high-earning brackets, suspect that the program is not a good investment for them as individuals. However, the program isn't optional and doesn't exist simply as an investment, but as a needed device for the minimum protection of the nation's populace (Ball 1978).

INSURANCE

The private practitioner must be insured against *financial loss,* which can come from a variety of origins. Unless she or her spouse has employment in an organization which has group coverage for health, income loss, or hospitalization, she might have to obtain coverage through more expensive programs. Virtually all psychotherapists belong to professional associations in which there are group health and hospitalization plans which are underwritten by private insurance companies. These are relatively low cost, but the extent and amount of even maximum coverages leaves the policy holder vulnerable to many possibilities. Many private practitioners supplement this insurance by purchasing individual coverage for their families through other companies. Many practitioners are covered by their employed spouses' policies and many others take part-time consulting jobs with organizations which offer group health coverage. In addition to insuring for medical and hospital expenses, the private practitioner needs to insure against loss of income. When she gets sick and stops seeing clients, her practice income completely stops. But office overhead continues to be just as expensive, whether she is working with clients or not. She cannot just shut down the operation and resume it when her health is better. Protection against loss of income due to illness is as important for the private practitioner as hospitalization and medical insurance.

The therapist also needs *liability insurance* for the office. This is not the same as malpractice insurance. Rather it is to cover against such possibilities as injuries to clients, maintenance people, or whoever enters the premises. This insurance should also cover damage or loss of property in the office. It is equivalent to a homeowner's policy. Since risks of this type in a private practitioner's office are rather remote, this form of insurance is inexpensive. Some homeowner's policies can be expanded to include office coverage, as well as loss due to burglary, weather damage, vandalism, or similar occurrences. These policies must be individualized and the practitioner should discuss her needs with an insurance agent even before she opens her office.

Malpractice coverage is another must. The group coverage

available through psychotherapists' professional associations is not expensive unless the therapist is a psychiatrist, although psychiatrist's premiums are lower than those of other medical specialists. The therapist should get the maximum amount possible and may even wish to supplement it with coverage elsewhere. Relatively few charges of malpractice have been successfully prosecuted against nonmedical psychotherapists. Perhaps some of this is due to the fact that psychotherapy is still so ill defined that it is difficult to litigate against its malpractice.

The therapist whose conduct with her clients is consistently within the framework of the code of ethics of her profession is minimizing the chances of losing a malpractice suit, but there are many situations in which the therapist can find herself having to defend against malpractice even if her behavior was within the ethical boundaries (Pope, Simpson, and Weiner 1978). More discussion about these risk situations will be found in chapter 8. The therapist should never attempt to see a client unless she is sure that her malpractice coverage is current, and even then she must exercise some caution if she is to avoid malpractice litigation. The therapist should not reveal to a client that she has malpractice insurance and certainly not indicate the amount of coverage she has. It is unpleasant to contemplate such possibilities, but seeing what happens all too frequently to members of other professions is ample reason to remain cautious and covered.

PROFESSIONAL INCORPORATIONS

Many private practitioners, especially in larger partnerships, establish professional corporations. Doing so is a somewhat complicated process which is expensive, requires legal assistance, and requires that the practitioner file corporate as well as individual returns each year. However, the advantages of incorporating make these inconveniences worthwhile for some. A major reason for incorporating is that more of the practice income can be set aside, held in the corporation assets, and therefore not taxed as personal income. The major asset of the corporation is, of course, the practitioner, so the corporation can pay to insure her out of its funds. The professional corporation also enables the practitioner in certain circumstances to set aside greater amounts for retirement than the $15,000 maximum now allowed in the Keogh program. But incorporating does not mean, as some seem to think, that the practitioner can have her corporation pay for most of her expenses, such as a car and fuel for it, cabin cruisers, and summer homes owned by the corporation. As a matter of fact, most management consultants indicate that unless the therapist's gross practice revenue is well over $50,000 annually, incorporating is not advantageous (Kilgore 1975). If the revenue is much below that figure, the expense and complications make incorporating a disadvantage. The only other reason for incorporating if revenue is less is that the members of a partnership wish to maintain a corporate identity. If the practitioner employs a management consultant, she can obtain the information which is specifically applicable to her about incorporating. In any event, it is not essential that she make this decision until after she has gotten well established as a private practitioner. The decision to incorporate can be made any time in the future.

THE CLIENT'S CASE RECORD

Another policy decision the therapist should make before seeing her first private client concerns the procedure she will use in her case recording. The case record is indispensable for any psychotherapist or other helping professional, even those with flawless memories, because in addition to storing factual data the record also gives focus, direction, and clarification to the transaction (McKane 1975). It seems even more critical for the private practitioner than for the agency worker to maintain thorough and efficient case records on all her clients. The record is going to be the private therapist's supervisor, her consultant, and her objectifier. In private practice she is likely to be more vulnerable to many problems and controversies with clients, insurance companies, and social organizations than would be the case if she worked under an institutional umbrella. The case record is going to be her major line of defense in any of these disputes. Many of the helping professions explicitly require that their members maintain thorough documentation and recording of each contact with their clients. The codes of ethics of some psychotherapy disciplines do not specifically state that record-keeping is required, though they indicate that clients must have reasonable access to whatever records are kept (NASW 1980). Perhaps it is taken for granted that case recording will be done, but it should explicitly be considered unethical for the therapist not to keep some type of ongoing record of the work with each of her clients.

The therapist uses her own judgment about what types of data and formats the case records will include. She is not bound by any agency policy about case records, so she is able to make better use of her own individual style and method. Some therapists use thorough process recording in their own shorthand, while others are highly selective about specific relevant facts. Some include information about the business aspects of the therapist-client transaction, and others keep the personal information and business data separate. Whatever style one uses, most therapists use a "face sheet" for keeping the most basic and objective facts about the client. Each private practitioner should develop her own face sheet form and fill it out on each client in the initial meeting. The information would include the client's name, address, telephone numbers, name of spouse, names of children and others living in the home, employer's name and address, educational background, name of family physician, date of last physical examination, names and dates of any previous contact with other helping professionals, names of any diagnosed current diseases, a list of current symptoms or problems and the date of their onset, and any other information that is relevant to the area of the therapist's specialization. For example, if the therapist deals primarily with alcoholics, information about the drinking history of the client or that of his progenitors may be included. Or if the therapist deals with children having school problems, some information may be included on the face sheet about the academic background of the child and his family. The face sheet is then stapled to the front side of the client's chart and used thereafter for ready reference.

As to the contents of the case record, many private practitioners are now using a modified version of the Problem Oriented Medical Record (POMR) format developed by Dr. Lawrence Weed in 1969. The method was developed to better facilitate assessments of care for physicians and to enable the information in the record to be computerized. It is particularly useful in task-centered and behavioral modification methods but also works well in the other forms and levels of intervention. Some therapists refer to the modified system as the Problem Oriented Record (POR) (Kane 1974a). It contains four elements, the data base, the complete problem list, the initial plans, and the progress notes. The first three of these components are organized in the initial interview sessions and the fourth represents the ongoing summary.

The data base material may include information gathered from various people in the client's background, and consists of such things as medical history, laboratory reports, social history, and school records. The problem list is compiled by the therapist and placed in the front of the chart immediately beneath the fact sheet. All the client's problems are listed and assigned a number. The initial plan contains the diagnostic considerations, therapeutic plans, and methods which the therapist and client establish as means to reach the goal of eliminating or reducing the problems.

The bulk of the POR will be the fourth component, the progress records. Unlike traditional progress records in which all factual information, opinion, and observation are combined, the POR progress notes are divided into four distinct sections: subjective, objective, assessment, and plans. The progress notes are dated and indicate the title and number of the problem which is being considered. The therapist's entries are grouped under four sections: subjective statements by the client, objective findings, therapist's assessment, and plans. For purposes of abbreviation in the record, only the first letter of these four headings is placed in the margin; they form the acronym SOAP.

The practitioner writes the date of the interview, in the margin writes S (for subjective), and then lists all the factual data which the client presented during that session. Then beside the O (objective) designation the practitioner writes her observations about the client—the mannerisms, appearance, ways of interacting, and attitude. This is the therapist's description of the client's behavior. The next area is designated *A* (assessment) and includes the diagnosis and any statement about the psychosocial meaning of the client's behavior or situation. Finally next to *P* (plan) category is the therapist's statement to indicate where the client is going and what methods are going to be employed to get there. All tasks on which the client is going to work during the subsequent period are listed here, as are all agreements.

The amount of time it takes to record this way is possibly less than is required for the less structured traditional way, once the therapist becomes accustomed to it. Each session can have a SOAP entry to constitute the process recording, and the data base, complete problem list, and initial plans list can be added to (with dates added as the new entries are included). This recording system, while it takes no longer to use, gives considerable focus to the work and makes for much more efficiency. It is reasonable to give copies of the record to the client whenever they are requested, and using this format makes it possible to feel more comfortable about being open, since objective data are separated from subjective material (Houghkirk 1977).

ANNOUNCING THE OPENING

Tradition and to some extent professional codes of ethics have decreed that the fee-for-service practitioner should be discreet and low keyed in getting out the word that she is now available to provide services. The most conservative and traditional way of making the announcement is to print and distribute 4″ by 5″ announcement cards which usually say something like:

Janet L. Young, M.D., Psychiatrist
Announces the Opening of her Office for
the Practice of Psychotherapy with Children

1100 West Twelfth Street—Suite 1001
New York, New York 10011

(212) 433-1121   By Appointment

The cards are usually sent to one's friends, social acquaintances, members of various professional associations in the same neighborhood, and anyone else who might be considered a referral source. Most send such cards to their former employer, former clients, other social and community agencies, crisis centers, hotlines, and medical institutions. Practitioners generally and realistically do not expect that these cards will lead to a plethora of referrals. The announcements are merely the initial step one takes to become known and must be followed up by other activities.

This traditional way of making the announcement was based on the rationale that anything more was the same as advertising. The simple announcement would lead other professionals to make referrals based on their assessment of the practitioner's credentials. The announcement cards, therefore, are not designed to be eye-catching or flashy. While it is possible that an ostentatious announcement card may be remembered by the recipient, it seems just as likely that the therapist will be remembered as being someone who may be unprofessional or more inclined to unethical practice.

There are other ways of announcing one's opening that may be more personalized as well as more effective. Personalized letters of introduction, written by or in behalf of the therapist have been used with considerable success by some therapists. Also the use of pamphlets and printed brochures describing one's services in attractive detail can be useful. Therapists just starting out usually keep an ample supply of business cards handy which they pass out to people with whom they come in contact. The repetition of the message is more effective than the message itself.

Personal letters are not easily written to everyone who may be interested in knowing that the therapist has opened for practice. Doing so is not a cost-effective way of announcing oneself. However, carefully pinpointing a small number of people with whom the therapist hopes to establish a working relationship can be very useful. A few letters, written to key physicians, lawyers, teachers, social workers, and selected others who might eventually become good referral sources can be far more effective than announcement cards, even though they won't reach nearly as many people. But they won't reach anyone unless the letters are very short, pointed, and attractive. They should be typed and contain a personal reference to the recipient of the letter. They should emphasize that quality or skill which the practitioner possesses that is likely to be of most relevance to the recipient. They can be accompanied by the less personal announcement card and/or a business card. An example:

> Dear Mr. Jones,
>
> I have heard that your legal practice includes work with divorces and family breakdown. You have a reputation for great skill and integrity in such work. I have just opened an office near you at _____ and am planning on working with couples who are experiencing conflicts in their marriages and with their families. I am a psychotherapist and registered nurse-practitioner who has specialized in this field by extensive graduate education and ten years' experience at the _____ agency. I aspire to achieve a reputation for knowledge and integrity as you have done. I hope to send some of my clients to you for legal services and to communicate with you in person about them. I hope you will feel free to contact me anytime about these people. Looking forward to meeting you and possibly working with you, I am
>
> Sincerely yours,
Kathleen Tadewald, R.N., M.A.

One does not need to be very perceptive to note the implicit request in such a letter, that one hopes to receive referrals. But since it is only implied it gives the recipient an opportunity to respond or not, without a feeling of pressure. Such a letter is not likely to lead to many referrals and should not be expected to. It is just another in a series of reminders of the presence of the therapist. It must be supplemented as time goes on with more compelling reasons for making a referral.

Printed brochures and pamphlets have also been used by psychotherapy private practitioners to announce the opening of their offices, especially in group practices. The pamphlets are usually large enough to permit the therapist to describe in some detail what services are being offered, often at what cost, and to include information about the qualifications of the persons providing the service. They are sometimes printed on glossy, colorful paper with bold print, and sometimes even with pictures or graphics. Pamphlets tend to be seen as being in poor taste if they merely describe an individual practitioner, but if they describe a range of services offered by a group of workers they seem more tasteful and effective. Printing costs for such material are not great and a widespread distribution is possible. Sending pamphlets at bulk business rates means that the distribution costs are moderate also. Many recipients keep a file of such brochures so that they have a ready reference file when they want to refer someone. Some practitioners send a small packet of the pamphlets to selected persons in the hope that they will be able to give them to clients who may want to consider the practitioner's services.

Personal telephone calls are also used to announce the psychotherapist's opening. It is important to pinpoint the recipients of these contacts too. A phone call, followed by a pamphlet or announcement card, could go to all the organizations in the area that keep referral lists. If the therapist notifies these groups and requests that her name be included on the list it is a convenience to the organization called as well as to any potential client.

Organizations and institutions which might maintain such lists are many. They include hospital emergency rooms, where people go when they have anxiety episodes or crises but don't require hospitalization, and legal aid bureaus, where people impulsively call for help to get a divorce or try to disown their children and the legal staff realizes that legal services aren't what the caller needs. Guidance departments of colleges and high schools often see students for assistance with emotional problems or decisions about family crises, but find that the department staff isn't able to provide such services. Mental hospital social service units keep referral lists too because they deal with patients who are about to be discharged and need aftercare or follow-up of a kind which the hospital is unable to provide.

Sometimes juvenile court staffs also have referral lists because they recognize a need for more intense family intervention and treatment than is provided through the court staff. Many families prefer to go elsewhere and avoid the punitive connotations of that setting. County welfare offices and public social service agencies are another possibility, because they are often contacted by people who, because of too much income, or because they have not lived in the area long enough, are ineligible for the public service. Public and private employment bureaus keep referral lists because their staffs see applicants who are having trouble getting and maintaining suitable employment because of some emotional or social difficulties which can be handled by social service intervention. Personnel departments of large businesses sometimes maintain lists.

Many types of organizations keep the names of people to whom referrals can be made. The crucial thing is for the therapist who is entering private practice to get on as many lists as possible, even before she opens the door to greet her first client.

SIX

BUILDING A CLIENTELE

PSYCHOTHERAPY has an image problem which the individual practitioner must overcome, or at least deal with, in order to be viable in a business sense. Therapists are seen as being excessively costly or as catering only to the needs of the affluent. They are often seen as being not very helpful or in some cases harmful. Many believe psychotherapy or mental health practitioners are deranged or obsessed with sex or overtly seductive to clients. Therapists are often put in the same category, in the minds of many potential consumers, with practitioners of the occult—with palmists, astrologers, and witch doctors. In view of the origins of psychotherapy this is perhaps understandable. Those potential consumers who have a more enlightened perception about psychotherapy and its practitioners are still faced with many confusions and uncertainties. Many find it difficult to decide if therapy is really the answer to their particular problems. Such a question is certainly valid in light of problems psychotherapy has in objectively demonstrating its effectiveness.

Those who do accept that it has something to offer are still faced with another quandary: which of the many types of therapy to select. There are a staggering number of therapies being offered, and the number keeps growing dramatically. Each therapy can and does cite statistics and testimonials ad nauseum to show the consumer that it is most worthy (Garfield 1981). Thus, consumers are confronted with many subtle and hard-sell approaches by various therapy proponents.

Those who provide the various forms of psychotherapy are becoming increasingly competitive. They are devoting considerable energies and resources toward building a substantial clientele.

Advertising is becoming more prominent, and chain-store therapy organizations are more prevalent. The number of people and organizations which are providing psychotherapy services is growing at a rate far in excess of the population growth, and even faster than the growth in the number of problems addressed by psychotherapy. The time will come, if it hasn't already arrived, when the number of psychotherapy practitioners in independent work will be greater than the demand for them. This will result in difficult adjustment problems for many therapists, especially for those who have not learned the intricacies of building and maintaining a clientele.

What are the skills involved in doing this? The psychotherapist cannot depend solely upon the fact that he is well-trained, highly skilled, competent, or honest to be assured of having a sizable clientele. These are necessary prerequisites, of course, but they are not in themselves sufficient. It helps to belong to the more established mental health professions, particularly psychiatry and psychology, but this is not sufficient either (Wilensky 1977). Psychiatrists as a group have been the most successful psychotherapy discipline in gaining public sanction and referrals, but even they have been expressing concern about the potential decline in their referrals ("Annual Report" 1980). The psychotherapy and counseling professions which are of more recent vintage or those whose traditional role in the public consciousness has been institutional have had an even more difficult time obtaining referrals. Many of these professions, such as clergy, nursing, social work, and counseling, have not been able to get public licensing to practice their version of psychotherapy in all states. They have been even less successful in getting insurance companies to reimburse them for providing psychotherapy services.

Part of this phenomenon is due to the inability of these professions to establish exclusive responsibility for anything that is not done by some other professional group. If exclusive responsibility is established it is usually accompanied by public sanction in the form of licensing. A license is required in Illinois to shoe horses, and in Maryland to dig wells, and in North Carolina to deal in scrap tobacco, but psychotherapists must belong to the "right" profession before they can obtain legal sanction to practice. At any rate, the psychotherapist in private practice needs to exert more effort than he perhaps once anticipated toward expanding his clientele.

Where does the psychotherapist's business originate? What can he do to build clientele? What must be done by the nonmedical therapist to overcome the obstacle of not belonging to a profession which will, of itself, draw clients to him? These are crucial questions. The inevitable answer is that the therapist must sell himself and his service to his potential clients. If he finds this degrading or is not willing or equipped to do this, then he would be more comfortable and more productive working in an institutional setting or social agency.

Private psychotherapy practice has been seen here as a business, and the techniques which reputable businesses use to gain more customers have much applicability to private practice. How business persons achieve success is worth attention. They make clear, first of all, what it is they have to sell. No business would long survive, for example, selling "widgets" or "lycanthropy elimination services" unless it devoted some of its resources to telling about the nature of these services and explaining why the consumer should have them. Second, they present the product or service attractively to the potential consumer. If the particular widget or lycanthropy service seems unpleasant or ugly, customers will go elsewhere.

Third, they give consumers reasons why the purchase would be of value. They show how others have had their lives improved by the transaction and imply that without the purchase the same unhappy conditions as before will exist in the customer's life. Fourth, they attempt to convince the consumer that the product or service which they offer is better in some way than the offerings of everyone else. Why should anyone pick anything that is inferior when someone else can provide it better at the same cost? Then they make it convenient for the customer to partake of the offering. Accessibility can occur through good location, convenient business hours, and "openness" of the establishment, and by the proprietor making the customer feel his patronage is wanted.

Finally, the successful business person seeks to build a reputation for honesty, sincerity, and good service or product delivery, by satisfying the customers. Repeat business, and word-of-mouth recommendations by satisfied customers to potential customers are the cornerstone of any reputable business, including psychotherapy practice. Every one of these goals should be sought as much by the private practitioner as by any other business person.

The private therapist must clearly define his service and show his potential clientele what it is that he has to offer. Psychotherapy is a "widget." It may be of use to people, but very few will pay for it unless they are told what it is. Since it has unsuccessfully grappled for more than 3,000 years with the problem of defining what it is, the single private practitioner is not likely to be able to develop such a definition on his own. His best bet is to define a specific area of specialization within the realm of possibilities in psychotherapy. Then, he must show his potential clients and his sources of referral that his service is attractive. The process of exploring oneself, of knowing oneself better, or of becoming a contributing member of society can be presented in a way that is appealing to potential consumers. The private practitioner can also show how the investment will be worthwhile for the client. If the client is a more productive person or able to accomplish more of his goals as a result of the psychotherapy, then the client knows he has purchased a valuable commodity.

The therapist should also be able to demonstrate that partaking of his services has more advantage to the client than partaking of the services of someone else. Showing those who make referrals that one's training and skills are just what this particular client needs is one approach. Developing enough satisfied former clients is another. The therapist must be accessible too. His existence must be known to the potential consumers and referral sources, and it must be easy to reach the therapist and make an appointment at the client's convenience. Most important, the private psychotherapy practitioner, like any business person concerned about building a clientele, wants to build a good reputation. He does this by satisfying the client, giving skillful service, and delivering on his promises, and the result is that his former clients will tell potential clients about him.

SPECIALIZING

One of the major activities of a psychotherapist should be to develop a focus in his work. He would do well to concentrate on a specific kind of problem or treatment method, learn all he can about it, practice the techniques that are proven in that area, and inform everyone possible of his particular area of expertise. Specializing is the best possible way he can make clear to potential clients and referral sources what it is he has to offer. Even if this were not the most practical way of increasing the client load, it would still be a good idea. It is, of course, important the therapist have a fundamental general overview of psychotherapy, but he cannot be conversant with all the particulars. If he tries to be, (and this is an admirable effort to be sure), he will inevitably have to sacrifice depth. He will be confined to more superficial aspects of the therapy process. He will never achieve the preeminence and recognition that would be accorded to an authority.

The challenge is to select that area for focus which is compatible with the therapist's long-range interests, talents, values, and background. Many therapists who develop a specialization after they have completed their formal educations do so on the basis of short-sighted economic considerations. They might choose, for example, a specialization in treating drug abusers simply because there seemed to be considerable public financial support for such efforts. This might prove to be disastrous for the therapist who finds that his interest and skills are in another area entirely. The selection should be based on a view the therapist takes of his whole career, and he should not be swayed by public fads and short-lived interests in one or another emotional or social problem.

This is not to say that the therapist who specializes should give up all other interests and become narrowly devoted to his own limited realm of expertise. There is no surer path toward burnout, boredom, and indifference to one's work than to avoid variety and the perspectives of others (Freudenberger 1975). Ideally, the therapist should carve out his area of specialization and devote considerable time to learning and practicing it, but should also maintain a generalist interest in the activities of his colleagues. This will keep him fresher longer, and even contribute to his improving in his area of expertise.

His work should also include some time for involvement in the social causes of the individual problem with which he is concerned. If drug abuse is his concern, for example, he would do well to become involved not only in the clinical aspects of treatment of abusers, but also in a social effort to address the problem. Engaging in political or educational programs or preventative efforts rather than restricting oneself to clinical work would be beneficial for all concerned. The therapist thus has the opportunity to address problems from both sides of the spectrum and avoid the tedium of overconcentration and the superficiality which comes from being too spread out.

Actually most psychotherapy practitioners have established a specialization before entering independent work. The typical route for them is to become sufficiently expert in some area that leads them from organization to the private practice. Some get diverted from this route after hanging out their shingle when they start accepting referrals for virtually any type of work. This is understandable, if short sighted. It must be very painful for a struggling young therapist newly entering private practice to turn away referrals when he is barely able to meet his overhead expenses. Yet this is precisely the best thing to do. Otherwise he is not conveying to the referral sources that he is a specialist. His alleged expertise is diffused. His time, which could have been spent further refining his own area and convincing others that he has done so, is spent seeing anyone he can. This will help him meet his overhead and perhaps provide him with an adequate income, but in the long run his colleague who focused on one type of problem will be far better off, as will be his clients.

WHO REFERS TO PSYCHOTHERAPISTS
IN PRIVATE PRACTICE?

The foundation of any private practice in therapy is the group of people who steadily and continually refer new clients to the practitioner. Referral sources are unquestionably the most valuable assets of the private practice, apart from the therapist himself. They must be developed and cultivated because if they wither away, so does the business. This solid foundation rests on consumer satisfaction, because people who refer others have either utilized the services themselves or are conscientious professionals who follow up on the outcome of the people they refer. If they are satisfied with the therapist's results the first time they make a referral, they are likely to send others and extol the therapist's virtues in a manner that no amount of public relations, advertising, or professional exhortations could possibly duplicate.

The essence of a private practice is stability, which relies on the establishment of a reputation for trustworthiness, honesty, and worthy service. Private practice could never be like a storefront business which is having a going-out-of-business sale every month or like a movie that uses saturation advertising and mass distribution of the prints before the word gets around that it is a bomb. These are self-defeating activities for the reputable professional, because they don't lead to consumer satisfaction. Nor, for that matter, do they lead to riches for the purveyor, because they require enormous amounts of energy simply to hustle up the next case.

The following eight groups are the major sources of psychotherapy referrals and they are listed here in the order of their importance. First are former clients of the practitioner and members of the client's family and immediate circle. Second are physicians, particularly those who specialize in general medicine, internal medicine, gynecology, and pediatrics. Third are social agency staff members who have had personal experience with the practitioner's work. Fourth are self-referrals, those people who see the practitioner's name on the door or listing in a phone book. Fifth largest sources of referrals are other psychotherapists who seek assistance in conjunction with cases or family members with whom they are working. Sixth are lawyers, particularly those who specialize in domestic relations issues such as marital breakups, custody fights, adoption procedures, and so forth. Seventh are school counselors, who have worked with students but find they must refer them out because of the nature of the problem or the limitations on their time. Eighth are clergymen and church laypeople. Then comes the inevitable "other" group, which comprises people from every walk of life who might have had some contact with the psychotherapist and remembered his expertise. A little more about each should be said.

Former clients and people close to the client are the predominant referral source, at least if the therapist is competent and ethical. Naturally, the client and those close to him have to be pleased with the results and feel that the service was worthwhile. For the client to be convincing in recommending others, he probably needs to have achieved objective improvements in his situation, as well as simply feeling internally that he has achieved good results. If the client feels much better but now everyone else sees him as a narcissistic, inconsiderate, surly lout, others will not be inclined to follow his lead. When he feels he has achieved good results and when his objective behavior is desirable to those he sees, he is a walking testimonial. Other people may well be eager to find out the origin of his newfound well-being. Many of them seek the therapist's services themselves, but many more of them tell of the remarkable improvement and attribute the results to the therapist.

Physicians, especially general practitioners, gynecologists, and pediatricians are the major *professional* referral source. The doctors who deal with the "whole patient" tend to have insufficient time to give to their patients who have emotional disturbances and problems in social relationships. Most such doctors report that a significant portion of their patients have no medical illness but need a professional's concern, attention, advice, and focus. Physicians in these circumstances are more likely to refer such patients to psychiatrists because they are obviously more familiar and comfortable with the education and techniques of their medical colleagues. So psychotherapists who are psychiatrists consider other physicians to be their most important referral source. Nonmedical therapists receive fewer referrals from physicians, at least until they have established that they are competent and honest. When they develop a closer, perhaps personal relationship with the doctor they might obtain referrals in their area of expertise. At least the first referrals from physicians are going to be monitored very carefully, and if the results are poor or equivocal that doctor will be less likely to refer for some time to come.

Social agency staff members, particularly those who previously worked with the private practitioner, are also a very important referral source. If they know the work of the independent practitioner, or if they have provided services together to a single client, it is likely that a feeling of unity and cooperative trust has occurred between them. Referrals come out of this relationship very naturally. The practitioner's skills and ethics are known by the agency workers. Then when the agency is contacted by a client who is not eligible for their services, or when the agency has a long waiting list, or when the client simply asks the agency for a good private practitioner, the response is predictable. Some agencies maintain referral lists as part of their channeling function. Realistically, even when a client is given such a list he is likely to ask the agency staff members if they personally know any of the names on it. The private practitioner is well-advised to maintain his contacts with the agency for these very reasons.

Self-referrals are another important source of new business for most private psychotherapists, even though this can often be a source of some difficulty too. Self-referrers come to the therapist from a variety of origins. Some have been in the building where the practitioner's office was located and simply walked in. Others looked through the yellow pages and called the therapist's number. Others have come because they heard about the services from others in a circuitous way, through a friend or a friend of a friend. The self-referrer tends to be somewhat less motivated than those who are referred by others. Often he seeks the therapist's services as an impulse after an explosive confrontation with someone else, and the impulse has abated before the appointment arrives. These clients sometimes don't return for second sessions. Frequently they don't follow the therapist's suggestions and attribute their resulting failure to the therapist. Such people are thereafter anything but good referral sources. The self-referrers also tend to have more reluctance to pay the therapist's bill, either at the time of the interview or afterward. This is not to say that the therapist should not ever consent to scheduling self-referrers. Many are as motivated and conscientious as any-one. All of them have the same rights to receive help. But the therapist would do well to exercise a little extra caution in initial dealings with self-referrals.

Other psychotherapists in private practice are another source of referrals. While there is indeed healthy competition among therapists, so too is there a great amount of cooperation. Often a therapist wants a member of his client's family to engage in therapy with someone else. Sometimes two therapists might refer to each other because they acknowledge that each has expertise in a specific area. This cooperative effort works most effectively and efficiently when the therapists are specialized and not simply mirror images of one another. If the therapist's image is that of a generalist, then another therapist will see no reason to refer to him. If the therapist is seen as providing unique or supplemental services, other therapists will become an important referral source.

Lawyers, especially those in domestic relations, also refer some of their clients to psychotherapists. They utilize the services of psychotherapists a great deal in helping to resolve conflicts be-tween spouses on the verge of divorce. They refer frequently when they are serving a client who is about to go to trial, in or-der to convince the jury and the authorities that the client is at-tempting to make improvements on his own.

Many lawyers are themselves beginning to become interested in performing counseling and therapy roles for their clients. Many are acquiring special training and experiences which pre-pares them for this endeavor. In this role they would not be good referral sources because they would want to work with the clients themselves. But they might refer to another therapist whose specialization is needed. Other attorneys who have no in-terest in performing therapy themselves are equally uninterested in seeing that their clients resolve their conflicts except in a legal manner. It is sometimes against the lawyer's short-term interests to refer his clients to a psychotherapist. He would have a lucra-tive case to resolve if the problem persists, but not at all if the therapist restored the family to harmony. But when the lawyer is himself secure, conscientious, and sensitive to the needs of people rather than to the needs of his own pocketbook, it is quite possible that he would refer some of his clients to therapists just as a psychotherapist might well refer some of his clients to the lawyer.

One way lawyers first come in contact with psychotherapists is when they feel such contact will strengthen a case in which they are involved. The therapist might have worked with the lawyer's client in the past and is now sought to give a professional opinion about the emotional or social damage done to the client by others. In this instance the therapist may be called upon to testify in court. For example, in a custody controversy between divorcing parents, the child may become the client of the psychotherapist owing to emotional problems incurred as a result of the conflict. This therapist may be called upon to give his opinion in court about the best type of environment for the child. This is a perfectly appropriate role for the psychotherapist and for the lawyer.

Out of such encounters it is possible that other referrals are made, not only for forensic reasons, but also to assist with marital therapy; conflicts with children; and runaway, vandalism, and delinquency problems. A therapist in private practice could establish a specialization of just working with attorneys in these ways. But lawyers are not generally the major source of referrals, unless the therapist's special interest and expertise interfaces with the interests of the legal professional.

School counselors can be a major source of referrals to those therapy private practitioners who are recognized for their work with school-age children. This is particularly true if the specialty is in those trouble spots which come to the attention of school authorities. If a therapist is noted for his work with dyslexic children, delinquents, truants, underachievers, or drug abusers, to name but a few possibilities, he is likely to get referrals from school counselors. These people come in daily contact with children and their families who have the very problems concerning which psychotherapists have long claimed an expertise.

School counselors are usually dedicated and motivated to helping students resolve such problems themselves, but often the large numbers of students they are required to see precludes their spending enough time with any of them. Some counselors feel so much desire to serve their students themselves that they do not refer them to others. They often have the skill and training to provide the needed work, but not sufficient time.

When the counselor refers students to other professionals, it is more likely to be to a social service agency than to a private practitioner. Counselors often develop close working relationships with social agencies, with good results. If the private practitioner has made himself or his work known to the counselor he is likely also to be the object of referrals.

Clergymen often refer members of their flock to psychotherapists, though it is sometimes difficult for them. This is because many clergymen, regardless of denomination, feel they must provide the same services to their congregations as do psychotherapists. Many clergymen have extensive training, or feel that they do, in marital and family counseling, and many are indeed excellent providers of this service. Furthermore, as described in chapter 3, groups of clergymen have formed pastoral counseling centers, fee-for-service private counseling agencies. Many clergymen would, naturally, rather make referrals to members of this group than to nonpastoral therapists. Still, when a psychotherapist has developed a good relationship with a clergyman, perhaps through attendance at the church or through participation in church panels and discussion groups, the clergyman can become a good source of referrals. It is extremely important in working with a client referred by a clergyman to make the clergyman feel and be an integral part of the helping and therapy process. Frequent collaborations and mutual discussions about the client will help ease the clergyman's conscience about fulfilling the psychotherapist role himself.

Other people, too numerous to describe separately here, are also occasional sources of referrals to psychotherapists. Bartenders, beauticians, barbers, taxi drivers, nursing home operators, morticians, day care workers, hot line workers, librarians, volunteer workers, and many others are frequently asked to provide emotional support or advice. If these people know about the services of a psychotherapist they often can and do make referrals. In any case, there are many people who can become important sources of referrals to the therapist. The question now is, how does one get them to do it?

CULTIVATING REFERRAL SOURCES

The prime ingredient in encouraging people to refer to the therapist is visibility, especially to the targeted clientele and their service community. The targeted clientele may be anyone who lives in a certain geographic area, or anyone in the area who has a certain kind of problem. The service community consists of all the professional and service people who may be called upon to assist members of the targeted client group. For example, the therapist may seek to work with elderly persons, the target clientele, and their service community, which includes doctors, nursing home proprietors, landlords, druggists, and senior citizens associations. Visibility means that the therapist becomes known to these groups. He becomes known as an honest, motivated, well-trained, and skillful person, an expert in working with the problems of the elderly. It is clear to the target and service groups what kind of work he is actually doing, why he is doing it, and how well it is being done. If this visibility exists, the psychotherapist will have little trouble getting as many referrals as anyone. Keeping in the limelight too can prove to be most beneficial to the clients and to the service community as well as to the therapist.

Psychotherapists have used a multitude of techniques for keeping visible, as have all other successful purveyors of products or services, but certain ones seem more effective for them than for other businesses, and of course some techniques which have proved highly successful in other businesses have been colossal failures in private psychotherapy practice. Some of the techniques that have proved useful to some therapists include (a) informing referral sources, (b) consulting with referral sources, (c) following up, (d) expanding the helping network, (e) prospecting, and (f) utilizing telephone directory listings, advertising, and public relations activities.

INFORMING REFERRAL SOURCES

When someone refers a client to a psychotherapist for the first time, it is especially important to keep that person informed as to the client's problem, prognosis, course of treatment, and when the work was completed. This is good practice advice anyway, but it is an important way for the therapist to keep his name and work before the referring person. It is a good idea for the therapist to send several letters to the referring person at various stages, (a) to inform him that the first appointment has been made and thank him for the referral, (b) to indicate the assessment and diagnosis as well as treatment plan, (c) to indicate at intervals of three months what progress is being made, (d) to indicate that the treatment has concluded and specify the outcome and possibilities for the future, and (e) to inform him of any subsequent contacts with the client. The progress letters should be sent even if the course of treatment is going poorly. It would be tempting only to describe successes, but then the referrer would question the therapist's veracity. Besides there is a good chance the referrer will see the client anyway. It is better for the therapist to reveal what has been happening. Then, when progress is made, the success seems all the sweeter.

Of course, all these letters are done with the client's consent and should not be sent without it. But it is likely that most clients will be glad that such interest is being taken and gladly give their approval. It is also worthwhile to give copies of the letters to the clients so there is no misunderstanding about these communications.

It seems like a lot of work for the practitioner to write all these letters, but most of them will be brief, almost form letters with the therapist's name, address, and phone number prominently displayed. Many psychotherapists find that phone calls to the referring person to accomplish this same purpose are equally useful and much less time-consuming. However, one disadvantage of the telephone is that it often interrupts the referring person's own work, which can be an irritant. Furthermore, the call doesn't permit the communications to be kept on file for future reference.

And the call doesn't keep the psychotherapist's name and number before the eye of the referrer. On the other hand, the letter does that, it can be written and read at the leisure and convenience of both, and the client is privy to this exchange of information about him.

CONSULTING WITH REFERRAL SOURCES

People who make referrals are generally sympathetic, caring people. Otherwise the clients would not have revealed their troubles to them in the first place. Being sympathetic and caring, but without the time or skill to provide the needed help themselves, they recommend the psychotherapist. If they never hear from the client again, or from anyone else about the client's situation, they are left in a quandary. Did they do the right thing in making the referral? Did it help or does the client still have the same problem? If they see the client and he indicates satisfaction and improvement, it can be reassuring to the referring person, but he is still likely to feel left out, unneeded, and perhaps no longer as important to the client as before.

If the referring person has not been involved with the therapist in the course of the client's treatment, it is difficult to measure the conflicts, and anxiety which he might experience (Selvini-Palazzoli et al. 1980). It is also difficult to be certain that more referrals will come from him, no matter how successful the course of treatment. It is far better, for the client as well as for the therapist's goal of encouraging further referrals, to be in consultation with the referring person during the course of the treatment. Again, it should go without saying that this is done with the approval of the client and, whenever possible, with his participation in the consultation.

For example, if the referrer was a clergyman, an occasional telephone call or letter, made in the client's presence, asking him to do certain things for the client or asking him for certain information about the client's behavior in the past, will be of considerable worth. The clergyman then feels he is being helpful, that he has not abrogated his responsibilities to a member of his church. He is going to be far more likely to remember the therapist for subsequent referrals. The client will also have positive memories, because of the extra care and concern which was demonstrated in the treatment.

Consulting with the referring person seems appropriate when that person is a professional or a member of the service community, but when he is himself a former client there are some additional reservations. The therapist still has an obligation to his former client and must do nothing that would interfere with that person's continued improvement. For example, if the therapist reveals to the former client any sensitive material about the current client, the former client may come to believe his own confidentiality is jeopardized. The best thing for the therapist to do in consulting with former clients about a new referral is to call them, preferably in the client's presence, thank them for the referral, indicate that the work was indeed needed and will get started, and that the therapist will call the former client in the future. Sometimes, when the former client is a member of the new client's family, it is appropriate to seek additional information about the new client, but otherwise it is better to keep this consultation rather minimal. Much more is unnecessary anyway, since the therapist is going to be following up his former client periodically and will be keeping in contact that way.

CLIENT FOLLOW-UP

The next technique for maintaining visibility to potential referring persons is the follow-up phase of the helping process. This is a most important procedure, not only as a way of assuring quality service for the client, but also to implicitly encourage continued referrals. It is important because the former client is going to be the major referral source, and if he is aware that the therapist is still interested, and still in practice, referrals are more likely. At the conclusion of treatment the therapist may encourage the client to keep in touch, but this is difficult for most clients to do. They don't know if the therapist is really interested, or if he just makes the request perfunctorily. They don't know if a subsequent call or drop-in visit would be welcome or an inconvenience to the therapist. It is therefore necessary for the therapist to initiate the follow-up contacts. While it demonstrates his continued interest, it has the added advantage of making the contact come at the therapist's convenience.

Some therapists make it a routine practice to telephone as many former clients as possible at least once a year for the five years following treatment. The calls can be very brief, just one minute or so, and confined to merely saying hello and asking about the client's continued well-being, as well as that of the client's family. Other therapists fulfill this same function by periodically mailing the former client a brief note expressing the hope that all is well. This is often done during holiday times, or times which the therapist remembers as being of special significance to the client.

The therapist has several ways of keeping visible to his former client in the follow-up process. Some therapists establish networks of former clients who can look out for one another after treatment is concluded. The network might consist of several clients who have something in common. People with similar problems, or people who live in the same neighborhood, or those who are similar in age or ethnic origin or who share similar interests can be brought together by the therapist when the client has ended treatment. The resulting group might model itself after an Al-Anon group, a consciousness-raising group, a teenage gang, or a Neurotics Anonymous association. The therapist could subsequently contact the group together or make inquiries about the other members of the group when contacting any one individual. Members are advised to give support to one another and to keep the therapist posted if anyone is having serious difficulty.

Another way of maintaining some visibility to former clients is in providing them, upon termination of their active treatment, with copies of their case records or with audio or video cassettes of sessions they had with the worker. The client can be asked to review the copy periodically as a way of reenforcing that which was learned in the treatment sessions. If the client actually does this, he is further reminded of the therapist's interest and competence.

EXPANDING THE HELPING NETWORK

A highly effective technique for increasing one's visibility to potential referring persons is to contact people who have some professional interest in the client. Nearly every client already has a variety of professionals who have dealt with him in the past and may still have some concern for his well-being. The therapist can contact these professionals by letter or telephone, to obtain information, provide information, and coordinate subsequent efforts made in behalf of the client. For example, the therapist can ask the client who his family physician is and then write letters indicating the diagnosis and treatment plan to the doctor. The letters can be retained in the client's medical file in the doctor's office. Or, if the client is a student, the school counselor, principal, or teacher may be contacted for information and suggestions about what the student's needs are. If the client belongs to a church or synagogue, his clergyman may be contacted and given some information about the client which can be helpful. Or the therapist can ask for the clergyman's assistance and advice in subsequent dealings with the client. Again, this should only be done with the client's consent and, wherever possible, the client should be included in the exchange of information. It is rare that the client does not want and appreciate this extra attention, concern, and coordination.

Referring the client to other professionals for their assistance is another approach to expanding the helping network: "Mr. Wilson, my client has a legal problem and I've heard you are a very skilled attorney in such matters. I would like to refer him to you and keep in touch as the case progresses." "Ms. O'Brien, I won't be able to see my new client because she needs to come in the evening when I'm not available, so I want another social worker like yourself to see her. Could we talk about the case?" "Dr. Harrison, I've been working with this family but I've heard

that you are quite good at working on ____ problems. I was
wondering if you'd be interested in working with me on the
case." These quotations illustrate approaches therapists might
take to serve their clients better and expand the contacts one has
with other professionals. They do not detract from the work
with the client and they enhance further contacts with other
professionals.

Using these approaches inevitably leads to an expanded referral resource base. Having thus worked with the professional person as a colleague on behalf of the client, the therapist has become established as one who is competent and professional. He
becomes well known to those who did not know him before, and
his treatment of his client is more effective than it otherwise
might have been. The beauty of this technique, in addition to expanding referral resources, is that it is so consistent with the psychotherapist's values and his understanding of the social forces
that effect his clients. The therapist does not see his client as existing solely in a clinical setting, completely detached from external or environmental considerations. Many professionals pay lip
service to the need for considering environmental factors, but are
then content to see their clients in a self-contained clinical setting. Psychotherapists must always take into consideration the
environmental factors, and it is professionally appropriate for
most therapists to engage others in work with the client. It is
only inappropriate and inadvisable for the private practitioners
whose practice is based on the analytic treatment approach.

For most therapists in private practice, this is an effective diagnostic and treatment technique. It invariably leads to greater
client satisfaction and well-being, more effective and concentrated efforts by others in behalf of the client, and greater exposure for the therapist, leading to an increased foundation of referral sources.

PROSPECTING

So far, the assumption has been that the therapist has some
clients to begin with, and encourages referrals on the basis of

work done with already contracted clients. But if there is no clientele to build upon, the private practitioner has to encourage newcomers who have had no experience with him, and no way of knowing whether the service would be of value. Insurance and real estate agents attempt to expand their clientele by what they call "prospecting" (Baumback and Lawyer 1979). They knock on doors, make blind telephone calls, send cards and letters at random promising free gifts, and generally find ways of introducing themselves to potential clients and to people who might refer them to potential clients. The professional person would be ill advised to use some of these techniques, but some of them have merit if used discreetly and with professional dignity.

The most common prospecting method for professionals in fee for service is to send announcement cards and letters of introduction to those professional people in the community who seem most likely to send referrals. As discussed in the last chapter, the cards are traditional, but they are not a very good referral source. Few professional people are likely to refer a client to someone they don't know, especially if they represent a profession about which they are uncertain. Letters of introduction are a slightly more effective prospecting method. These can be written to the potential referring person to include some details about the therapist's goals, treatment methods, specialization, and training. If they are personalized and obviously targeted to the potential referral source they will probably be read, and possibly the therapist will be remembered. If they are impersonal, almost form letters, they are less likely to be read and remembered. It is sometimes effective for the letter of introduction to be sent to the potential referring person a week or two after the announcement card was sent. This then may be followed up by more personal contacts.

Another prospecting technique is to personally call upon the potential referring person. While it is much more effective, it seems to be very difficult for many psychotherapists to do. If the therapist finds the idea uncomfortable, he would not project an image of confidence and skill in the meeting, so its purpose would be negated. For this therapist, personal meetings would not be wise. If he can comfortably make a personal call, it can be effective because he is then seen as a real person by the potential referrer. It affords an opportunity to answer questions the potential referrer may have about the therapist's background, skills, and special interests.

The therapist who intends to make personal contacts with physicians, lawyers, and other fee-for-service professionals who operate on tight time schedules may have to be prepared for interminable vigils in crowded waiting rooms. It is not worthwhile to wait for long. Doing so conveys the image that one's time is not important or well spent, and this is hardly the image to project to someone who is busy. It is difficult to overcome this by making an appointment with the potential referrer, because then there may be misunderstandings about the nature of the visit. The therapist might receive a bill for the time he spent with the other person and be remembered only as one of the many clients or customers seen that day.

It is better for the therapist to go to the potential referrer's office, armed with another letter of introduction and possibly a pamphlet describing the therapist and the service he offers. He states his purpose to the receptionist or nurse or secretary as simply to leave the information. He may talk with this person briefly, and give her an impression which she might relay to her employer. If the therapist spends a few minutes with this person she may be able to arrange a very brief introduction with her employer. In any case, the therapist has made something of an impression, left some information about himself, and not wasted his time or that of the referring person or staff.

Insurance and real estate agents who use prospecting as a major means to expand their clientele become inured to the fact that the vast majority of these contacts do not lead to the desired results. Their philosophy is that many such contacts will lead to a few referrals. The private psychotherapy practitioner should adopt a similar philosophy, and certainly not rely on it as anything but a supplement to his efforts to increase the number of his clients.

One other way therapists have to increase their visibility to potential referring sources is to get attention of the general public. Many people, if they are exposed to the therapist in the course of their daily activities, will keep him in mind as someone to consult or refer to in times of need. Any business uses attention-getting devices to enhance and maintain its visibility, and the psychotherapist or counselor does likewise. Telephone listings, advertising, and public relations are the major mechanisms for this purpose.

TELEPHONE BOOK REFERRALS

"Let your fingers do the walking," says the ad. It is advice that many people follow, even to find the names of professionals. It is the most important advertising tool available to many businesses, but it probably is much less important to professionals as a referral source. Nevertheless, it cannot be discounted. It is best considered by the private psychotherapy practitioner as a supplement to other techniques (Allison and Hartmann 1981). If, for example, a potential client has heard about the therapist through a friend, or heard the therapist make a presentation at a public conference, he might look up the therapist's name and number in the telephone book. Few people are likely to simply call up someone blindly: still, it does happen. There are potential clients who don't know whom to ask, or are too embarrassed to ask their doctors or other associates for such a referral. These people are more likely to look through the yellow pages for someone to contact.

They aren't as likely, however, to look up a *psychotherapist*. As we have seen before, the term is too ill-defined in the minds of most people. Many look under "Psychologists" or "Psychiatrists" in the "Physicians" section. Many others look in the section which deals more specifically with the problem they face. "Marriage and Family Counselors" (which comes right before "Massage Parlors" in most communities) is one place people look. Also, the yellow pages might have listings for "Group Psychotherapists," "Clinics," "Adolescent Services," and many other designations. The therapist will have more success in getting telephone book referrals if he is listed under these more specialized headings than if the listing is "Psychotherapists."

If the private practitioner is somewhat dependent upon the telephone book as a major source of referrals—which is extremely unwise—he would do well to make preparations for the listing well in advance. The yellow pages typically have deadlines of approximately six months prior to publication and distribution of the directories. So the therapist who just missed the deadline could have as long as a year and a half to wait before his name is included in the directory. The therapist could get the listing, even using his home telephone number at first, long before he has actually entered private practice, in order to be assured of the listing as soon as possible. It is more tasteful and professional if the therapist has a simple listing consisting only of his name, address, telephone number, professional degrees, and specializaton. Larger display ads seem less professional, and there is no evidence that they are more effective in drawing interested clientele. Many professional associations in local areas have unit listing in the yellow pages. All the individual members of the association who are in fee-for-service private practice, who desire it, list their names. This method of listing is somewhat less expensive and probably as effective as the individual listing.

Self-referrers who have called solely because of the telephone listing are likely to require a considerable amount of the therapist's time and attention even before his first face-to-face interview with them. Since they knew nothing about the therapist before making the call, they necessarily would have many questions which deserve to be answered. What are the fees? How must they be paid? What are the therapist's qualifications and credentials? How long has the therapist had his practice? What is his theoretical orientation? What are his typical treatment techniques? How exactly does one find his office? Can appointments be canceled at the last minute? Since the caller is, at this point, likely to be shopping around, he is going to have many questions, and there is no certainty that the time spent with him will result in an appointment. And if an appointment has been set, there is far less likelihood of his keeping it than if he had been referred by someone who knew the therapist. As we have already seen, many self-referrers call on impulse and then do not keep the appointment. Naturally, the therapist cannot charge the client he has never seen before for the missed session.

Sometimes the therapist may be tempted to call back the person who made the appointment and then failed to show up. This is usually a futile and frustrating exercise. He may want to call because of concern that the client had further troubles and may need help more than ever. Or he may call simply because he is slightly piqued at having been "stood up" and wants to convey that to the caller. In either case a return call would only add to the therapist's frustration. It will probably sound like this:

> THERAPIST: Hello. Mr. Ryan? I'm sorry we weren't able to meet for our appointment today. Was there a problem about coming?
> CLIENT: What? Who did you say this was? Oh, yeah, I—well, I couldn't come today. I couldn't get my wife to come with me and—I guess we really don't need to see you now.
> THERAPIST: I made an appointment with you and had to wait for you for an hour. I wish you would call if you change your mind.
> CLIENT: Well, yeah—you're right. I just forgot. I'm really sorry. Actually maybe we really should see you. You've been pretty nice about this, spending all that time on the phone with me the other day. Do you think I could make another appointment with you? I'll keep it this time. Or else I'll be sure to call you if I can't make it.

Now the therapist is in a difficult position. Should he reschedule? If not, how does he now defer? What is the caller's motivation? Is he requesting a new appointment just because the therapist has tweaked him a bit and now he feels guilty? If the caller was impulsive before, is he now being impulsive again in asking for another appointment? Once the caller has hung up will he again forget about the appointment he wanted to make?

Everyone concerned would probably be better off if the therapist did not call back about the failed first appointment. The response the therapist gets from the person is not going to feel satisfactory to either of them. Another appointment scheduled would be too haphazard. The potential client's motivation in treatment thereafter might be pretty dubious. If the caller truly did have another problem that precluded his keeping the appointment, the caller is himself quite likely to initiate a subsequent call. Then the therapist is able to use his judgment about whether he should schedule the person another time.

THE QUESTION OF ADVERTISING

"Beware of quack doctors who advertise to scare men into paying money for remedies which have no merit," proclaimed a typical ad in 1902. "Dr. Hammond's Nerve and Brain Pills are absolutely guaranteed to cure you of any disease, including low spirits, poor memory, nervousness, weariness, and a constant feeling of dread as if something awful was going to happen" (Sears 1969). The public of that era was exposed to a plethora of claims, all purporting to cure anything. Many people who partook of such remedies were harmed to an appalling extent. The excesses and suffering experienced by naive or gullible people who trusted this advertising caused a public reaction for more controls. This led to a social norm, which predominated for the next sixty years.

The movement, backed by considerable government legislation and growing enforcement of professional behaviors, stressed that all advertising was unethical. Practitioners were limited to small discreet signs listing their name and degree. Physicians and lawyers were not allowed by their professional associations to even indicate their areas of specialization. Beyond a very discreet announcement to fellow professionals to indicate the opening of one's office, the fee-for-service professions took a dim view of any self-promotional activities. Anything that even remotely gave the appearance of advertising was met by harsh inquiries from the profession's committee on ethics. The professions came to feel that the only way to protect the public from false claims and harm was to forbid any type of advertising at all. The way for a potential client or patient to get to the suitable specialist was to be referred there. One had to trust the judgment of someone else.

Things began to change in 1962. President John F. Kennedy gave a special message to Congress which was the beginning of today's consumer movement. In the message he proclaimed the existence of four basic consumer rights. These were (a) the right to safety—protection against the marketing of goods hazardous to one's health; (b) the right to be informed—that is, to be protected against fraudulent advertising, or misleading information about products and services, and to be given the facts needed to make an informed choice in the marketplace; (c) the right to choose, that is, to have reasonable access to a variety of producers and services; and (d) the right to be heard, to be assured that the consumer will get a sympathetic hearing by the government and that the consumer laws will be enforced.

What has happened since that proclamation can be honestly described as a revolutionary change in the American marketplace. Numerous laws have been passed, and the norm in the nation is to give information to the consumer so that he can make his own decisions (Herrman 1980). The right to be informed and the right to choose have had a strong influence on the professions. Consumers asked, "What right do the bar associations have to prevent lawyers from publicly stating what their specialties and fees will be?" The question was asked of the psychotherapy professions as well (Feldstein 1971).

Consequently, in the past several years there has been a marked softening in the zealousness with which professional associations and their ethics committees have looked at the promotional efforts of their memberships. One can scarcely open a newspaper anymore without seeing ads for lawyers who specialize in divorce, wills, accidents, or malpractice, and whose fees are spelled out in the text. Now one can seek physicians listed in the yellow pages under their specialties. The 1980 convention of the American Medical Association, partly because of pressure from the U.S. Federal Trade Commission, voted to allow physicians to advertise in the media of the general public. Dentists are on the radio extolling their professional virtues, and television has sold time to members of many professional groups, along with ads for deodorants, beer, and vegetable choppers. The softening does not mark a return to the days of Doc Hammond's cure-everything pills, but the trend seems definitely toward more rather than less advertising.

What then, should be the stance taken by the private practice psychotherapist? Presumably advertising should now be acceptable if it makes only truthful claims and is discreet. But each practitioner must decide for himself if it is in his interests to advertise. Since there are no longer any legal or professional sanctions against it, the decision has to be made individually. Those who argue in favor of advertising, which is not the same thing as publicity, public relations, or self-promotion, make the following claims: Advertising defines for the public what it is psychotherapists and counselors do. It can describe how their services are provided and at what cost. It puts the therapist in the public eye and thus makes it possible for the uninformed layman to know about the available services. It sometimes increases the interest one might have in seeking those services. Advertising can clarify the specialty of the therapist to the public and to other professional groups. It can be directed through the relevant media to the target population. Finally, advertising can list fees, which will lead to a more competitive situation for the consumer. This makes it better for both client and practitioner.

On the negative side are those who argue that advertising is basically a disreputable, sordid activity that is forever associated with ambulance chasing and quackery. "If a person is competent, why should he need to advertise?" is the frequent response at first sight of an ad for a professional person. Some fear that advertising may lead to false claims of expertise or abilities. If this happened it would lead back down the road to the Doc Hammond era. Another argument is that the practice is still in its infancy and hasn't gained anything like general acceptance among most professionals. A private therapist is therefore likely to receive some subtle or explicit disdain from colleagues or members of other professional groups.

The most compelling argument against advertising, however, is that it is a very expensive procedure to achieve what can be done just as well or better by using other means. The average independent practitioner is only going to be able to provide services for a relatively small number of people. Advertising is inevitably targeted to a large population. A full-time clinical practitioner only needs to add a few new cases to his workload every month.

Other approaches to obtaining referrals will therefore be more successful and cost effective for his more limited needs. Public relations activities are the best of these other approaches.

PUBLIC RELATIONS ACTIVITIES

Public relations is far more effective than advertising, less expensive, and ultimately more satisfying and reassuring for the client, the worker, and his profession. Unlike advertising, it has always been acceptable to all the professions. Public relations activities don't explicitly ask for the client's business. They don't ask people to refer clients to the therapist. Instead, the activities are designed to project a positive but general impression about the therapist and his type of work. Nearly all professions have engaged in public relations in an attempt to enchance society's impression of them. Some professional associations have hired public relations firms to achieve this improved image (New York Psychiatrists 1980). The individual can rely on his profession to do this or he can engage in his own public relations activities. In so doing he is likely to expand his referral resources. The following are ten of the major activities which individual psychotherapists have used successfully in public relations.

Providing Free Consultations to Social Agencies or Self-Help Groups. The psychotherapist is in a unique position to enhance his professional image and identity and help in a valuable and necessary way. He can work with social agencies or self-help groups which have the need but not the finances for his professional expertise. There are a multitude of agencies, many of which are poorly funded and not even professionally staffed. There are even more groups of people who get together to help themselves, or their communities, which have virtually no financial resources. They could be more effective if they received some training from a professional person, or at least some advice on specific situations. They can do more than they otherwise might attempt if they had the reassurance that a professional person would be available for difficult situations. The practitioner, especially one whose orientation is clinical, can help fulfill his obligation to help improve society and its institutions by becoming involved in such consultations. The therapist could meet with one of these groups periodically or regularly at no cost. He could discuss specific cases or general principles, or perform direct services to demonstrate skills and techniques. This aids the agency or program and provides positive feedback for the private practitioner. It helps him refine and keep up his skills and reduces his sense of isolation.

Serving on a Social Agency Board of Directors. Private practitioners can also serve the better funded, more formally organized social agencies by becoming members of boards of directors. Often the membership of social agency boards consists wholly of business persons or socialites, with an occasional physician or lawyer. The social agency board establishes the policy and oversees the methods used by the staff, but sometimes the board members have different values or priorities than psychotherapists might have. The private therapist can be a valuable asset as a board member because he can represent the values and methods embodied in his profession.

Psychotherapists aren't often enough members of social agency boards. They sometimes become so immersed in their clinical interests that they feel they haven't the time for such distracting pursuits. But when they do participate in board activities their involvement proves to be very valuable for themselves as well as for the agency. It acquaints the therapist with the other board members, and thus another referral source is developed. It affords him a respite from his day-to-day clinical responsibilities. It gives him exposure to new ideas and approaches and it helps him fulfill his obligations to society.

Giving Talks to Groups. Civic associations, wives' clubs, educational associations, church meetings, special interest groups, and ad hoc committees are constantly seeking speakers whose interests and expertise appeal to the group. One need only indicate to some of these groups a willingness to speak publicly, formally or informally, and there will be ample invitations to do so. The talks serve a multiple purpose for the therapist. His views are expressed and some of his values are made known. He might convince others of the merit of those values. He educates his audience to the problems and possible solutions within his area of expertise. He helps bring about greater understanding within one segment of the public. He displays his own knowledge and concerns. The contact also exposes him to the views of members of his audience, thus giving him greater insights and awareness of community concerns than he otherwise would have had. It helps him to sharpen his own thinking about the issue at hand as well as to give more focus to social problems in general. All this goes far to leading the therapist toward more effective delivery of his own services.

Participating in Panels or Discussion Groups. It is almost as productive for the therapist to participate as a discussant or panel member in workshops or meetings where someone else is the featured speaker. Again, the demand for such volunteers is great, and a mere expression of interest to such groups will result in ample opportunity to participate. As a panelist, the practitioner is introduced and his credentials and specialties are presented to the audience. His role is that of a counterbalance to the speaker, and as such he has opportunities to present his own views and values as well as to demonstrate his knowledge and skill in making presentations.

The advantage of serving as a panel member is that there is little time-consuming preparation involved, if any at all. The therapist is not expected to have a polished speech, and yet he is given ample attention in a less formal context. A discussant has almost the same opportunities as a main speaker to achieve the same objectives.

Campaigning for and Holding Political Office. Psychotherapists seem underrepresented among those who hold or even run for political office. Engaging in the political process as a candidate for office and as an officeholder gives the therapist or counselor a major opportunity to express and carry out the values of his profession. The mere act of campaigning will give him considerable exposure and subject his views, values, occupation, and methods of working to considerable public attention and scrutiny. It is almost a tradition among some young lawyers that they run for political office, not even for the purpose of winning, but to have an opportunity to raise people's consciousness about their existence. They indicate that in so doing, win or lose, they have helped their private practice careers by the exposure thus gained. The psychotherapist in private practice has the same opportunity.

Leading or Participating in Normative Change Crusades. Social causes abound. Psychotherapists should be at the forefront of movements to bring about needed change. If they prefer not doing it as active political campaigners or officeholders, they still have the opportunity to become involved in grass roots movements. Being a crusader is not every psychotherapist's predisposition, but all of them have strong belief and value systems. Many therapists find they need to avoid taking strong political stands. They avoid involvement in social action or political events because they wish to appear politically neutral so as to not influence their clinical clients. But in most situations and for most types of psychotherapy and counseling such constraints are not necessary. On the other hand, actively seeking to bring about some change in the legal system, or in the norms of the society, or even of a small community, is a significant way for the therapist to continue to be in the limelight. As a public relations effort this will not appeal to everyone who might disagree with the cause toward which the practitioner is working, but to those who agree with his views, his esteem is immeasurably increased.

Using the Media. An articulate psychotherapist or counselor who is strongly identified with a special interest, or is recognized as having a particular expertise or leadership role in any issue of social importance, is likely to be called upon by radio, television, and newspaper interviewers. Local television and radio stations frequently interview therapists on the subject of a social problem or helping technique. Participating in such ventures seems to lead to calls from other media interviewers, and the therapist can rapidly convey to the general public his expertise in the area of interest. To get on the media circuit, it is important that the therapist actually is highly knowledgeable about the subject and that he can present it in a clear, jargon-free way. The therapist who can show some humor and irreverence for the established or traditional way of thinking, and can present himself in a colorful way with professional dignity, will become a popular "reliable source" for reporters and interviewers. This type of attention also affords the therapist the opportunity to be publicly visible and bring credit to himself and to his profession. Of course, it is possible to go overboard. Some communities have been deluged by the remarks and opinions of therapists who crave the limelight and become overly zealous in their efforts to get public attention. They become known to newspaper editors and television station producers as "media hogs." Such people do not bring credit to their profession and are often an embarrassment to their colleagues. Moderation in the use of the media is in order for the reasonable psychotherapist.

Writing Articles and Columns for Newspapers and Popular Magazines. The general public seems to enjoy articles, columns, and essays in the popular print media from experts who can present themselves in a clear, easy to read, but knowledgeable way. Often these columns use an advice-giving format, or question-and-answer style. The bigger magazines and newspapers are usually booked up with expert column writers, but there are a large number of small papers, newsletters from various interest groups, and local magazines which welcome such material. The therapist can get established in the popular print media at first by doing free-lance material on subjects within his area of expertise. If he continues to submit such articles, and if they are readable and worthwhile, the publisher is going to seek more.

Another way for the therapist to use the print media to be in the public eye is through letters to the editor. When newspapers publish stories on subjects about which the therapy practitioner has professional knowledge, if the article contains factual errors, or if the viewpoint is contrary to the therapist's values and ethics, it is his duty to write to the editor. If the letter is well presented it may be published along with a list of the writer's credentials to establish that the letter has credibility.

Writing Articles for Professional Journals. Public relations is also important among one's peers and other professional groups. Recognition of expertise by other professionals comes when the therapist presents new findings, or demonstrates new ways of considering things of professional interest. Publishing in journals which are read by fellow professionals enhances one's position in the professional community. The self-discipline that comes from writing such material—focusing one's thoughts, gathering and analyzing data, and enduring the resulting scrutiny and possible criticism from one's fellow professionals—is bound to lead the therapist to greater self-awareness, skill development, and competence.

Being a Good Community Role Model. All the public relations activities one can imagine will be for naught if the psychotherapy private practitioner behaves in the community in ways that discredit him and his profession. Violating the ethics of his profession or his own individual standards is one way to discredit himself. Another is to use shoddy business practices. And another way is to subordinate his professional values to more mercenary considerations. The psychotherapist who presents himself in his community as a contributing member, a value to his neighborhood, a person to look up to because he cares and is competent, is being a good role model. This is worth all the other public relations activities combined.

This chapter has been concerned with ways the therapist may employ to expand his clientele. Certainly no therapist can do all the things suggested here all the time. If he did so, he no doubt would be deluged with clients and referrals, but he would not have time to see any of them. Some of these techniques are more useful than others for some therapists. One must be selective in the approaches used. One must choose those techniques which are compatible with one's personality and special circumstances. All of these things have been proved useful for many private therapy practitioners, but none of them has been useful for everyone. The therapist's use of these techniques will not only expand his referral sources and numbers of clients, but will also enhance the quality of his practice.

SEVEN

VALUES AND MONEY

M ONEY is not, as some people suggest, the raison d'être of private practice in psychotherapy and counseling. But it is important enough to the practitioner to merit objective scrutiny. It is a subject which tends to raise the anxiety level of many in the psychotherapy professions. It has this effect because many entry-level psychotherapists in private work don't know enough about it in a theoretical or a practical business sense.

This lack of knowledge is a natural result of the training, experience, and values most therapists seem to possess. Professional schools and academic programs in the psychotherapy disciplines offer virtually no courses in business management, economics, or accounting. Of course, this is appropriate in view of the far more important task of acquiring as much as possible of the immense amount of knowledge about human behavior and treatment techniques which competent therapists need. Then, most young psychotherapists and counselors begin their work experiences in institutional settings where the financial management aspects are controlled by specialists and administrators. Even those therapists who have had training and experience in administration and management find they are dealing with an entirely different set of problems when they conduct a small business such as a psychotherapy office.

Another reason psychotherapists become anxious when their attention turns to money matters is that their value set appears to be antithetical to the values which seem inherent in business and enterprise. Therapists entered their professions, for the most part, because they wanted to help people. They want to give of themselves. They want to enrich not their own pocketbooks, but the lives of their clients. The professions which they choose—medicine, nursing, social work, psychology, religion—had the care of people as the foremost consideration. It seems somehow contrary to this value to ask these people for money. It must be done if the therapist is to earn a living as an independent practitioner, but it is not a favorite activity for anyone (Keefe 1978).

Maintaining a private practice in psychotherapy or counseling necessitates many behaviors which seem crass, mercenary, or unprofessional. The therapist must directly ask the client to pay. She must sometimes remind clients that their bills are overdue. She must regularly confront clients and third-party payers about financing the therapy, and often these people are not pleasant about it. She must employ bill collectors and credit bureaus, and she must make it clear that her concern for the client is not entirely altruistic.

The private psychotherapy practitioner could not take a lofty stance even if pure altruism were the major tenet of her profession's value system. If she overlooks concern about receiving payment for her services, the client is likely to as well. But the practice would not long survive if this continued to happen. Actually, most clients would be likely to bring up the subject if the therapist avoided it for very long. Often they have less trouble dealing with the subject than the therapist might. They don't tend to entertain illusions about the therapist's motivation. They recognize that an inherent part of the transaction is the exchange of money for the service rendered. Without a fair exchange, the client feels or is made to feel subordinate, dependent, inferior to the giver (Kerson 1978). One of the first things most clients ask in their initial contact with the private practitioner is the charge. They do not expect therapy to be free and do not consider themselves charity cases. If the therapist could be as matter-of-fact and businesslike about money matters as her clients often are, there would be far fewer problems for her in the financial aspects of her private practice.

The following scenario illustrates this issue: A psychotherapist has just entered private practice after several years of agency work where money matters were dealt with by other members of the staff. She is eager to show her private client that her primary concern is for the client's well-being. In the initial contact there is discussion about goals, symptoms, and the problems the client faces. But nothing is said about fees. By the end of the second interview the therapist still has not mentioned her charges. The client, naturally concerned that his bill might be excessive, raises the subject. The therapist becomes uncomfortable. Other professionals she has dealt with don't discuss money with their patients or clients because they have staff members to do that. But she doesn't have a staff. She mumbles something about her rates. Her manner, body language, and verbal tone convey that the money issue is virtually irrelevant or of minor consequence compared to her concern for the client's resolution of his problem

The therapist planned to simply bill the client at the end of the month and not have to have any direct communication about it thereafter. But perceiving that money is of secondary importance, her client consciously or unconsciously doesn't get around to paying the bill. Months go by. The therapist is well aware of the growing unpaid bill. The therapy continues but the therapist's reticence keeps her from bringing the issue up. But finally she asks the client about the bill.

The client's response could have been predicted after the second interview. The client simply minimizes it, explains it away saying he just forgot or hasn't gotten around to it but that he will do something about it as soon as his next paycheck comes in. More time goes on in therapy. The therapist's increasing anxiety interferes with her ability to be effective with the client.

Eventually, the client terminates therapy with some or all of the goals reached. He promises to pay soon, but since the bill is so large he wonders if he can pay a part of it each month. No problem, the relieved therapist assures him. Monthly statements are sent. No response. Now the therapist has a renewed source of anxiety. She now must call her former client and confront him about it. Or she must get third parties to do it, people like lawyers, bill collectors, or credit bureaus.

Whatever she does, the therapist by now realizes that her actions will interfere with her grandiose illusions about the nature of her relationship with the client. Some negative feelings will now exist between the two. If she uses a third party to collect she will receive only a small part of what is due. Her only other option would be to ignore the bill and consider in her own mind that this will be a gratis case. She rationalizes that it is important that she see some of her clients at no charge. But she is deceiving herself when she entertains such a notion. The self-deception leads her to feel more anxiety which is reenforced when it comes time for her to deal with her next client about money matters.

This illustration may seem like an exaggeration, but unfortunately it is not. It is an experience shared by many in private practice, especially those just starting out. Obviously there are few veteran private psychotherapists who still have the conflict, because most of the ones who cannot resolve it cannot financially or emotionally remain in fee-for-service private work for very long.

Most experienced therapists have learned that there is a far more simple, straightforward, less anxiety-provoking method of dealing with this issue. It begins with a mental process. The therapist must look within herself to understand the nature of her conflict. Does she feel that playing down fees will improve the relationship with her client? Or will it make the client feel she is more sincere about her desire to help? Will it cause the client to like and respect her more? Or does she simply doubt that her services are worth the charges she is asking?

An objective analysis, removed from any neurotic conflicts, would reveal that the relationship will not be improved and that the client will not have greater liking or respect for the therapist for the lack of attention to money. And if the therapist doubts the worth of her services she should take action. She should either lower her charges to that point which she feels is deserved, or she should improve her skills so that she feels she merits the charges.

If she believes her charges should be less than those in a subsidized agency, she probably should seek a different profession and/or psychotherapy for herself. Once the therapist has come to recognize that her services are worth her charges she will convey this to her client. The client may have doubts about this too, and the therapist's confidence in herself will be reassuring. The client certainly wants his money's worth and if the therapist doubts the worth, so too will the client.

The next step in dealing with the conflict is for the therapist to establish an explicit policy about money. The policy should be clear in her own mind and presented clearly to every one of her clients. The policy should include answers to at least the following questions: How much is the charge? Is the charge based on amount of time the therapist spends with the client, or other factors? How must the fee be paid? Will insurance cover the fees? Can payment wait until insurance reimbursement occurs? Is the charge greater for the same amount of time when two or more members of the family come in at the same time? Are the fees based on a flat rate, or on a sliding scale? Is there a charge for the first interview before an agreement is reached about continued treatment? If the client can't pay by the agreed-upon time, how long can he have before paying? What will the therapist do if payment isn't made? Can the fees be raised or lowered during the course of treatment? What about professional courtesy? Is group therapy less expensive than individual therapy? Are charges made for talks on the telephone? Are charges made for the therapist's time when she communicates about the client with other professionals in behalf of the client? What is the best way to bill or collect from clients? Should charges be higher for more desirable times, such as evenings? Can fees be split with other professionals working with the client? Are charges made for missed appointments? What about seeing some clients for free?

There is no single right answer to these questions. Each practitioner must think about each question carefully and decide herself what her policy will be. Whatever decision she makes, she should then be prepared to maintain and enforce it consistently throughout her practice. Any changes she makes in the policy should be done only after careful consideration, rather than after impulsively bending her own rules to suit the circumstances of an individual client. Part of the policy should be presented in writing to the client at the beginning of the working relationship, perhaps as a part of a contract agreement similar to the one presented in chapter 4. Having a clear policy enables the therapist

to be somewhat personally detached about money matters thereafter. It is the policy of the organization, not the whim of the
therapist, that imposes the money rules into the relationship. It
is now time to discuss the decisions that the private practitioner
must make concerning her own money policies.

THE INITIAL UNDERSTANDING ABOUT MONEY

When is the right time to bring up the subject of money? The
therapist owes it to the potential client to inform him about some
things *prior* to the first interview session. At the very least, the
potential client needs to know what the therapist's charge will be
for the initial session, how long that session will last, how the fee
is to be paid, and when it should be paid. Any further discussion
about money should be made during that first session. If the
client begins the first interview without being informed of these
requirements, the situation is already fraught with the danger of
misunderstandings and of money problems interfering with the
relationship.

One reason for misunderstanding at this point is that many
clients do not expect to have to pay for the first interview. These
people reason that no agreement has yet been established, and
that the interview is merely a sizing-up process in which both
therapist and client decide whether to go ahead with the treatment. They might base this notion on having seen attorneys who
don't charge for initial interviews until a decision is made to take
the case. They might feel the visit is analogous to having a car-
penter give an estimate of the cost for adding on a room, or a
caterer interviewing the client to determine how much to charge
for a party. One would not expect charges for these initial eval-
uations, and many potential clients do not expect charges for the
initial interview. Those who don't aren't prepared to make payment after the first meeting, if ever. Virtually all fee-for-service
professionals engaged in psychotherapeutic services charge the
same for the first interview as for any subsequent one.

Most private psychotherapy practitioners have some contact
with the potential client prior to the first "official" interview. For

the most part, such contacts are made by telephone. Less often, clients will enter the office and talk with the therapist or her receptionist. However, when the initial appointment is made the client must know if there is a fee for the first session. He must be told whether the fee is to be paid at the beginning of the session, at its conclusion, or by the end of the next month's billing period. If the potential client has this information in advance, there is less likelihood of subsequent misunderstandings, and if the appointment is made, the client is more prepared to comply with the financial arrangements.

Any other questions about money should be answered during the first interview, when the contract or agreement about whether to engage in treatment is decided upon. This is an important factor in making the decision and thus it cannot be left out of such a consideration. The client may not raise the issue during the first meeting, especially since he is likely to be far more concerned about the reasons that led him to see the therapist. However, whether or not the client raises any questions about it, the therapist must make clear what the money policy is. It should be presented clearly and understood thoroughly before any further appointments are made. Sometimes this discussion may take several minutes of the scant amount of time available in the session, but it still must be done. Rather than take up much time on the issue, some practitioners give clients a written policy statement about money, perhaps as part of the written contract or agreement, and ask them to read it carefully before they make any further appointments. Then if the client decides to continue the work he calls the therapist for a further interview. Psychotherapists and counselors reveal that this policy sometimes loses clients, but by far most return, and those who do are better motivated and likely to maintain their financial obligation.

HOW MUCH TO CHARGE

The appropriate fee depends on a number of considerations, including such things as the type of clientele one hopes to reach, the prevailing rates for comparable services in the area, the comparable income range of the therapist if she were based in an institution, overhead costs, the cost of living in the area of the practice, and the therapist's assessment of her own drawing power. Whenever a fee is charge for anything, some people are unable or unwilling to avail themselves of the service, and it follows that the higher the fee, the fewer potential clients. So the therapist must find the optimum fee to charge to help her reach her financial goals and still appeal to a large enough group of people so that she can maintain a stable practice.

There is, however, some skew in the correlation between amount of fee and potential clientele. If the fees become very low many people become as anxious and possibly repelled as if the fees were very high. Clients and everyone else seem to believe in the maxim that "you get what you pay for," whether or not it is always true. So if the fees are very much lower than the norm, the therapist is likely to be seen as inferior, less well-trained, or somehow second-rate. If, for example, attorneys in the area typically charged between $50 and $75 per hour, the attorney who sees clients for $19.95 per hour will be suspected of incompetence, regardless of her true worth or merit.

Most private psychotherapy practitioners set their fees in the beginning on the basis of what other members of their profession in the area are charging, or using as a baseline the charges of other disciplines for performing comparable services. The therapist is subsequently able to increase or decrease the set fee.

Psychiatrists are at the bottom of the spectrum of physicians' earning power but they are the highest paid of the psychotherapy professions (Sharfstein and Clark 1980). Psychologists who have Ph.D. or Psych. D. degrees typically charge between $5 and $10 per hour less than psychiatrists with the same experience in the same geographic region. Insurance companies' statistics, however, are beginning to show that psychologists are charging virtually the same amounts for insured clients as psychiatrists. (Sharfstein and Clark 1980). Social workers with Ph.D. or D.S.W. degrees are still relatively few in number, but in cities where they are well represented their charges match doctoral level psychologists. M.S.Ws as well as nurses and clergymen with master's degrees are all charging approximately the same fees, about $15 to $25 less than psychiatrists in their areas. Psychotherapists from other disciplines are not so easily ranked. Their charges are more related to their unique drawing power and experience, or ability to appeal to the public.

Most therapists charge the same hourly rate if they see an individual alone or with other members of his family. The minority of therapists who charge more to see couples or families for the same amount of time have strong justification. Their view is typified by one therapist who said.

With a family, I have to keep track of several people instead of just one. All of these people are my clients. I have to keep notes on all of them. My records and bookkeeping are more complicated and time-consuming. I have to keep in touch with all of the people in their role-sets, like the kids' teachers and the wife's doctor and the husband's boss. More people here means more wear and tear on my furniture. It is more cost-effective for a family to see me together than one at a time. They would be really getting a good deal if the charges were the same for the whole family as for the individual. It's like a hotel charging more for a family using a room than for an individual using it.

This justification is not shared by most practitioners, who feel that they keep track of the family of an individual client anyway, that additional wear and tear is miniscule, and that it is less complicated in record keeping and in every other way to merely charge for the time spent.

There is one exception to the notion of charging just for the amount of time. That is in group therapy or group work encounters, where each client pays. Charges for group therapy participation tend to be less than for an equal amount of individual time. The therapy group in private practice is traditionally 50 to 100 percent longer than an individual session, and the individual client in a therapy group is usually charged between 25 and 50 percent of what the practitioner charges for an individual hour. So, for example, if the therapist's individual fee is $60 per one hour (fifty minute) session, her group rate is likely to be $30 for an hour and a half or two hour session. The time spent in group is different from the time spent with an individual or with mem-

178 VALUES AND MONEY

bers of the same family, and this is why the exception is made. Each member of the group is treated as an individual client, while the family is treated as the single client. Each group member requires individual records and billing. Also, the intensity of the treatment experience is so much greater than in the individual sessions that the basis of fee charging is different.

Of course, the therapist's charges for individual sessions vary if the amount of time spent varies. Some therapists have full sessions, usually consisting of an hour, half sessions, half an hour long, and double sessions, lasting two hours. These are usually established in advance with the understanding that the fees are proportionate to the amount of time the therapist spends with the client. Some therapists also have open-ended sessions with no set time limits. Usually these sessions are prorated from the hourly charges. Open-ended sessions may have some merit from a theoretical viewpoint, and they may be worthwhile for some clients, but they cause the private practitioner a great deal of administrative headache, and are thus very rarely used. The therapist who has open-ended sessions has a difficult time being able to schedule a client to follow, and her personal activities after the workday are disrupted.

Some practitioners charge higher rates than their standard charges at prime time, or lower rates when the appointments are at less desirable times. Prime time for private practitioners is usually in the evenings and on weekends, and sometimes during lunch hours. Many clients seek these hours because of their own work schedules. Many practitioners are in the position of having to turn away some potential clients because there is no time available after work, even though the therapist may have many open hours during the workday. These surcharges or lower rates can help to balance out the practitioner's schedule of appointments, but they raise other questions. Insurance companies who might be helping to pay the expenses of the treatment may take a dim view of the practice. One wonders if it isn't discriminatory for those people who work during nonprime time hours. And the practice is an administrative problem in requiring the therapist to keep track of different fee schedules.

FIXED RATE CHARGES OR SLIDING SCALES

Are all clients to be charged the same amount for the same service or is the therapist going to charge some clients more and others less depending on their resources? The question has been debated for decades and still hasn't been completely resolved. The norm in therapy clinics, social agencies, and medical settings at first was to use a sliding scale, charging less for those whose means were limited (Fizdale 1957). Today the fixed fee system is becoming more popular even though the sliding scale is still the implicit policy for many hospitals and social agencies. Many advocates are now saying that clients should be expected to pay the full costs of service, unless they *demonstrate* an inability to pay the total amount (Goldberg and Kovac 1971). The assumption is that the family is able to pay unless there is explicit information to the contrary. The private practitioner has followed the lead of clinics and social agencies on this issue. Most private psychotherapists once used a sliding scale basis of fee charging in the past. Now most private practitioners have explicitly fixed fees, but they tend to be very flexible in individual instances.

The psychotherapy professions have had trouble deciding which of these two possibilities is best. Each is based on a value set which is consistent with most therapists' values and principles, even though they come from contradictory and mutually exclusive points of view. Those who advocate the sliding scale make the following arguments: It emerges from the tradition in which fee formulas are based on the client's resources, expenses, and expected frequency of the use of service (Goodman 1971). It is consistent with the principle of individualization. The policy makes it possible to provide services for many who otherwise would be unable to afford them. Since most agencies and clinics use the sliding scale formula, clients have come to expect it when they seek such services in the private sector. Finally and most important, say the proponents of the sliding scale policy, a client's inability to pay a substantial sum for services should not preclude his or her receipt of the needed assistance. Letting money be a criterion of whether or not to aid a client is completely antithetical to the most fundamental values in the helping professions.

Those who advocate charging a fixed fee have an equally compelling argument. They contend that the sliding fee is discriminatory and unjust for the "nonpoor." In effect, these clients would be subsidizing those with inadequate resources. Subsidization, they argue, is necessary for the less affluent, but such payments should be borne by the public at large rather than only people who happen to have problems and seek the therapist's services. Fixed fee proponents also point out that the sliding scale interferes with the therapist-client relationship in its initial stages more than does the fixed policy. The proper fee has to be determined in the very beginning, and in the sliding scale the client is subjected to a means test. Most helping professionals believe that the means test, in which the therapist scrutinizes the client's finances and resources, is degrading and unfair to the client. Social activists have, for years sought to end the means test because it is so contrary to democratic values (Theobald 1966). Yet it is always a necessary element in the sliding scale formula. How else could rates be established? In the sliding scale format, the therapist must make extensive inquiries about the client's finances in the first contact, leaving considerably less time to discuss the client's problem. It suggests that money is the major interest the therapist has in the client.

Fixed fee proponents also point out that during the course of treatment the client's fortunes frequently change, and consistency to principle would thus dictate that the fee be adjusted accordingly. It is likely that the client would improve his financial position as he overcame some of the problems which led him to the therapist. But if the therapist keeps varying the fee, an intervening variable is introduced into the therapy situation, which may confound the course of treatment. For example, some clients may have less motivation for improving their financial situation, or revealing that it has improved, if they know that doing so will lead to greater costs.

Private practice psychotherapy faces another conflict in the use of the sliding scale that is eliminated with the fixed rate. Since many referrals come from former clients, there can be some awkward moments for the therapist in justifying to a client why he must pay more than did the person who referred him. The client's expectation might have been that his fee would be the same as that of the referring person.

Third-party payments are becoming highly influential in the trend toward fixed fees. Insurance companies already look at psychotherapy with a highly skeptical eye when it comes to reimbursement. (Lesse 1979). The companies would find it intolerable if they saw that fees varied from client to client. If the fees charged to insured clients were higher than for those of non insured clients, the insurance company would raise many questions about the ethics and legality of the practice. The practice would be, from their point of view, as serious as embezzlement or fraud. So therapists who seek insurance coverage for their services must unquestionably establish a flat rate for service regardless of the economic circumstances of the client.

The consumer movement is also a strong factor in the trend toward fixed fees. Psychotherapists as individuals and as a professional group, are generally very sympathetic to the consumer movement and strive to support it wherever possible. Thus, it would be highly inappropriate for therapists to deviate from adherence to consumer principles in their own provision of services to the consumer. A major doctrine of consumerism is that the user of services must know what he is getting for his money and that his dollar is worth the same as anyone else's (Hermann 1980). Most psychotherapists would be appalled if a department store varied its prices on goods depending on how affluent the customer appeared to be. Price adjusting and other bait-and-switch practices are serious consumer issues and do not seem that different from sliding scale formulas. Consumer advocates stress the need for openness about costs and prices and uniformity in setting them. Let the consumer decide, based on available facts, whether to purchase the service. And once the price has been established, it should not be changed. It seems clear, in sum, that the fixed fee for services will be the norm in private practice, and perhaps in clinics and social agencies, if not for value reasons then for practical ones.

THE METHOD AND TIMING OF PAYMENT

Experienced professionals in fee for service have learned a hard truth about client payments: the likelihood of payment increases if the client is billed or expected to pay immediately upon provision of the service. Conversely, the longer after service provision the bill is sent or the client is expected to pay, the less likely it is that payment will ever be made. It is for this reason that many professional's offices or waiting rooms are equipped with signs saying that payment for services may be made immediately upon receipt of the service. Many such offices have secretaries or receptionists who ask each client, "Could you leave us a check today, or how do you want to pay?" If business considerations are the only ones, then immediate payment is the best policy. However, there are many other factors that influence the policy. For one thing, it is unethical for any profession to withhold needed services because there is no immediate payment. For another, the therapist-client relationship has been based on trust and individualization, and demand for immediate payment, for some clients, obviates this policy.

The available options about timing of payment are (a) to pay before the service is rendered, (b) to pay immediately thereafter, (c) to pay before the month is ended, (d) to pay before a certain number of days has elapsed into the next month, (e) to pay after paychecks or insurance reimbursements are made, or (f) to pay on an individualized basis of installments over a period of months. It is appropriate for the therapist to have a different policy about the time of payment for each client. If a client is known to have problems managing money and needs controls, it would be logical to require that he pay immediately after each session. Another client may be asked to pay just *prior* to each session when there is reason to believe that he wouldn't pay at all if he were permitted to wait until the session was over.

Most practitioners who don't receive immediate payments present bills or statements to the client at the end of each month, either personally or by mail, with the expectation that full or partial payment will be made within a prescribed amount of time. Usually the length of time and terms before payment is due are stated on the bill. These expectations, of course, would have already been discussed in the initial contract setting, but the bill eliminates any misunderstandings. Some practitioners find that *personally* giving a statement to the client at the end of each month is the most effective way of assuring payment. Therapists who prefer to use the mail find that their return rates are higher and faster when they also enclose a self-addressed envelope. Before first class postage stamps became so expensive, it was found to be cost effective to stamp the self-addressed envelope, but this is now more conjectural.

Many practitioners work out arrangements with their clients to defer payments. This is in keeping with the individualization principle and makes allowances for the financial limitations of clients. Making smaller payments each month over a longer period of time is one popular arrangement. However, when a client does not pay or is not required to fulfill his obligation for a prolonged period of time, it is tantamount to being given a no-interest loan by the therapist. In the medical profession and in many other fee-for-service helping professions it is explicitly unethical to charge interest on unpaid bills. Other therapy professions have not yet established a policy on this matter, so these practitioners need to decide about interest.

The preferred method of payment is by check or money order. Checks serve as receipts for the client, who may then use them to document expenditures for personal budget and income tax purposes. When checks are not used, the therapist is frequently asked, before the next year's income tax deadlines, to provide clients with records of payments. Cash payments are very problematical. When thus paid, the therapist must provide a receipt for the client. The cash must be handled just like checks. That is, it must be kept with checks until time for making bank deposits, and it must be recorded carefully. It is too easy and tempting to pocket this cash and spend it before it is fully accounted for in the office accounting system.

Skimming, taking money out of the business operation without declaring it as income, is illegal and rules against it are vigorously enforced (IRS 1982a). Internal Revenue Service investigators audit the records of fee-for-service practitioners on a frequent and random basis, even when there is no ostensible problem in the reported tax forms. When they do so, according to their manual of instructions, they are to give close scrutiny to the possibility of skimming, as well as the more usual problems of deducting inappropriately (*U.S. Master Tax* 1982). IRS agents sometimes seem to assume that skimming occurs unless the practitioner is able to prove otherwise. Acceptable proof is likely to be a thorough record of all income, kept in a daily ledger, a record in each client's chart of his payments, and bank statements which indicate that each deposit adds up to exactly the same as office receipts for that time. If cash payments were discouraged and made infrequently these problems would not occur.

Another method of payment that is increasing in popularity among practitioners is the use of credit cards (Kilgore 1975). Credit card companies are eager to enter the professional fee-for-service market because they experience fewer problems of collection than with many of their other clients. Therefore, it is a simple matter for the practitioner to become a participant in one of their programs. It is advantageous to the practitioner because he is assured of collection when the client signs the credit card expense receipt, and the client is then able to negotiate terms of payment with the company. The terms can be flexible with the credit card company, and the issue about interest on the unpaid balance is no longer a problem for the therapist. The disadvantage is that the credit card company deducts a substantial portion of the total payment, thus reducing the therapist's earnings for that particular transaction.

BILL COLLECTING

The most unpleasant aspect of any business is trying to obtain the money the customers agreed to pay and for which they have been billed. The problem is very sensitive for businesses which provide services or intangible commodities whose value is less visible to the customer. It is even more touchy when the essence of those businesses is a relationship based on trust, mutual respect, concern for the consumer's well-being, and compassion.

Most businesses and fee-for-service professionals minimize the problem by collecting as soon as possible, but this isn't always possible for many clients. Every private practitioner has some clients who do not and will not pay the agreed amount for services.

In medicine, office-based private physicians have a collection ratio of 92 percent (Kauffman 1980). A collection ratio is the total practice receipts divided by billings. To put it another way, 8 percent of all patient billings made by physicians go unpaid. This ratio has remained fairly constant in the past twenty years, even during periods of economic recession or relative affluence. The ratios vary only slightly according to the doctor's location and specialty. The collection rate is somewhat lower in the West and Midwest and higher in the middle South and the New England states than the average. Family practice doctors have slightly higher ratios than do physicians in general. The doctors who provide more free services to patients tend to collect less than doctors who provide less. Comparable figures for psychotherapists have not been established, but it seems unlikely that the collection rates would be any higher than those of physicians.

It is appropriate for the psychotherapist or counselor to be concerned about bill collecting and to do everything possible, within the constraints of her professional ethics, to increase her collections. She is not only doing a disservice to herself when she fails to enforce the agreement made with the client, but she is also doing a disservice to the client. When "relationship" is the essence of any treatment, and when that relationship is thereafter tainted by the realization of both parties that the trust and respect were violated, the treatment gains are also jeopardized.

There are several steps the therapist can take to minimize the problem. First, of course, is for the therapist to reiterate the terms of the agreement when it appears that the client is not adhering to them. If, for example, the bill has not been paid by the agreed time, something is said about it during the next interview session: "Mr. Jones, I haven't received your check for last month's sessions yet. Is there some problem about it that we need to discuss?" The response will determine the next step. If that response suggests that the client didn't feel this was an important part of the agreement, then this becomes the opportune time to discuss its importance.

If the client explains that he thought it would be all right to wait until his paycheck or insurance reimbursement payment came in, the therapist must clarify this point. The therapist's office expenses and her own obligations must be met at prescribed times. Landlords do not wait to collect rent depending on when the client's money is received. But if the client response indicates that he is having unanticipated money problems, the therapist has several options. She could decide to lower the fee until the financial circumstances improve again, or she could decide to provide needed services for free during this time. Or the therapist could make a new agreement about the financial terms, and perhaps put it in writing. The agreement might indicate that payment will not be required until some specific future date, or that a small amount will be required monthly until payment has occurred. In some circumstances it might be advisable to postpone the treatment until the financial situation is improved (Wolberg 1977).

In any case, when the financial agreement is violated, it is a propitious time for the therapist and client to reassess the goals and the nature of the agreement, the nature of their relationship, and the motivation of the client. If this action is taken at an early stage, before the bill has mounted up, both the therapist and the client will be more comfortable with whatever eventual decision is reached.

But following these steps will by no means assure that every agreement about money is fulfilled. There will be times when the private practitioner will be confronted with the realization that her client is not going to pay. Usually this realization occurs after treatment has concluded and bills are sent to the client for several months with no response. Nice notes are included in the bill. ("No doubt this bill has escaped your notice. Please disregard it if you have already sent in your check.") Then the bills are sent with more emphatic messages. ("Every patience has been extended to you. If we don't receive a check soon we will be forced to . . . ") Then the therapist telephones the former client. ("Hello, Mr. Jones. How have you been? I was wondering about your bill.") Psychotherapists must be careful about telephone calls concerning bills. Recent consumer protection laws are designed to protect people from harassment about bills, and the therapist could find herself in legal trouble if her calls are too zealous.

What is left for the therapist to do? Her options are to (a) forget the whole thing, (b) take the matter to small claims court, (c) engage an attorney, (d) hire a professional bill collector, or (e) use a credit bureau. Most practitioners who want to pursue the matter choose the last option, a credit bureau. Small claims courts can be very time consuming, and there is considerable difficulty getting the court to enforce its decision. And it is by no means certain that the court will decide in favor of the therapist if there is no letter of agreement signed by the client. Engaging an attorney is very costly and usually achieves the same results as small claims courts. Professional bill collectors often engage in tactics that are alien to the values of the psychotherapy professions. Furthermore, when they do successfully collect from the client they typically keep 40 to 60 percent of the collected amount for their services.

Credit bureaus, the favored option of private practitioners, also leave a lot to be desired. Credit bureaus are private organizations located in most larger communities, financed primarily by commercial businesses and banks to keep and provide credit files on the populace. As an adjunct to the major service of providing information, the bureaus often employ people to contact those owing money and stress to them that failure to pay will result in a new entry in their credit bureau data. The client is then asked to pay the credit bureau directly. The bureau typically remits 50 percent of its collection back to the practitioner and may or may not make an entry in its records about the client. Using credit bureaus is possibly the best of the last resorts, and while it is unsatisfactory its use is a necessary fact of life for every person in business.

CHARGING FOR INDIRECT SERVICES

Effective psychotherapy includes what are called indirect services. These activities include such things as communicating with others in behalf of the client, providing information about clients who give consent, writing letters, giving testimony, interviewing members of the client's community, or even discussing various matters with the client on the telephone. There is no question that these activities are necessary, but there is question among private practitioners as to their financial status. The institutional therapist performs these activities as part of her duties, and her annual salary is paid on the assumption that such activities are performed. The private practitioner, on the other hand, might have some problem billing her clients for such services. It behooves her to establish a policy concerning such matters and making this policy as clear to the client as any other financial matter.

The other fee-for-service professionals are not entirely helpful in providing guidelines on this issue. Lawyers bill on the basis of the amount of time spent *in behalf of* their clients, unless they are working on a contingency or percentage basis in suits. They have an imaginary meter which they turn on whenever they do anything for the client, including writing letters, talking to the client on the phone, preparing briefs, dictating, or whatever. The amount of time thus spent, multiplied by the established charge per hour, is the amount the client is billed. The physician has a fixed fee for various medical procedures, including office visits, which is not entirely based on the amount of time spent with or on behalf of the client. Other service people simply charge an agreed flat rate.

Most psychotherapists in private *clinical* practice charge only for the time spent in interviews with the client or collateral interviews with members of the client's family. Some have used the lawyer's meter analogy, but find that it leads to unnecessary complications and requires constant clarification with the client. The rationale is that the fee for the direct interviews includes the fee for any ancillary activities such as letter writing, providing or obtaining information, and telephone calls with the client. Most clinical practitioners find it wise to minimize the amount of time spent with the client on the telephone anyway, since such communications are rather limited and sometimes more harmful than helpful in maintaining the relationship. Therefore, the amount of telephone time is minimal and charges need not be made.

Charges for extraordinary indirect activities can be negotiated prior to performing them. Thus, if the therapist is asked to testify in court, or contact other organizations, schools, agencies or institutions in behalf of the client, it must be established at the outset what the fee for such service will be. Most private practitioners in all specialties charge "portal to portal," if such activities involve travel. This means the standard hourly rate is charged from the time the therapist leaves her office to the time she returns to her office. But aside from these time-consuming activities, the psychotherapist or counselor is better off charging only the fixed charge for the face-to-face contact.

CHARGING FOR MISSED APPOINTMENTS

A practitioner receives a call two hours before her client is expected to arrive at the office: "I'm very sorry, but I just can't come in today. My wife is ill." The practitioner, even if she has a full workload and is turning potential clients away or referring them elsewhere, is soon going to have an empty hour on her hands. It is too late to schedule anyone else and she is caught up on her paper work. Does she bill the client who canceled? If she does not do so her own income is lessened by the amount of her hourly rate, through no fault of her own. If she does bill for the session, some complications will possibly arise in working with the client. The client's bill cannot be reimbursed by the insurance company if the interview was not conducted. Yet, the client's reason seems valid, and his actions in view of those reasons seem appropriate. What is the policy about charging for missed appointments?

It depends. The policy, whatever it is, should be made clear to the client in advance. Most private psychotherapists establish that charges will be made for appointments canceled less than twenty-four hours ahead of time, unless there are compelling reasons for exceptions. If the client tells the therapist that he will not be able to meet next time, and if the information is given at least a day in advance, the therapist has enough time to fill the hour or to make other plans. If it is less than a day's notice, the therapist may not have enough time for alternative plans. But the principle of individualization is again operative.

The decision to charge or not can be based on the client's reason for canceling, and on the therapist's judgment about the underlying reasons for it. It means one thing when the client has never before failed to keep an appointment and has fulfilled all parts of the agreement, and quite another thing when the client has repeatedly canceled appointments and continuing to do so seems part of a pattern. Whether or not the client had a particularly difficult session last time may be related to the reasons for cancellation. The therapist must certainly exercise some judgment and take into account certain circumstances that inevitably occur in the client's life. However, for the purpose of consistency and clarity in the therapist-client agreement, it is useful to make explicit that charges will occur if no notice was given a day in advance, and not mention that special exceptions will be entertained. Then when and if the issue ever comes up it can be dealt with in the next session. If the decision is made to charge for the missed appointment, it must be understood that the client cannot expect the insurance company to reimburse him for the session. Furthermore, he cannot expect the therapist to fill out any insurance forms which would enable the client to be reimbursed for that appointment.

The policy for attendance in group therapy may be different than for individual sessions (Berne 1955). In group therapy the norm is to charge the individual for every time the group is in session, whether or not the individual attends. The rationale is that the session is available to the individual whether or not he attends and that the worker must conduct it anyway. The client's failure to attend does not make it possible to have someone else take his place for that one session. He is still holding a position in the group. When he returns to the group he usually must be brought up to date, at the expense of the group time. It is equivalent to a student paying for classes at school, whether or not he attends all the classes. Of course, here again discretion may be made by the therapist. Some group therapists allow no exceptions to the policy of "pay for every session," but some give the clients a certain number of sessions off for vacations if notification was well in advance.

DOES GROUP THERAPY INCREASE INCOME?

Some members of the therapy professions feel that their economic rewards will be enhanced considerably by using group therapy as a supplement to, or instead of, individual work with clients. "After all," say this rationale, "if you see one person an hour you can only charge so much but if you see a whole group of people in that time you increase the return a great deal."

Since time is all the therapist has to "sell," there are only three ways to increase income: to charge higher fees; to spend longer work hours with more clients; or to see more than one person at a time. Charging higher fees might lead to a diminution of clientele and a deviation from the psychotherapist's principles about accessibility of her services. Increasing one's work hours means the individual will have to sacrifice more of her time with her family and friends. Thus, for many, group therapy seems like an ideal way to increase income without giving up anything else.

This view has solidified because of the original justifications for the use of group therapy. When it was first struggling for acceptance and recognition, group therapy was sold as an economic expedient as much as for its treatment effectiveness (Slavson 1947). Institutions often used it because it appeared to be a good way for limited staff to treat more people, thus keeping costs lower. Now, of course, group therapy is established and documented as a treatment method that is very effective and useful, at least for many clients, as any other treatment method. It is now advocated more for its treatment effectiveness in institutional settings than for its economic considerations. But private practitioners still see it as having interesting possibilities as a revenue producer. Is it as remunerative as believed?

Suppose the private practitioner charged $50 per hour of individual work. As we saw earlier, the standard group therapy fee is about half that amount and the group is usually 50 to 100 percent longer than the individual session, or 90 to 120 minutes. Private practice groups, depending on their orientations and goals, tend to have from six to ten members. Thus, the typical situation would be to charge each individual member of the group $25 per 120 minute session. If this group contained eight members, the proceeds per group session would be $200. But the group is twice as long, so the income is $100 per hour compared to the individual charge of $50 per hour.

However, the therapist must spend eight times as long in preparing case records and insurance forms for the group as for an individual. Each group client deserves and is ethically entitled to as much care in record keeping and other administrative procedures as the individual. It is reasonable to expect the therapist to spend 10 minutes in case recording with each group member if he spends 10 minutes with each individual client. He gets the 10 minutes from his individual client's 50-minute hour. The 80 minutes he spends on the group record-keeping is his own time. Instead of 120 minutes for the group, then, he spends 200 minutes. This effectively reduces his hourly rate to the same as the rate for the individual client.

But there are other cost considerations too. The therapist receives telephone calls from his group members as often as from individuals. The therapist who has groups must have larger amounts of space, which increases his monthly rent. The same is true for furniture costs, as well as greater wear and tear. And how about wear and tear on the worker? The single therapist has to keep track of more dynamics and intricacies in group than in individual sessions. If this extra effort and stress causes the therapist to need longer vacations, or more time off from work, or if it causes his health costs to increase, money is lost from the group income. Many groups, because of these extra demands, have cotherapists, or assistant group leaders. This further reduces the income down to one-half what it would be if the therapist treated the group alone.

Also, there are often times in groups when a full complement of members is not attending. Considerable care must be taken to assure that the right new addition is made to an ongoing group and finding this person can sometimes take weeks. The group then would not have eight members and the resulting income is still less.

Many of the factors in reducing the estimated proceeds from group therapy are hidden and therefore not easily recognized or acknowledged by many therapists. Many group therapists cut corners too, by not spending nearly as much time in recording and administering for their group clients, but the ethics of this seem questionable. Therapists don't think about extra wear and tear on their equipment or on themselves. They are more inclined to think that if eight group members don't increase revenue by that much, why not have very large groups?

Large groups usually have a different purpose and orientation than more intensive, smaller therapy groups (Spotnitz 1972). They can be quite remunerative, as organizations such as Life-springs and est have discovered. But all in all, the therapist would do well to consider that traditional group therapy is not necessarily going to increase his income significantly. Group therapy should be utilized because it is an effective treatment technique, and because it can offer the therapist an opportunity for a change of pace from his individual work, rather than because of financial considerations.

PROVIDING FREE SERVICES

A typical case illustrates the issue of providing service at no charge. A middle-aged woman begins weekly sessions with the psychotherapist to assist in resolving marital problems. Her husband refuses to participate in the sessions but does agree to pay the fees. The wife suffers depression, insecurity, and anxiety. The three children are grown and living independent lives. The wife hasn't worked for twenty-five years and feels she has no marketable skills. She suspects her husband is having an affair. She says her husband thinks she is "crazy" or "menopausal."

After the sessions have progressed on a weekly basis for two months, during which time some of the symptoms have improved and some of her self-confidence is restored, her husband leaves home. He notifies her through his attorney of his intention to divorce. Her lawyer advises that she should continue her therapy. He also tells her that she will not get enough money from her husband in a future settlement to live on. At this point, while frightened, even more insecure than ever, confused and depressed, she tells the therapist that she can no longer afford her services, at least not until a settlement is reached and she is able to get training and enter the job market. What is the private practitioner's response? Does she agree with the client and discontinue the treatment? Does she refer the wife to an agency which charges an amount she could afford? Or does the treatment continue on a gratis basis?

One thing is certain in a case such as this one and the plethora of similar ones that all private practitioners encounter. Under no circumstances does the practitioner have the ethical or moral right to discharge the client without seeing that treatment continues. When services are needed and contracted for, it is the private therapist's professional duty to meet those needs until service is completed. Anything less is a violation of professional values, ethics, and principles and should be a violation of one's personal moral standards as well.

In some cases it might be advisable to refer such a client to an agency whose fees are appropriate to the client's financial circumstances, but for the most part such referrals are of questionable merit. Referring "undesirable" clients to others is a frequent practice which is very dubious ethically (Lindenberg 1958). Many clients, after being referred around enough times, simply give up trying to obtain help (Lantz and Lanahan 1976).

Even though the practice is questionable those who do it are quick with their rationalizations. They say that this is simply a part of the therapy process of providing the client with the information and resources to obtain help from someone who is able to provide it. They also say it is similar to starting treatment for depression and then learning in the course of treatment that the cause of the depression is organic. It is appropriate to refer the case to a neurologist, if that happens. New information justifies the transfer, they say.

This, of course, is based on faulty reasoning. If the therapist contracts to treat the client and if she wanted to discontinue because of money problems, then money would be the most important part of the agreement. This is hardly consistent with the notion that the relationship is also based on trust, respect, and concern. Clearly it is essential that private psychotherapy practitioners recognize that there will be times when they will need to see and work with such clients, through to the conclusion of treatment.

But what about the person who inquires about obtaining private psychotherapy services but indicates an inability or unwillingness to pay the stated fees? Here is an entirely different issue. Until the contract between the therapist and client has been established, there is no obligation by the therapist to provide service, even if it is deemed to be needed. The therapist is within her ethical and value boundaries if she refers such a client to an organization which is able to provide subsidized treatment. Of course, the therapist may choose to work with this client on a reduced rate basis if she uses the sliding fee scale format, or she may choose to see the client on a gratis basis.

It is a common practice among the fee-for-service helping professions to see some clients at no charge. A predetermined proportion of the clientele is seen for free. This is quite in keeping with the values of the helping professions. It is recognition of the private practitioner's social obligation, is virtually institutionalized within the professions, and is explicitly or implicitly part of their codes of ethics.

The criterion one may use in determining who should receive gratis services is rather uniform among those who provide it. The clients have limited financial resources which prevent payment. The practitioner has probably allocated a predetermined number of hours per month for this purpose only. Gratis clients are usually only taken on when there is a vacancy in this segment. Many practitioners see gratis clients when the client demonstrates a particular problem which is of particular interest to the practitioner, or when the client seems likely to present information which the practitioner is seeking as part of a research interest. Providing services for free to some clients is an important part of the private psychotherapy practitioner's responsibility. The therapist will be amply reimbursed in many nonfinancial ways.

PROFESSIONAL COURTESY

One form of gratis service is the practice of professional courtesy. Providing services to one's professional colleagues for free or at a reduced rate is a custom as venerable as the Hippocratic oath from which it is derived. The tradition exists, at least to some extent, among all professionals in fee-for-service practice. It is done ostensibly to tangibly demonstrate the professionals' bond of fraternity and thus it rarely extends from one professional discipline to another (Owens 1980). Physicians often do it for physicians and lawyers for lawyers, but rarely do lawyers do it for physicians or vice versa. Since psychotherapy is not one but many different professions, it is rare that this courtesy occurs between psychotherapists. Even when therapists do extend it to their fellow professionals, there is an implicit, or sometimes explicit, understanding that the courtesy doesn't extend for the full length of the required treatment. In a profession where a single client takes up a significant proportion of the practitioner's time, and an even more significant amount of personal involvement, it is necessary to establish limits about courtesy. As a practical matter, therefore, the norm is to not charge for the first interview and thereafter charge the same amount every other client pays. Professional courtesy by private practitioners is highly individualized, and that is as it always should be.

FEE SPLITTING AND COLLABORATION

Fee splitting once was considered a heinous act in the medical and legal professions. It was the practice of referring a client to another professional who would then pay the referring person part of client's fee. It was considered to be a serious abuse, because practitioners would often refer not to the best person for the client's need but to the person who paid the highest referral fee. The client often had to pay more for the service in order to cover the practitioner's charges and the referral cost. It is most appropriate that such a practice be explicitly forbidden by psychotherapists. But it closely borders other practices which are reputable and sound so similar that clarification is warranted.

When a therapist sees that her client has problems that can best be served in a cotherapy situation, how is the billing done? For example, in sex therapy, the treatment of choice is for both husband and wife to work with a male and female therapist (Masters and Johnson 1970). If the therapist calls upon another therapist of the opposite sex to assist in the work with the couple, both therapists require payment. Is this fee splitting? If the therapist sends his client to another practitioner for an evaluation and consultation to refine diagnoses, does this result in fee splitting? If the therapist refers the client to another professional, and the other professional refers another client to her, is this considered fee splitting?

Sharing fees in cotherapy, consultations, and collaboration is a valid activity in private practice and not the same thing as fee splitting. Collaboration is an extremely valuable and important tool in providing improved service for the client (Spitz and Spitz 1980). Unfortunately, it is used less often than most private practitioners would like, because of complications about fee charging. The client may be expected to pay twice as much for an hour when it is done with cotherapists or on some collaboration basis. Difficulties about insurance payments are inevitable. It is often easier to merely see the client alone and thus not run into such billing problems as exist in these formats. In any event such practices are not the same as fee splitting, and rather than being considered unethical, as is fee splitting, they are very positive experiences for the therapist and the client.

INSURANCE REIMBURSEMENT

Before concluding this chapter it is necessary to look at the influence of insurance reimbursement on money matters in psychotherapy. The effect of insurance companies and third-party payers on the entire field of psychotherapy has been profound, and the consequences are not yet fully felt. Third-party payments influence the kind of psychotherapy that will be offered and probably will determine which psychotherapy professions will survive and which will not. It will lead therapy methods to develop more tangible ways of demonstrating their efficacy. The third-party system of payment will make it possible for many people in need of psychotherapy to avail themselves of it for the first time. Because of the seriousness of this issue, all the therapy professions are engaged in lobbying efforts with federal and state legislative bodies and with the insurance companies themselves (Fisher 1981).

Several studies have recently been conducted about the effects of third-party payments on the psychotherapy process, and the findings are not encouraging (Enoch and Sigel 1979; Meltzer 1975). The six worst consequences are as follows. First, there is a drain of skilled therapy manpower from the public institutions, as professionals enter private practice fields which are covered by insurance payments. This is already evident from the vast increases in the numbers of new psychotherapists in private practice. It is also evident in looking at the labor statistics in public facilities. For example, the great majority of the nation's 25,000 psychiatrists are now in private practice, while the mental hospitals are experiencing a terrible shortage of psychiatrists (NCHS 1978). Even though the number of psychiatrists has quadrupled in this country since 1950, there are fewer now employed in mental hospitals, per patient, than there were then (NCHS 1978). The shortage of nurses in hospitals and clinics is also well known and is occurring in the face of many of their number entering independent counseling practices. Social agencies are not now suffering from labor shortages as they were in the 1960s (Barker and Briggs 1967) even though many social workers are entering private practice, but only because the agencies have been faced with declining public support and funding, resulting in personnel cutbacks.

The second negative consequence of third-party payments is that there is an imbalance in the distribution of services, so that those illnesses and treatment methods which are eligible for coverage get more attention than those which do not. Need by clientele becomes a secondary consideration. If, for example, an insurance company would pay for an adolescent to receive psychotherapy, even though the young person would benefit more significantly and for a longer period of time if she could receive vocational training, she likely would get the therapy and not the training. There is no way to prove that training would be more beneficial than psychotherapy, so no one could adequately argue the case. Also, the health insurance company is not in the business of providing vocational training. Common sense and some research reveal that some people can benefit greatly from preventative programs, training experiences, and education, yet for many there is only psychotherapy instead.

A third negative consequence is an overuse of psychotherapy services by a relatively few people, preventing others who could benefit from getting treatment. Not only the affluent but also the well insured are partaking of therapy, and there is, unsurprisingly, a correlation between the length of treatment and the extent of insurance coverage (U.S. Congress 1980). Insurance companies are beginning to combat this phenomenon by establishing time and frequency limits on treatment for certain diagnoses. Miraculously this has so far led to a shift in the kind of diagnoses being made. But psychoanalysis and intensive psychotherapies, marathon encounters, and long-term treatments are under increasing scrutiny. Their practitioners are being asked for extensive justifications for the treatment method utilized (Gelwin 1981).

The fourth negative consequence of the insurance reimbursement system is that marginally trained or untrained people in both public and private sectors are attracted to mental health delivery. Some of them had been reimbursed by insurance companies, at least in the first few years that psychotherapy became covered. Now insurance companies are becoming very restrictive about which professional groups are covered. But even so, as more people partake of outpatient psychotherapy in the expectation that insurance will cover their needs, more poorly trained therapists are being consulted. Often these people work under the supervision of a therapist who is covered, or the covered therapist submits the claim to the insurance company and divides the proceeds. It is difficult for third-party payers to deal with this unethical practice.

Fifth, the fees which psychotherapists ask of their clients are rising faster than the rate of inflation, and so are the premiums which must be paid by the insured ("Health Insurance" 1981). The increase would not be so great, owing to the increasing competitive situation, were it not for the foundation provided by the insurance companies. If all psychotherapy services were reimbursed directly by the consumer, or by public support through social agencies, then the price of therapy would fall dramatically. A total cutoff of third-party payments for psychotherapy seems unlikely but there may be a diminution of payments by insurance companies to psychotherapists.

Finally, the sixth negative consequence of third-party payments to psychotherapists is that treatment strategies are more often determined by economics than by mental health principles. If therapists are asked to justify at length the choice of one treatment method but not another, they are likely to use the *covered* method. Or if therapy of one kind is covered and not therapy from other disciplines, then those disciplines will not have opportunities to contribute to the mental health care delivery system, no matter how much they might have to offer.

Nevertheless, the third-party payment system is needed and is likely to remain in some form as long as we remain a viable socity. The physical health part of the system will certainly continue ("Health Spending" 1981). The mental health coverage aspects might undergo substantial changes in the next few years however. At present, most insurance companies discriminate against mental health consumers in that their coverages are usually less, if they exist at all (Mueller and Piro 1976). Some insurance programs don't cover for mental disturbances or psychotherapy. Others reimburse only a small percentage of the total fee charged by the therapist, and some only begin paying after a sizable deductible has been met. For example, a client might have to pay the first $100 or $200 of the therapist's bill before the insurance begins coverage, while the same insurer might begin paying for physical care after only a $50 deductible has been met. Also, companies cut off payments after a certain length of time, whether or not the need for treatment still exists.

Insurance companies are also rather careful about which professional groups they do cover and which they do not (Garfinkel 1976). Of the companies which do cover for psychotherapy services, all cover for the treatments administered by a licensed psychiatrist. Almost all cover licensed psychologists, too. Some companies still require psychologists to practice under the supervision of the psychiatrist, but this is becoming rare. Most of the major health insurance companies reimburse social workers and nurse-practitioners if they are licensed and practice under the supervision of a physician, but the reimbursement amount is less than for the psychiatrist. Licensed or certified marital and family therapists are reimbursed by CHAMPUS, the Civilian Health and Medical Program for the Uniformed Services, but the federal government has been challenging this requirement vigorously ("Recent Problems" 1981). The other psychotherapy professions are less successful in getting reimbursement from health insurers. For them, there are two alternatives. Many of them simply work outside the third-party payment system, requiring direct reimbursement from their clients. The others become affiliated with physicians, often working in the same offices, and letting the physicians bill the clients and their insurance companies.

Insurance companies and other third-party financing organizations maintain records about the fees which psychotherapy providers are charging. On the basis of this information they establish their own fee scales for the different professions, which they call "reasonable and customary" charges for that particular geographic area. However, the amount they say is the reasonable and customary one is usually less than what psychotherapists are actually charging. The third parties say they must keep a lid on charges and that the fee increases are going up so fast that they do sometimes fall behind. The gap between what the companies say are reasonable and customary and what therapists are charging seems to be growing, but it would undoubtedly be growing even more rapidly if the third parties did not set these limits (Herrington 1981).

All the psychotherapy professions are coming under increased pressure by the public and by third-party financing organizations to demonstrate that what they offer is worth the money provided (Gelwin 1981). As we have seen, psychotherapy has had a difficult time giving such proof of efficacy so far. The professions have depended on their quality assurance programs rather than their proven cost-effectiveness to justify receiving third-party funding. But health insurance for psychotherapy is no longer guaranteed for any providers even with quality assurance ("Health Insurance" 1981). The next few years will reveal the direction the third parties will be taking.

EIGHT

MALPRACTICE, SOCIAL CONTROL, AND OTHER DILEMMAS

ONCE upon a time there was a young man, a young woman, and, as often happens in true modern tales, a psychotherapist. The young woman's name was Tatiana Tarasoff and she was bright, popular, attractive, and eager to experience life to the fullest. For some time she had been dating the young man, but she eventually decided that it would be best to end their relationship. He was very upset about her decision, confused and terribly angry. Somehow his feelings would not diminish, and their intensity even seemed to grow. Finally he decided he needed help. He was a graduate student at the University of California, so he went to the university's mental health clinic, where he was assigned to a staff psychologist. He told the psychologist about his feelings for Tatiana, about her decision to break up with him, and about how he found the decision unendurable. She had just left the country for a tour abroad, he said, but when she returned he planned somehow to resolve the matter. With growing emphasis and conviction he told the therapist that he was going to kill her.

The psychologist was a conscientious and competent professional who could see that the student's thoughts were serious and that he had the ability and determination to carry out such a threat, so he promptly told the staff supervisor, a psychiatrist, about the new client. They agreed that the situation was critical and that it required immediate action. The therapist called the campus police and indicated that his client was very dangerous and should be committed for observation and treatment, involuntarily if necessary.

The police picked up the student and interrogated him. They questioned him at great length, particularly about his relationship with Tatiana Tarasoff. The police officers noted that he seemed sincere, rational, and in control of his faculties and he promised them that he would stay away from her. The officers gradually became convinced and they finally released him. Predictably, the student broke off his treatments with the psychologist because of the police investigation. But a few weeks later, after the young woman returned home from her trip abroad he carried out his threat. He ended the life of Tatiana Tarasoff.

In the subsequent investigation it became publicly known that the student had been in treatment at the university clinic and that the psychotherapist had alerted the police that he was a danger to the victim. Tatiana's parents brought suit against the psychologist, the psychiatrist-supervisor, the campus police, and their employer, the University of California. They were sued for failure to warn Tatiana or her parents of her peril and for failing to suitably detain the student for treatment. The suit was dismissed in lower courts, but on appeal to the California Supreme Court the finding was against the psychotherapist and the others at the university. The judges concluded that regardless of the psychologist's attempt to confine the student, and since he and the others at the university knew he was at large and dangerous, the "failure to warn Tatiana or others likely to apprise her of the danger constituted a breach of the therapist's duty to exercise reasonable care to protect Tatiana" (*Tarasoff* 1976).

The *Tarasoff* decision was handed down in July 1976, making it illegal in California for a therapist not to warn anyone when a client makes a threat. Other state courts are using the *Tarasoff* decision to justify similar rulings, so that the "duty to warn" is becoming virtually a national requirement. There is, of course, a storm of controversy and uncertainty in helping professions as a result of *Tarasoff*. Therapists are being pressured to an ever increasing extent to subordinate their principles of confidentiality in favor of various forms of social control.

PROBLEMS, RISKS, AND MALPRACTICE
IN PRIVATE PRACTICE

The *Tarasoff* ruling illustrates the kinds of dilemma confronting members of the helping professions, but it is only one of the many risks and problem areas with which they are now faced. State laws are increasingly requiring professional people to notify authorities of conduct which is deemed illegal or harmful. Insurance companies and government agencies which are underwriting and subsidizing mental health care are more rigorously looking into the practice methods of therapists to determine if their work is effective and worthwhile. The therapists' records are essentially becoming open to the public, accessible to the clients, to insurance companies and government agencies, and to law enforcement officials. Further, there is an explosion of malpractice suits. Conflicting responsibilities place the therapist in a no-win situation. For example, if he complies with the *Tarasoff* judgment and warns someone who is threatened by his client during an emotional outburst, the litigious client would very probably be able to win a lawsuit for violating confidentiality and for defamation, if no harm is actually done.

The private practitioner is not the only professional who is confronted with problems of this type, but he is perhaps more vulnerable to them than practitioners in institutional settings. His work with the client is more visible and the results, good and bad, are more easily traceable to him alone. There is no one to give him backing in problem situtations. There is no one to help diffuse some of the pressure that might come his way. He is less likely to have access to other professionals who can provide immediate and objectifying consultations and data which might be necessary to properly serve the client. It is therefore imperative for the private practitioner to be congnizant of the risk situations to which he is vulnerable. He has to learn to spot potential malpractice situations before they get out of hand.

It is unfortunate but true that many professionals have become exceedingly cautious and conservative in the methods they are now employing in helping their clients, because of these risks.

They are becoming reluctant to experiment with new techniques or deviate much from traditional methods. In a defensive mood, many are not seeing clients until an extensive battery of psychological and physical examinations have been given, to cover even the remotest of possibilities. This caution necessarily adds considerably to the costs of providing needed services and removes much of the creativity, ingenuity, and growth that any scientific method must utilize. Such caution is probably extreme, but when the discerning practitioner considers the risks to which his is vulnerable, especially in malpractice situations, it is easy to understand.

SOME MALPRACTICE EXAMPLES

It would be naive to assume that if the practitioner adheres to the highest standards of his profession, conforms to his profession's code of ethics, conducts his treatments in accordance with the traditional methods used in his profession, and always achieves what he considers a successful therapeutic outcome with his clients, there would be no risk of malpractice suits. Most practitioners would be hard pressed to say that they have been able to adhere successfully to all these elements at all times, but even if they did, they could be liable. Consider the following examples in which practitioners have found themselves having to defend against malpractice suits.

A forty-year-old woman is married to an alcoholic. She has supported him for the last ten years of their eighteen-year marriage. She has self-destructive tendencies and is very insecure, typical traits in people who are married to alcoholics. Because of her insecurity and self-destructiveness she has not been able to influence her husband to work on his illness. Nor has she been able to terminate the relationship. She is a member of Al-Anon, the support group to help spouses of alcoholics, and is encouraged by her fellow members to seek therapy. They tell her that her internal problems keep her from ending an intolerable situation. She enters therapy, works diligently and successfully, and eventually resolves many of her conflicts. Her self-confidence is restored and her self-destructiveness is vitiated. Again she attempts to influence her husband to get help, and this time threatens to leave him if he does not do so. He still refuses to work on the problem. She finally decides on divorce and sues her husband to leave the home. He then goes to a lawyer and explains that his wife decided to leave him as a result of her therapy. The husband's source of livelihood is jeopardized because of the therapist. He and his attorney sue the therapist for the harm that he has allegedly caused the husband.

A twenty-two-year-old man has just been discharged from military service because of severe and chronic depression. He returns to his parent's home and they urge him to seek treatment. The young man does well in therapy for the first four months. He gets a job, starts making friends, and shows signs of reintegrating into the community. Many of his depressive symptoms are diminished. He then decides he wants to get a place of his own away from his parents. He decides to terminate his therapy in order to save money. The therapist tells him that his depression may return and advises against ending treatment. The therapist even offers to reduce or postpone the fees in order that the young man might continue. But the man stops anyway, by failing to keep the next appointment. The therapist calls to see why he didn't come for the session and the client again stresses that he wishes to discontinue. The therapist never sees him again. Three months after the call, the young man commits suicide. His parents, feeling that the therapist did not do everything possible to alleviate the suicidal tendencies and either keep him in treatment or get him hospitalized, seek compensation from the therapist through a lawsuit.

A woman has been in group therapy for several months. She is an attractive young married mother of two, in treatment because of conflicts about her sexuality. She reveals to the group that she had recently had an affair with a married man but that they broke it off because they both felt guilty and fearful about its effect on their marriages. A fellow group member is very interested in the woman's revelations. He is a man with severe characterological problems who has had various troubles with the law, difficulty holding jobs, many unsuccessful involvements with women, and a deep-seated anger and resentment toward authority figures. Even though everyone in the group is admonished to honor and respect each other's confidentiality and to not see one another outside the group, the man secretly starts following the woman to her home after group sessions. He starts learning more and more about her personal life. He finally calls her on the telephone and attempts to get her to meet with him in a motel. She rebuffs him and calls the group therapist to report the man's behavior. The therapist contacts the man and reiterates the group rules about confidentiality and about no outside contact. The man becomes enraged at the therapist and refuses to continue his sessions. The woman also refuses to return to the group, despite the therapist's attempt to get her to continue. The man now begins calling the woman and harassing her. He threatens to reveal her secret to her husband and to her ex-lover's wife, if she doesn't meet with him. When she still refuses, he writes letters to both families. This results in a considerable conflict between spouses. They all seek legal assistance and attribute much of the blame for their troubles to the group therapist. They contend that the therapist should never have put the man in the same group with her and should have exercised more control over the man. This therapist had to defend against suits from two parties.

The final example concerns a thirty-four-year-old man who is referred to a psychotherapist by a friend who had previously been successfully treated by the therapist. For six months, the man had been taking three five-milligram tablets of Valium daily because of anxiety and tension. He tells the therapist that the anxiety seems to have begun in the past year and is increasing. It becomes so severe, he says, that his heart pounds and he sweats profusely. He seems insightful and articulate and attributes his symptoms to the growing pressures of his job and to some unresolved conflicts about the death of his mother two years ago. He assures the therapist that his last physical examination was normal and that he had no health problems. After treatment begins, catharsis seems to help the client tremendously, and there is a marked diminution of the anxiety symptoms. But after three months the symptoms return and seem to get worse. The therapist recommends increasing the number of visits to twice weekly.

Again there is a reduction of symptoms for awhile, but then they return with even more intensity. One day at work the man becomes so upset he is taken to a nearby hospital. Tests follow. The consulting physicians at the hospital discover that the symptoms are caused not by functional neurosis, as was assumed by the therapist. The diagnosis was "mitral valve prolapse syndrome." The client's lawyer eventually sues the therapist for misdiagnosis, for inappropriate treatment, and for not insuring that the client get proper attention for his medical illness.

Even though the therapists in these four examples were able to win their suits, defending against such charges was extremely expensive for them both in legal fees and in time away from their jobs, to say nothing of the harm which inevitably occurred to their reputations. All four therapists had adequate malpractice insurance, which helped to pay for some of the legal expenses, but there were many hidden legal fees which were not covered. Nor was there any insurance coverage for the loss of time from employment and loss of esteem they experienced, even though the results were favorable. The group therapist even had to fight her insurance company, which wanted to settle the claim out of court because any defense would be more costly than the possible judgment would be. The therapist of the suicide victim eventually left private practice.

It is easy to see how these things could happen to the most well-meaning and competent of psychotherapists. Every therapist encounters situations daily which have malpractice overtones. Many clients don't achieve successful results no matter how competent the therapist is or how reliable the method is. And when there is a successful outcome, the client very often has a changed relationship with others, who might not feel very grateful to the therapist for bringing about the change. Furthermore, it is not possible to keep clients in therapy against their wishes, no matter how much they might need it. It is becoming increasingly difficult to get clients confined or incarcerated against their will, no matter how serious their problems. It is not possible in every case to rule out every physical ailment that can cause a client problems. Nor is it possible to control or be responsible for the client's actions and behaviors after treatment ends, even if the therapist wanted such power. Nevertheless, such expectations are held regarding therapists, and when they aren't met, malpractice liability can result.

MINIMIZING MALPRACTICE RISKS

What then can the private psychotherapist or counselor do to minimize these risks? How can he provide services effectively without becoming defensive, unimaginative in his approach, or so cautious that the desired results become even more difficult to achieve? There is no certain way to avoid malpractice suits, but some things will reduce the risk. The therapist is going to be less vulnerable if he conforms to standard professional conduct at all times in his dealing with the client. He is also going to reduce his risks if he knows what the malpractice pitfalls are and how to avoid them whenever possible. He must accept, however, that he could never completely avoid them, because the pitfalls are contradictory. As we have seen, he may be liable if he doesn't warn an intended victim of his client, but if he does he may be liable for defamation. He may be liable for not reporting a client's illegal behaviors but also liable for not conforming to his profession's standards about confidentiality. To an unfortunately great extent, he must simply play the odds.

What are the odds? Thus far they are better for therapists who belong to some professions than to others. They are worse among those who deal with the physical care of clients, especially physicians, and to a lesser extent nurses and physical therapists. There is now on the average one malpractice lawsuit in the United States for every five to seven years of practice for every physician. Some physicians' specialties are much more vulnerable to lawsuits than others. Neurosurgeons are the most likely and psychiatrists least likely to be sued (Schaeffer 1981). There is one suit for every one to two years of neurosurgical practice and one for every fifty to one hundred years of psychiatric practice (Trent and Muhl 1975). Most malpractice incidents, however, do not result in payments. More than half the malpractice incidents (55.5 percent) are closed prior to initiation of lawsuits, and only

6.5 percent of the initial incidents ever reach a verdict. When payments do occur, they have usually been relatively small. A 1973 study of claims paid, for example, showed that 59.5 percent were for under $3,000, 34.4 percent were awarded for $3,000 to $39,000, and only 6.1 percent were for over $40,000 (*Medical Malpractice* 1973).

While it is no longer unusual to read about million-dollar judgments against physicians and practitioners who treat for physical problems, it is still uncommon for anyone involved with caring for emotional disturbances to achieve such judgments. Several psychiatrists have been sued successfully for six-figure amounts, but these were mostly in connection with incarceration issues and controversies arising out of drug reactions. Amounts awarded for nonphysical damages or confinements have tended to be for much less (Shear 1973). The highest award against a psychologist was $170,000, in 1973. One case was settled out of court for $60,000, against a social worker and the worker's supervising psychiatrist ("Social Workers' " 1978). Insurance companies report that it is difficult to develop actuarial tables about the risk of malpractice for nonphysician psychotherapists because there are so few claims or suits. Nevertheless, they are still urging therapists of all disciplines to purchase great amounts, such as one millions dollars' worth of professional liability coverage. The risks may not be as great as those faced by medical practitioners, but it seems inevitable that some nonmedical psychotherapists will also be sued for a great amount of money.

This is certain because of two increasingly important trends. The first is the greater numbers and visibility of private practitioners who are engaged in psychotherapy and counseling. As discussed in chapter 1, the growth and increased autonomy of therapists is accompanied by their movement away from host agencies which no longer deflect the risk of malpractice claims.

Even more significant, however, is the second trend, the exploding increase in the numbers of lawyers and the correlating increase in litigiousness among the public. The American legal profession is growing faster now than at any time in its history, and there are already more lawyers by far in the United States per capita than anywhere else in the world (*New York Times*

1981). All of them want to make a living, and most will seek to maximize their income potential wherever possible. They are often willing to represent any party which feels aggrieved and will frequently do so on a contingency basis. That is, they can represent clients for free provided they receive one-third of any amount won in the suit, plus expenses. If the lawyer is otherwise unoccupied, as is certainly the case with many because of the increase in their numbers, contingency lawsuits are an attractive possibility (Stone 1978). Since the client doesn't need to be concerned about any financial risk there is hardly any reason not to enter suits. If the lawyer feels a case has merit he has nothing to lose but his time in pressing the issue.

Some physicians' associations are now advocating that doctors countersue any lawyers who make claims for damages without just cause. This seems to have had some effect in reducing the number of frivolous or nonserious cases. But physicians are advised not to threaten lawyers with countersuits merely in an attempt to persuade the lawyer not to go ahead (Rosenberg 1980). Lawyers expect such threats. Often it only makes them more determined to build a strong case to insure that they will win. If they win, no countersuit would be successful. Even if they lose, if they get enough material in the court record that leads to valid questions, the success in winning a countersuit is very remote.

Another trend in some states is to reduce the number of malpractice suits. Because several state courts have been deluged with frivolous suits in recent years, their legislatures have adopted statutes which deter the less substantiated claims. In North Dakota, the law requires the loser in a negligence case to defray some of the winner's costs. Thus, if a psychotherapist is sued and wins, he may ask the court to reimburse him for his expert witness fees and court costs, and the court will determine how much of the loser's money will be awarded. In Florida, the client who sues and loses will have to pay a portion of the professional person's attorneys' fees. Of course, if the professional person loses he will also have to pay these costs to the winner. But, of course, the best defense is for the practitioner to avoid behaviors which might lead to damage to the client, or eliminate causes of malpractice claims wherever that is possible.

THE CAUSES OF MALPRACTICE

To recover damages in any malpractice action the plaintiff must prove that the professional owed his client a duty to conform to a particular standard of conduct, that he breached that duty by some act of omission or commission, that because of the breach the client suffered actual damage, and that the professional's conduct was the direct or proximate cause of the damage (Bernstein 1978; Pope et al. 1978). The key is breach of duty, but the standard of care which is breached is hard to define. It is likely that breaches in standard of care will be determined by expert testimony by other members of the profession, who will tell the court whether the behavior was or was not in accordance with professional standards.

On the basis of experiences of physicians and mental health care providers, it is possible to identify eleven specific types of conduct which have led to successful malpractice claims. Damages have been awarded because of each of these behaviors, which have been considered breaches of professional standards of care. They are (1) treatment without informed consent, (2) failure to advise the client of the danger of treatment, (3) faulty diagnosis and inadequate treatment, (4) failure to refer the client to a specialist when necessary, (5) misuse of psychotherapy, (6) physical restraint and bodily harm, (7) abandonment, (8) limitations on ability, (9) termination of treatment, (10) breaches of confidentiality and defamation, and (11) failure to warn others who are threatened by the client. Of course these are not discrete elements, and usually the behaviors which are seen as malpractice breaches overlap two or more of these elements.

Treatment Without Informed Consent. The client must agree to the service offered and willingly and explicitly must consent to any methods to be employed. Violation of this standard is more likely to occur when clients are institutionalized. Consent problems would be rare in the private practice setting. The private practitioner's clients come to him voluntarily, which itself is evidence that consent has occurred. Only when the client is unable to consent because he is a minor or judged legally incompetent because of mental illness or other incapacity is there likely to be a consent problem for the private practitioner. In such instances consent is obtained from the parent or person legally responsible for the client. The risk for private practitioners is in the client not being *informed* enough to give consent. Malpractice damages can be awarded if the client was not properly informed about the methods to be used and therefore not in a position to give consent. For example, if a client has a misperception about the nature of the treatment and is not told about the methods before he undergoes them, the therapist may be held liable. Some clients may have expected that positive results are a certainty or that they can be achieved in a very short time at a minimum of cost. A claim could be upheld unless the therapist could prove that no assurances, guarantees, or claims were expressed or implied.

Failure to Advise the Client of the Danger of Treatment. This is an important component in the *informed* part of informed consent. There are risks in any treatment or intervention that the therapist may undertake, and of course, the client has a right to know this. Several court cases have determined that the person offering treatment is required to tell the client or patient of the potential adverse effects and dangers of treatment. If adverse effects later occur, and if the client wasn't warned of the possibility, a malpractice claim could be made. Some exceptions to this occur in the case of emergency treatments where the client is in no immediate position to evaluate the prescribed treatment. Nonmedical psychotherapists are rarely in these emergency positions, so the emphasis for them should be on simply discussing the possible risks and being sure that the client understands and accepts them. Failing to do this, the therapist does not have informed consent.

Faulty Diagnosis and Inadequate Treatment. Most malpractice suits of this type have concerned clients who were incarcerated because of diagnostic assessments that were later found to be invalid. Only physicians should make diagnoses which lead to commitment.

However, the nonmedical psychotherapist can be involved if he provides information to the physician which leads to an improper diagnosis. One of the largest settlements against a nonmedical therapist involved a situation of this type. A social worker evaluated a client and prepared a report for a psychiatrist to use in court. The report said the client was not dangerous, but shortly thereafter the client shot several people including himself. Both the psychiatrist and the social worker were sued, but they settled out of court for $60,000.

If a nonmedical therapist gives facts or recommendations to a physician and later those facts prove to be incorrect and contribute to a misdiagnosis by the physician, the therapist may share liability. For this reason it is crucial for the private practitioner to maintain accurate and complete records of his client's history, as well as of any tests or interview findings. The client's file should contain a current diagnosis, treatment plan, and prognosis at all times in order for the therapist to avoid a compromising situation. Inadequate treatment suits have been entered against staff psychotherapists of institutions in which the client is not treated in accordance with professional standards. The famous *Wyatt* v. *Stickney* class action suit, in which patients in an Alabama mental hospital were not given proper treatment, is but one example (Johnson 1975).

Private practitioners are less vulnerable to charges of inadequate treatment when the client is not being held involuntarily. But as seen in the examples of malpractice, it is also possible to be sued when the therapist treats and diagnosis inappropriately. This makes it imperative that every client be required to undergo a thorough physical examination before proceeding with psychotherapy or counseling.

Failure to Refer the Client to a Specialist When Necessary. This breach of professional standard can be very serious for the private practice psychotherapist who is not also a physician. It could lead to charges of practicing medicine without a license. The expected standard of conduct is clear on this point, because of many successful suits brought against people, particularly chiropractors, in fee-for-service practice. The standard is that the practitioner must tell the client whenever he knows or should have known that his form of treatment will not or might not be effective, and that more effective treatment is available that he is not trained to offer.

For example, if a client is suffering from anxiety or depression, the therapist might consider medication first, and if this has proved unsatisfactory then the longer, drawn-out forms of "insight therapy," or behavioral modification techniques may be used. Only physicians are in a position to prescribe drugs for such illnesses, so if these criteria are used, physicians must be consulted. However, it is debatable whether drug therapy constitutes more effective treatment than psychotherapies without medication. In any event, the nonmedical psychotherapist should consider psychiatric consultations whenever there is a question of which type of treatment to use (Green and Cox 1978). The therapist could be liable to malpractice claims if he has not had some form of consultation with a physician about the client and the client is thereby damaged.

The "required standards regarding consultation are met if, in the judgment of a medical specialist (psychiatrist), nonmedical treatment would be effective in a given situation. An unlicensed person found to have violated state statute by practicing medicine as defined by the statute is held strictly liable for any damage suffered by the patient as a result of that practice" (Green and Cox 1978: 103). What constitutes medical practice in nonphysical treatment areas is always questionable so the worker must be very careful in this area, especially in dealing with clients who exhibit somatic complaints.

Misuse of Psychotherapy.   If the therapist utilizes the treatment process to serve his own ends at the expense of the client, the resulting misuse can constitute a valid malpractice judgment. The most common breach in this regard is in sexual activities with clients. There have been a number of successful suits against practitioners who have had sexual relations with clients ("M.D. Condemns" 1981). When sexual or social relationships occur and are judged harmful to the client, the court will likely hold the therapist responsible for mishandling the transference phenomenon (Serban 1981). The various disciplines practicing psychotherapy are all clear and explicit on the point. The therapist must always effectively manage any transference-countertransference situations or he is deviating from professional standards. It would also constitute a misuse of psychotherapy to use information which the client has presented in a way that it enriches the therapist at the client's expense. For example, influencing a client to include the therapist in his will, or purchasing properties from the client, especially without giving proper remuneration, are other examples of the misuse of psychotherapy. The obvious precaution is to avoid any social, financial, or any other relationship with the client that is not explicitly therapeutic.

Physical Restraint and Bodily Harm. Some therapists can be vulnerable to malpractice damages when their clients have become institutionalized because of the therapist's actions, or when the therapist's therapeutic processes directly or indirectly lead to physical harm. Providing information to authorities or physicians which leads to improper commitment is one area of vulnerability. Another may be found in some of the more active group therapy encounter techniques. For example, in some of these encounters the clients, under the therapist's supervision, are encouraged to push or hit each other with paper bats or otherwise give vent to repressed feelings. Should a client by physically injured during such activities there is a possibility of legal action. Care is necessary wherever actions are taken to commit clients or otherwise deprive them of their liberties, as is care in activities where clients are subject to physical activity as a form of treatment.

Abandonment. When a psychotherapist or counselor is no longer available to the client who still has need, malpractice is a possibility. Of course, there will inevitably be times when the therapist is unavailable to his client, when he takes vacations, is ill, attends professional conferences, or retires. At such times he must be careful to insure that his behavior is not construed as abandonment. He must insure that someone else is covering his clients during his absence, particularly if a client has suicidal or violent tendencies. A therapist has protection if the professional covering for him can make a valid diagnosis and maintain a treatment plan from the available record, but if the record contains misleading data or the information is insufficient, it is the original therapist who is negligent. Abandonment liability can therefore occur if the therapist has not informed the client of his planned absence, has not arranged for the client to see someone else if the need arises, and if the covering person does not have sufficient information to provide proper care until the worker returns.

Limitations on Ability. If a client develops a more serious emotional or social dysfunction after being in psychotherapy, there is a possibility of malpractice litigation against the therapist. Sometimes, for example, a client's problem requires the expertise of a neurologist because there is a disturbance of the central nervous system. If the therapist treats for anxiety when neurological treatment is needed, major difficulties can arise for the therapist. Some states now have laws which stipulate that both physical and mental health care should be given professionally only by physicians, unless specific exceptions are included in the statute. Often these exceptions are made for nurses and others under the physician's authority. Therapists should be clear as to the state statutes so that they do not perform professional activities which are the legislated responsibility of members of different professions.

Termination. Problems concerned with ending the treatment relationship are also a source of potential malpractice liability. There must be an orderly and professionally prescribed process by which the client discontinues therapy. Treatment continues until both therapist and client agree to end it, or the client explicitly decides to conclude, or the therapist decides to conclude because he feels the client is no longer in need of service. If any of these occur the treatment is thereby terminated. It is sometimes wise to put the decision in writing with a summary letter or a termination of treatment notice. Sometimes the client forms a transference-based attachment to the therapist, or the therapist feels attached to the client through countertransference, and these feelings cause the treatment to extend beyond the point where it is productive. If the client wants to continue because of the attachment but is not in need, the worker must use care to terminate without making the client feel rejected or personally abandoned. Sometimes if the treatment seems no longer productive, the therapist should acknowledge the fact and refer the client to another professional for treatment or at least for consultation. Failure to do this is potential proof of negligence. Termination of treatment may also lead to liability if therapy is no longer necessary but the psychotherapist continued to collect fees. This happens sometimes when therapists unnecessarily prolong the treatment, or even stop seeing the client and continue to submit claims to the insurance companies. Another problem around termination occurs when the therapist ends treatment prematurely, resulting in the client's relapse. Of course, if an error is to be made, it is better to see the client longer than really necessary than to conclude too soon.

Breaches of Confidentiality and Defamation.   The therapist is privy to his client's thoughts and behavior, and this information may not be shared with anyone without the client's written permission. This is explicitly stated in the codes of ethics of all the psychotherapy disciplines and any violation could easily result in malpractice suits. Not only would the therapist be negligent because of deviation from the standards of his profession but, unless his disclosures could be proven, the client could sue him for defamation of character, slander, or libel. Usually this is not a difficult issue for therapists, who tend to be rigorous in their devotion to confidentiality. However, there are situations which make it difficult for therapists to always adhere to confidentiality. For example, in the *Yoder v. Smith* case, a doctor was asked by his patient to give medical information to an employer. The information indicated that the patient was unable to perform some of his former duties on the job, so the patient felt harmed by the doctor as a result (Slovenko 1966). Therapists are also asked to breach confidentiality when a client reveals he has committed a crime and the police are attempting to find him. Possessing such information and failing to reveal it to legal authorities puts the therapist in a precarious position. He can be in difficulty if he does and if he does not violate the principle of confidentiality.

Failure to Warn the Potential Victims of Client Threats. The therapist is in a dilemma about breaches in confidentiality and protecting the public. The *Tarasoff* decision, which, as we have seen, requires therapists to warn anyone who is threatened by his client, causes this dilemma. Malpractice suits can be successful against therapists who hear their clients make threats and then fail to reveal the information to the intended victim. But if they do issue the warning and the client does not harm anyone, the client can sue for slander or defamation as well as breach of confidentiality. The balance between confidentiality and the duty to warn is a delicate one, and the therapist who must negotiate it is in a precarious, highly vulnerable situation, no matter what course of action he chooses (Simmons 1981).

THE CONFIDENTIALITY–DUTY TO WARN PARADOX

The therapist's paradox cannot be eliminated because the laws and legal interpretations are still contradictory (Simmons 1981). If he issues warnings he violates some confidentiality standards, and if he doesn't do so he may be breaking the law. But there are some actions he may take to minimize the paradox and protect himself as well as his clients. He must first look at his dilemma in an objective way and consider all the possible consequences of his actions. He cannot predict which clients might present such a dilemma to him.

Psychotherapists, because of the nature of their work, can never avoid clients who might make threats about others. A major part of therapy is to help people deal with the conflicts they have with others. Therapy clients are more often than not at odds with others and seek the therapist's assistance in resolving such problems. For example, people having marital problems frequently ventilate their frustrations about their spouses in the form of threats. Many clients fantasize about punching their employers or teachers. The therapist uses this material to understand the client and help him find more socially acceptable as well as more personally effective ways of relieving social frustrations. But if the therapist is required to tell each client that any threats he makes must be reported to the intended victim, he may be hampering treatment.

If the law holds any therapist liable for failure to warn an intended victim, then the client will be less likely to confide his feelings to the therapist. A basically antagonistic relationship between the therapist and his client may develop. Clients who disclose information about themselves could be incriminating themselves and thus be subject to legal action. Psychotherapists and counselors who act in accordance with the principle of informed consent may well deter clients from seeking their services. Ultimately fewer and fewer people will seek psychotherapy because of the fear that they may talk about the "wrong things" or express unacceptable feelings or desires (Noll 1974). Unless such feelings are revealed, the therapist is in no position to help the client find more effective, nonviolent ways of revealing his problems. Thus, potential victims may be in greater danger because of such rulings as *Tarasoff,* specifying the duty to warn, than without them.

The *Tarasoff* decision is based on a premise of questionable merit. Inherent in it is the belief that therapists can reliably predict the likelihood of a client's future violence. But the bulk of expert opinion and research data indicate that none of the helping professionals have such powers of precognition. If the professional person is willing to make such judgments, he will inevitably be uncertain about the accuracy of his predictions. It is also likely that he will overpredict that which he fears is possible. If he adheres to the *Tarasoff* judgment and his only consideration is to protect himself from any violations of the law or from suits by victims, it is likely that he will be warning almost everyone who is close to his client. If his primary considerations are to serve his client well, rather than to protect himself, he may be doing so at his own peril. Most psychotherapists in private practice will be highly concerned about the well-being of their clients and devoted to the principle of confidentiality, despite *Tarasoff*. It is therefore in their interests to know how best to deal with situations which have *Tarasoff* implications.

Psychiatrists Loren Roth and Alan Meisel have prepared some guidelines for dealing with such situations (Roth and Meisel 1977). These guidelines, modified here to include all psychotherapy disciplines, are as follows.

First, the therapist should not be stampeded by the *Tarasoff* ruling into providing frequent warnings to third parties. Serious threats are infrequent, and the ones made are less frequently carried out, so it is senseless for the therapist to compromise his confidentiality standards or usual treatment methodology.

Second, all of the psychotherapist's clients, upon entering into a treatment contract, should be informed of the confidential nature of the relationship and the various circumstances under which confidentiality may have to be breached. It would seem to be overly cautious to go into the *Tarasoff* considerations with each client because this might interfere with a meaningful therapeutic relationship, or even deter clients from treatment. However, the psychotherapist must be candid with the client who speaks convincingly about his intent to do harm to someone. When the practitioner becomes fairly certain that the threat is serious, he must express alarm and describe what the law requires him to do if the client persists in the threats.

Third, the therapist who is convinced that danger seems imminent can use some social or environmental manipulations to reduce the client's "dangerousness" without compromising confidentiality. For example, other persons such as the client's friends and family may be asked to participate in the treatment, or the client may be dissuaded from keeping lethal weapons.

Fourth, when the therapist has made it clear that the law requires him to warn potential victims, many clients are willing to give the warning themselves or to permit others to give the warning. When disclosing such information about the client to others it is wise to obtain the client's permission and if possible to reveal the disturbing information about the client in his presence.

Fifth, the therapist must evaluate the impact of the proposed intervention on any future treatment, and he must assess the likelihood of success in preventing violence. If disclosure is likely to interfere with future effective treatment, and if it is not likely to reduce the chances of violent behavior, he may want to rely on the odds and hope for the best. Rather than warning the potential victim or working to get his client hospitalized or incarcerated, he may feel it is more appropriate to treat the client so that such violence does not occur.

Following these guidelines may cause the therapist to feel that that he is falling short of his ideals of always complying with the law and with the highest standards of his profession, but sometimes social forces and conflicting exigencies make such pragmatic actions necessary. This will always be the case when helping professionals are required to serve clients and perform various social control functions as well.

THE SELF-DETERMINATION AND
SOCIAL CONTROL PARADOX

Tarasoff not only compels practitioners to suffer the risks of malpractice but it also pushes them into social control activities. More laws and courtroom decisions are being made to require practitioners to place social needs over the needs of clients. Yet it is inherent in the psychotherapy disciplines that the client should not have the therapist's values imposed upon him. When the law requires practitioners to exercise social controls on clients, it removes the practitioner's commitment to the primacy of the client's interest.

Thomas Szasz advocates less institutional or agency-based treatment because he sees it as a way for society to control any behaviors which the institution deems unacceptable (Szasz 1970). He values the "contractual arrangement" because the individual independently seeks psychotherapeutic help by making his own agreements with a mental health professional in private practice. In the contractual arrangement, he says, the therapist is presumed to place the interest of his client above any other outside interest, or the client would go elsewhere. As a consequence, Szasz concludes, clients need not fear that what they confide to

their therapist will be used against them. But Szasz did not anticipate subsequent court decisions requiring private helping professionals to report people to authorities and engage in social control functions. These rulings negate many of the advantages Szasz
finds in private practice contractual arrangements.

Social control functions are being increasingly forced on private practitioners in more ways than through *Tarasoff* considerations. One emerging example is in child abuse and neglect situations. No private practitioner or any other ethical professional
would simply sit back and attempt to do nothing about a client
who reports abusing his children, but professionals have always
assumed the responsibility for dealing with this in a professional
rather than a legalistic way. But professional judgment opportunities are being removed from the practitioner and given to legal
authorities. For example, many states have enacted legislation
which requires mandatory reporting by professionals of suspected instances of child abuse or neglect.

One state law says that "any physician, nurse, dentist, optom-
etrist, medical examiner, coroner, or any other medical or mental
health professional, school teacher or administrator, school
counselor, social worker, day care center or any other child care
worker, police or law enforcement officer having knowledge of
or reasonable cause to suspect that a child coming before him in
his official or professional capacity is abused or neglected shall
report the circumstances to the division" (Noll 1976). Such statutes include measures of enforcement and describe the penalties
that may be imposed on the professional person who does not
make his suspicions known to the proper authorities. In these instances the psychotherapist would be breaking the law to not reveal confidences which led him to the suspicions.

But laws and judgments of this type are ultimately short-
sighted. In child abuse cases the client, knowing that his actions
will be reported, is likely to conceal them from the professional
person who may be able to help him. If they remain concealed,
the behavior may lead to more harm than ever to the child. If the
practitioner reports the client to the authorities, the client is then
likely to be publicly reprimanded and humiliated but probably
not incarcerated. If placed on probation he is more likely to be
angry and frustrated and may take it out on his child.

If the legal process then requires that the person get professional help for the problem, as is likely, the person is in exactly the same situation he would have been without the incident having been reported in the first place. Reporting such regrettable episodes as child abuse, wife beating, threats of violence to third parties, criminal activity, or any deviant behavior is ineffective as social control. Worse yet, it vitiates the possibility of giving needed help through the therapeutic relationship.

PRIVATE PRACTITIONERS AS DOUBLE AGENTS

If the private psychotherapy practitioner is to serve his client and serve the public through exercising social controls he effectively becomes a double agent. He must serve two masters whose needs and interests are not always identical. He often must choose sides. In the private practice setting this may not be as apparent to the client as it might be in a host agency. Clients in social agencies or institutions probably expect that the therapist is representing the interests of society or the organization. In organizations where the client is not voluntarily seeking help, the nature of his disclosures is likely to be different than when he seeks the services of a private practitioner of his own volition. The psychotherapist must exercise considerable caution so that the client does not presume that the therapist has no social control responsibility. The client cannot be led to believe that the therapist serves him only. He must be allowed to know that the therapist is a double agent, and he must be informed about the extent and type of activity the therapist will engage in on behalf of the public or other agencies.

Some ways in which the private practitioner is required to act as a double agent, besides warning intended victims or reporting instances of criminal conduct, include the following: giving information to insurance companies about the nature of the client's problem, informing employers or potential employers about the client, and having one's case records scrutinized by others who seek information about the client.

Insurance companies intentionally or inadvertently put private psychotherapy practitioners in a double agent situation with clients. For example, clients and former clients are frequently faced with the question on insurance application forms: "Are you now or have you ever received treatment for emotional or mental disorders? If the answer is yes, please explain." It is quite possible that if the applicant acknowledges that he has had treatment his application will be rejected, no matter what the circumstances are. Or it is possible that if the application is accepted the client will have to pay larger premiums for the same coverage. At the very least the client will be required to give many further explanations, examinations, and additional statements. The insurance company may also ask the therapist to provide additional information.

Some clients decide to conceal their treatment from insurance companies, but this is risky. If those treatments were covered by health insurance it is a certainty that the insurance company to which the client is applying for new insurance coverage is aware of them. There is a central computer system funded by over 700 insurance companies to keep all kinds of information about insurance recipients and applicants. It is called the Medical Insurance Bureau, headquartered in Boston, Massachusetts, and it currently has files on millions of Americans. At the push of a button it delivers any information about an applicant which might help determine his risk category.

The psychotherapist who is asked to provide information to an insurance company about a client or former client is virtually compelled by the existence of MIB to give explanatory data, since the particulars of the treatment are likely to be known anyway. This is one of the risks of treatment, and the psychotherapist, in order to have *informed* consent, must tell his client of this possibility. Clients who realize this may then give their consent to treatment or may decide not to undergo treatment because of these consequences. The client may instead decide not to enter health insurance claims for reimbursement of treatment expenses, so that this information is not included in the MIB computer. Whether or not the client is concerned about this information getting to others, it does not obviate the necessity for the therapist or counselor to obtain his full and informed consent to treatment.

Giving information to potential employers about a client is another instance in which the therapist is a double agent. In recent years there has been a vast increase in the requests for information from therapists of all disciplines, emanating largely from employers who ask applicants if they have ever received treatment for emotional or mental problems. The practitioner who is asked by an employer about his client may be in a moral dilemma. If the client benefited from the therapist's assistance or was not too disturbed in the first place, the therapist can respond with a few positive comments and there will be relatively few complications. The psychotherapist will have a clear conscience and the client will probably get the job. But more often than not the issue is more equivocal. The therapist frequently knows that some of the things he might reveal could prevent his former client from being hired. Sometimes there is very little the therapist can say that is favorable. However he responds, or if he doesn't respond, the client loses (Bazelon 1974). Again, the client must be informed of this possibility before treatment commences and must give consent, in writing, before any such information goes to third parties.

Another double agent area concerns the therapist's case records. Due to recent statutes, court decisions, and the Privacy Act, records are becoming more and more open to the scrutiny of clients and public authorities. The client needs to be informed that there can no longer be any ironclad guarantees which protect him from having this file given into the hands of others. Furthermore, the client himself generally has the right now to review his own record and must be informed of this right. Therapists themselves are placed in a compromising situation about record keeping. Inadequate records can be considered a form of malpractice, but thorough records can lead to other problems.

PROBLEMS ABOUT RECORD KEEPING

In earlier, simpler times, case records were deemed as important as now, but there was no ambivalence about their confidentiality. The early psychotherapy writers made it abundantly clear that case records were for the eyes of the therapist, his colleagues, and the agency, and no one else (Richmond 1921; Hamilton 1946). Therapists were even given explicit advice on how to keep their records confidential when outside pressures attempted to make them visible (Resnick and Balter 1934; Castandyck and Fenlason 1936). Things are not so simple or unequivocal any longer. Even though private practitioners have had little difficulty in keeping records to serve their own clinical purposes, they have had considerable difficulty about being required to use records to serve social purposes. The therapeutic process is no longer just a matter between the private practitioner and his client. As seen above, the expansion of insurance coverage for therapy and the commensurate pressure by insurers to review the work to be sure that they are getting their money's worth plays havoc with confidentiality in records. Increased professional requirements for professional standards review organizations (PSROs) also intervene in the therapist-client confidentiality format.

Such pressures also come from the client himself. The trend is away from paternalism, in which the therapist or agency is seen as knowing what is best for the client to know. Clients increasingly feel they have the right to be protected as much from the therapist as from anyone else and therefore feel they have the right to know what is contained in their records. This has been accorded legal sanction with the passing of the Federal Privacy Act of 1974, giving people the right to review data kept about them by public agencies (Fanning 1975). The act has been used as a model in state and private settings too. When they conform to the Privacy Act principles, clients have a much higher degree of access to the records that the therapist keeps about them.

In legal terms it is now relatively easy for others to get their hands on the therapist's clinical records. Subpoenas, professional reviews, and client requests can all be used to do this. Institution-based therapists and counselors have long had to meet agency requirements related to accreditation and other third-party pressures. Now such pressures are becoming more evident in the private sector, so it is the private practitioner who most needs to enlarge his or her view of what adequate records might entail (Ganseroff et al. 1977).

Slovenko says that case records and anything in them cannot be protected by privileged communications agreements (Slovenko 1973). There are so many exemptions to the privilege among all the professional disciplines, that the privilege is a nullity. As a shield it provides very little protection. Aside from no record keeping, which could result in malpractice awards, the helping professional could do little to keep records from official scrutiny. One thing he could do would be to incorporate as a religious body, thereby placing services under constitutional protection. No helping discipline other than religion has this protection. Another possibility is to heed former Secretary of State Dean Acheson's observation, "A memorandum is written not to inform the reader but to protect the writer." It is an unfortunate commentary that such actions are considered, even facetiously, but it is understandable.

Confidential Records and the Zurcher *Decision.* The United States Supreme Court drove the last nail into the coffin of confidentiality in case records on May 31, 1978. On that day it handed down the controversial *Zurcher* decision, which prevents people or agencies from keeping their records from the view of authorities when there is reason to believe that the information therein can be useful in obtaining criminal convictions. The decision essentially removes any legal barriers to police searches of just about any filing system. The facts of the case are these: The Stanford University Hospital had incurred the ire of some of the campus student body and their supporters because of a new hospital policy. Demonstrations around the hospital building gradually escalated, and the protesters broke into the facilities and began damaging the premises. Police were summoned, and in the course of their attempts to evict the demonstrators a violent fight erupted. Many demonstrators and police were seriously injured. Photographers and reporters from the campus newspaper, the *Stanford Daily,* were present, reporting and photographing the events as they unfolded. Later the Santa Clara County prosecutor wanted more information to determine who the demonstrators were. The municipal court issued a warrant upon finding probable cause that the newspaper, although not involved in unlawful acts, had photographs which might identify the demonstrators who assaulted police officers. The newspaper refused to comply with the warrant, citing freedom of press protections. The prosecutors then issued Santa Clara County Sheriff James Zurcher a warrant to enter the newspaper office and search for the desired documents. The search occurred in broad daylight in the presence of the newspaper staff (Zurcher 1978).

Sheriff Zurcher also had in his possession a warrant to search the files of a psychiatrist who was thought to have information in his records about the assault, but this search was not made. The newspaper sued Sheriff Zurcher, and the suit made its way through various courts until the Supreme Court heard it on January 17, 1978. At issue was whether the Fourth Amendment provisions against unreasonable search and seizure were violated. The Court ruled that the Fourth Amendment did not bar warrants to search property on which there was probable cause to believe that the evidence of a crime was located, even though the premises to be searched were owned or occupied by a person who was not himself reasonably suspected of complicity in the crime being investigated. Since this ruling, if there is any reason for a law enforcement agency to think that a private psychotherapist has information in his files that might lead to the client's conviction of a crime, the practitioner's office and files may be legally searched and seized.

In subsequent years various psychotherapy professions and others affected by the ruling, notably newspaper and other media organizations, have appealed. Eventually journalists won some immunity, but few others have been successful. In fact, the American Psychiatric Association asked for immunity from Zurcher type searches in 1981 and their appeal was rejected. Psychiatry was then explicitly named in the current government regulations as not being immune. This ruling was published in the *Federal Register* on April 17, 1981. The law now says that if it is believed that a therapist or others have information about a suspect, the files may be searched after a search warrant is obtained through the Attorney General's office. If the information is sought under emergency conditions, a search warrant may be obtained in the local U.S. Attorney's office ("Regulations" 1981).

Avoiding Problems in Case Records. It is unethical and impractical for psychotherapists and counselors, regardless of discipline, to not keep thorough case records, and there is no guarantee that such records will not be available to the client and the authorities. The question is not whether to have case records but how to maintain them in such a way as to preserve and enhance the therapeutic relationship while at the same time to reduce the risks of lawsuits, misunderstandings, or public confiscation. There is no perfect answer to this question but the best one is to have records which are accessible to the client and completed with the client's assistance. This can be done by using the previously described Problem Oriented Record (POR) and letting the client see it on an ongoing basis (Houghkirk 1977).

Since the POR format uses different sections to contain data that is factual, subjective, and objective the client can easily determine what is being said about him. The client sees the notes which the therapist has written after each session, giving the client the opportunity to make corrections in factual material and to better understand how the therapist feels about him and his behavior. If the client acknowledges that he has seen and concurs in the notes, there is less likelihood of future problems between therapist and client (Roth et al. 1980). Also if the client knows what information is contained in his records, he can make an informed judgment about whether to permit those records or data contained in them to be sent to anyone else (Hartman and Wickey 1978).

If the therapist knows that his records are going to be read by his client, and knows that there is the possibility that they will be examined by third parties, they will obviously be written somewhat differently than if he were certain he alone would be seeing them. The therapist will probably be somewhat more judicious about the way he describes his client and in the way he uses jargon. The therapist will probably avoid making remarks in the record which are highly unflattering to the client or which could lead to legal disputes. For example, the record should not contain unsubstantiated remarks such as "client is drunk," or "client is lying." This is not to say that uncomplimentary statements should not be made in the record. It is just that the therapist should give the client an opportunity to review these statements and discuss them and their meaning.

Since records may be seen by third parties they should never contain any libelous remarks unless it is clearly indicated that they are opinions which the client expressed to the therapist in private. The record should always contain a current diagnosis and a statement that the therapist recommended whatever changes were necessary to preserve the client's health and well-being. The record should not indicate that the therapist made a mistake or inadvertently misjudged something. This would be tantamount to a guilty plea if a malpractice suit occurred. The record should also carefully document the nature of the termination. If the client ends treatment and the therapist has advised against it, the records must so state. The record should always note that a physical examination was recommended prior to the beginning of treatment and that after termination the client was also urged to get a physical. The record should mention that the risks were described and that the client gave informed consent. These inclusions in the record will do much to protect the therapist against any subsequent malpractice litigation and will do much to protect the client against any misleading information about him being available to others.

Obviously, keeping records in this way is not going to completely eliminate problems of the sort described above. Third parties will still attempt to get information about the client from the therapist or his records. If this information is later judged to be harmful by the client, the results he achieved with the therapist are likely to be diminished if not nullified. However, if the record is a document which has been written with the client's full knowledge, assent, and participation, any issues that arise from it can be dealt with during the course of the treatment. Any information that subsequently gets out has had input from the client and he is not the last person to know what is on record about him, as is often now the case. Issues which have *Tarasoff* or *Zurcher* implications can be dealt with by the client and the worker before any third-party involvement occurs. In this way, the therapist's responsibility to his client remains as paramount as society allows, and the accountability the therapist has to the public is still maintained.

OTHER TROUBLES FOR THE PRIVATE PRACTITIONER

As if malpractice risks and social control pressures weren't enough, private psychotherapy practitioners are also susceptible to a plethora of unpleasant situations which institutional-based therapists and counselors do not experience. Institutional-based professionals often view private practitioners as members of an elite corps who are freed from the mundane problems of bureaucratic life. Private therapists, they feel, don't have to work with clients they don't want to, spend time in excruciatingly boring staff meetings, or devote endless hours to case recording to comply with agency or institutional standards. Private therapists don't have to subsist on meager taxpayer-funded paychecks and endure the humiliation of low status and inadequate recognition for the skills and considerable education they have achieved. Private therapists don't have to resolve all problems that come to them if they don't want to, say institution-based therapists who themselves must find proper dispositions of any clients which their agencies have accepted. The private practitioner has it made!

This view is for the most part inaccurate. The private practitioner may not face all the same kinds of problems as those which the institutional counselor or therapist must endure, but he has a different set of difficulties of which the agency therapist is mostly unaware. These difficulties are sometimes enough to cause the private psychotherapist to give up his practice and return to institutional practice. When he does return to the institution, he is frequently seen as a failure. He is seen as being unable to get enough clients and financial remuneration to justify remaining in private practice.

Actually, many who have left private practice to return to

agencies have been quite successful in financial and professional terms. They decided to leave private work and give up financial success because they no longer want to deal with the difficulties which regularly confront the independent practitioner. Few institutional professionals have to endure the constant ordeal of getting insurance companies to reimburse clients. Agencies have covert ways of discontinuing service to clients who are considered by them to be "undesirable," but the private practitioner doesn't have such opportunities. Private therapists, like agency therapists, have career problems too. Where does the private therapist go after years of direct service? His promotion opportunities are nil. The private therapist, not serving under the institutional umbrella, sometimes feels as if he is in a fishbowl, with little opportunity to screen out people he doesn't particularly want to deal with. He is accessible at times when he doesn't want to be.

Another problem, not unique to the private therapist but certainly as insidious and perhaps more probable, is burnout. Without the supports and stimulation that exist in the contacts one could have with his peers, burnout is more likely to occur. Each of these problems deserves elaboration.

THE INAPPROPRIATE OR "UNDESIRABLE" CLIENT

It is anathema for helping professionals in either private practice or institutional settings to refuse service to anyone in need. Furthermore, it is against the code of ethics of all the therapy professions. Many psychotherapists feel that they have no right *not* to provide needed service. The criteria is need, not whether or not the therapist or counselor wants to meet that need. Yet inevitably there are going to be clients whom the therapist is not going to want to serve. Such clients may be highly unmotivated, unreliable about keeping appointments or paying bills, or dishonest with the therapist, or they may have needs which are not within the realm of the therapist's skill or area of interest. Sometimes the client dislikes the therapist or the therapist dislikes the client for no apparent reason. Sometimes the client is seen as undesirable because of the therapist's prejudices or unwillingness to work with members of certain minority groups or clients who maintain certain value systems. A therapist may, for example, find it difficult to work with alcoholics because of pain in his personal life in dealing with an alcoholic relative. Or a therapist may be racially prejudiced and find it difficult to accept clients who are members of another race.

Such problems are not as difficult to surmount for the institutional therapist as for the private practitioner. Most organizations would not assign a case to a staff professional who has such conflicts. Some agencies screen out clients which the organization does not wish to serve. Sometimes this is done when the agency is geographically inaccessible to certain clients. Sometimes the case is assigned only to agency professionals who are willing to accept them. Sometimes it is done by developing procedures which tend to screen out certain clients (Lantz and Lenahan 1976). For example, the institution might explain procedures to clients in such ways as to make them think they are not eligible for services. Some organizations place certain clients on waiting lists on which their names never seem to come up. Such actions are covert, and usually are integrated into the organization's procedures to such an extent that their existence is not even recognized by the workers themselves.

The private practitioner cannot screen out clients through bureaucratic obfuscations. If he cannot or does not wish to work with a certain client he must rather directly relate this fact to the person and give uncomfortably candid reasons for his decision. Rather than using the agency umbrella to preclude doing this, he must reconcile himself to the fact that it is personally and professionally acceptable to withhold service for no valid reason other than personal choice. Further justification is irrelevant. If he treats a client he doesn't want to see, he is causing that person to be harmed. He is keeping him from obtaining the help that he would get if he were not under the therapist's care. It is probably true that the therapist has some deficiency which keeps him from being able to serve this particular client. Perhaps it is based on prejudice, or irrational moods, or unresolved childhood conflicts. If such reasons account for the therapist's lack of interest in working with this client, it is likely that the client would be able to obtain better service elsewhere. Other therapists might not have such reservations and the client should have access to those professionals.

The therapist who recognizes that he has such deficiencies may be fully aware of such conflicts and may be attempting to resolve them. However, the client shouldn't have to wait for the therapist to resolve his own conflict before effective treatment can get under way. Why should the client be subject to the less than adequate service which would result if the therapist felt forced to see him? The therapist might feel so compelled because of rigid adherence to a value or standard which, while noble, is in conflict with an even more basic one of doing no harm to the client.

The private practice psychotherapist or counselor has his own criteria about what kinds of clients he will be able to work with. If these criteria exist for reasons which are discriminatory or not in keeping with the helping professionals' value of equal service for all, the criteria are most certainly not to be condoned. But if they exist, the client who is considered "undesirable" by this therapist would not be given the best possible service. The independent practitioner in this position must have a means of screening applicants for service. He must have a clear view of what his criteria are, and know what his reasons are for having them. He will hear sanctimonious proclamations from institution-based therapists, who decry practices which discriminate against certain clients, but he must not be pushed into seeing clients whom he knows he will not be able to serve effectively.

"Dumping." Some agencies and fee-for-service helping professionals engage in a highly unethical and callous practice which practitioners informally refer to as "dumping," or dropping a client. It works typically like this: A fee-for-service professional finds the client he has been serving has become too short of funds to pay for continued treatment. This might happen because of financial reversals or because the limits of the client's insurance payments have been reached. The practitioner cannot terminate the therapy if the need continues and if ending it would endanger the health and well-being of the client. Not only

would this be unethical but it is also negligent, with malpractice implications. So the practitioner "coincidentally" decides that someone else would be better able to serve the newly emerging problems which the client has been recently demonstrating. For the most part he refers clients to subsidized social agencies, but occasionally he might call another practitioner or write a letter justifying the transfer. A letter of this type might sound like this:

> Dear Dr. Kimball,
> I have been working with Mr. Blank for the past six months. He has made considerable progress and is well on the road to resolving the problems for which he sought my services. We have recently been uncovering material which I find is not within my realm of expertise. Having heard that you were highly skilled in this area, I asked Mr. Blank to contact you about the possibility of pursuing this aspect of his treatment. I am confident that you will be of great help and will find this to be a very interesting referral. If you are unable to provide treatment for Mr. Blank, he and I would be most appreciative if you would refer him to someone whom you may know who has your same high degree of skill in this problem area. Your cooperation is greatly appreciated.
>
> Sincerely,
> Maxwell Warbucks, Ph.D.

Such a letter might seem flattering and give the therapist the feeling that indeed his expertise is becoming well known in the community. When the client makes the first appointment the therapist discusses the problems and treatment possibilities. Then he learns about the client's financial circumstances. But the treatment relationship has begun, and it is difficult for him to avoid further responsibility to the client. Usually, however, referring persons are not consciously deceitful. They might make such referrals because of the impression that another therapist really does have unique expertise. It is possible, however, that the referring person was merely passing off an active client to someone else when he no longer proved rewarding, financially or some other way. Sometimes clients are passed off on other practitioners because they are becoming litigious, or threatening, or boring.

This practice is by no means restricted to individuals or independent fee-for-service practitioners. A surprisingly large number of private psychotherapists have experienced attempts by mental health care facilities to "refer" in this way. Such facilities have been known to keep clients in the inpatient facility as long as their insurance coverage remains in effect, but when it runs out the client is suddenly seen as improving. The client is deemed well enough to be discharged, provided some aftercare can be done. The institution gets one of its staff members to contact professionals in agencies or private practice about the possibility of continuing treatment for the client. Institutions often keep in their own aftercare programs those clients who have adequate financial resources, and refer the rest elsewhere. It is as though they were specializing in diseases of the rich.

While it is clearly unethical, the practice is easily justified as the best of the available alternatives. It is certainly less unethical than simply discontinuing service to the needy client because of money limitations. The practitioner who practices this form of referral can convince his client and himself that he actually was providing proper service. It is sound professional practice, he reasons, to refer the client to another with greater expertise.

The fee-for-service private practitioner should maintain a caveat in his thinking about receiving referrals from other fee-for-service practitioners or private institutions. The therapist should determine the manifest reason for the referral before agreeing to see the client the first time. One need not become paranoid about this, since practitioners do refer clients to one another frequently, with very successful results. Still, the therapist should inquire about the potential client's financial situation, unless the referring person is someone the therapist knows and trusts. On the telephone the therapist inquires about the reasons the client is being referred and he may casually ask about the financial situation. If it turns out that the client has financial difficulty or his insurance has lapsed, this is no reason to make the assumption that "dumping" is occurring. But it leads the therapist to make additional inquiries about why the referral was made. All people have the right to receive service but the therapist also has the right not to provide it unless he has already undertaken the responsibility. In receiving referrals from others the therapist is advised to exercise a little caution.

Problem Referrals. A more frequent experience for the private psychotherapy practitioner than being the recipient of "dumping" is receiving a referral that is inappropriate. Most people who refer clients make inappropriate referrals not out of malicious or malevolent motives but because they are not well informed about the type of service which the practitioner provides. Psychotherapy and counseling roles are often misperceived by the public. The therapist might have to spend an inordinate amount of time making sure that the client who has been referred to him is one whom he has the ability to help. Even though it may be rather time-consuming, any problems about inappropriate referrals may be reduced by obtaining a thorough evaluation and a complete history before the contract between client and therapist is established. Ideally, this would include a complete physical examination, some contact with the client's family members, and a rather extensive workup of the client. Naturally by the time this is accomplished, if it is accomplished, the relationship has probably already been well established and work toward the goals has already been explicated. If, by then, it turns out that someone else should be seeing the client instead of the therapist, a considerable amount of time and expense has been squandered.

A related situation of this type concerns the problem of the referring person himself. Often the person who refers the client makes an appropriate referral to the right person, but thereafter becomes an intervening variable in the therapist-client relationship. Perhaps the referring person is a close relative, the family physician, the client's clergyman, or a school counselor. This person may have been working with the client for years and has a considerable emotional investment in the client's well-being. Some studies have shown that these well-meaning persons often have a vested interest in keeping things status quo in the client's personal or situational life (Palazzoli et al. 1980). The referring person may maintain an interest with the client that second-guesses and undercuts the therapeutic transaction. He may unconsciously want to sabotage the therapist's efforts because he might otherwise feel that his own efforts to help the client were failures.

The thing to do, of course, is to involve the referring person as much as possible in the therapy relationship. If the referring person remains in the background he can undermine the treatment more effectively than if he has face-to-face positive interactions with the therapist. If he is an insider rather than an outsider in the treatment, his efforts would be more likely to enhance treatment efforts than diminish them. In any event, the worker should get to know the referral person to some extent prior to accepting the client referred. This enables the therapist's role to be more clearly revealed to the referring person and it enables the therapist to coopt any efforts which the referring person might make which could harm the treatment relationship.

BURNOUT

Burnout is a popular expression frequently heard in hospitals, social agencies, institutional settings, and organizations where professional people are asked to provide services in the face of great obstacles, little appreciation, and incessant frustration. It is a work-related syndrome whose symptoms may be physical (fatigue, minor illness, headache, insomnia); behavioral (quickness to anger, lability of emotions, irritability); and psychological (boredom, resentment, and discouragement) (Hartman and Wickey 1978). Its most common manifestations are a loss of concern and feeling for clients and subsequent treatment of clients in a detached and dehumanized way. It results in lowered efficiency and morale, and its victim is often found considering other employment possibilities. Many studies about burnout present a revealing picture of those most vulnerable to it. Therapists are more vulnerable to it when they have less opportunity to get away from the work and when they have fewer supports from their peers (Maslach 1976; Thompson 1980). Job satisfaction is related positively to several characteristics, including feedback from one's peers, supportive relationships from colleagues, and such organizational factors as work-sharing, time-outs from the workday, social feedback, and smaller caseloads. It seems that such factors as higher pay, autonomy, and variety had much less significance in contributing to occupational tedium and burnout.

One-way flows of emotion from the therapist to the client lead to emotional depletion for the therapist unless there is opportunity for him to have two-way flows, such as would exist in closer relations with peers and colleagues.

It should not be surprising, from these findings, that the private practitioner may be just as vulnerable (or maybe more so) to burnout as his agency-based counterpart. He has far less opportunity to get the feedback and social interaction which have been found to be perhaps the most important factors in preventing burnout. The lack of variety or respite in his work compared with that of institutional work is another important reason for his vulnerability. Higher pay has not proved to be adequate protection against burnout. The private practitioner may not even be aware that he is experiencing the burnout symptoms, since there is not likely to be anyone to point it out to him or encourage him to take corrective measures before the problem gets more intense. Vulnerability to burnout can be reduced if the private practitioner maintains his contacts with his peers and puts himself in a position to get regular feedback and positive learning experiences from his colleagues. Doing so is consistent with the highest principles of his profession, and such contact is the most reliable way he can have to insure that he is maintaining professional standards. As he works toward keeping himself stimulated, growing in his knowledge and skill, interacting with his colleagues, and continuing to learn through formal and informal education, he will reduce or avoid the problems faced by all psychotherapists and counselors in private practice.

NINE

ACCOUNTABILITY, PROFESSIONAL STANDARDS, AND QUALITY CONTROLS

WHEN someone needs help, what determines that the helper has the ability, the knowledge, and the experience to do the job adequately? There are, unfortunately, too few reliable ways of telling and never any guarantees. Consumers cannot be certain. They certainly don't want to put themselves in the hands of someone who hasn't worked with their particular problem before. They don't want the services of someone who isn't aware of new and effective techniques for resolving the difficulty. They want some assurance, some way of judging whether they are requesting help from a proven expert or a malevolent charlatan. But what is or can be their basis for judging?

On some occasions there may be very obvious clues that a person hasn't kept up: the TV repairman who only services American-made televisions; the dentist who uses a drill powered by a foot-pedal; the lawyer who doesn't have access to a computer for case information retrieval; the neurologist who hasn't heard of primodone therapy for epilepsy; the psychotherapist in a phobia clinic who is unfamiliar with behavior modification techniques. But mostly clues about competence and currency are obscure and probably deceptive at that, such as the decor of an office, the shininess of the equipment in the shop, or the personality of the provider. The consumer's recourse is to use a caveat emptor caution until he finds some tangible indicator of the provider's capabilities.

This indicator may be based solely on word-of-mouth testimonials by others who have been helped. Or, it may be based on the consumer shopping around on a trial and error basis until he finds a provider who *seems* to have the answer or *seems* to be able to meet his vague criteria. Or, it can be based on the provider's membership in an organization which is sanctioned to meet the need and which has clear qualifications for membership. When the consumer relies on the service provider's membership in a professional association, he still needs to know what the organization's membership qualifications are. What are its educational requirements for inclusion? Are its members tested by objective bodies to measure their competence? Are they required to pass tests periodically to demonstrate that they haven't fallen behind in their knowledge and skill? Are there any supervision requirements or quality controls? Unless such information is available to the consumer, the provider's membership in organizations is meaningless. Without such data the consumer's situation would then be similar to that which existed in the nineteenth century. Then there were few, if any, standards or requirements for those who would practice such professions as medicine or law in the United States.

AUTONOMOUS PRACTICE AND QUALITY CONTROL

Quality control is the term industrialists use when they talk about pulling sample products off their assembly lines and analyzing them to see if they are as good as they are supposed to be. If the analysis reveals that the product is not as good as intended, or if some defects are starting to creep in as part of the production process, then adjustments can be made. The design can be improved or the production line can be refurbished, or at least the consumer can be informed that the problem now exists. People who are in the mental health care delivery system are like the products produced on the assembly line. Their training, experience, and skills need to be constantly reviewed in order to determine if they are as good as they are supposed to be. If it is shown that they are not, adjustments can be made, through more training or different kinds of training, or at least through notifying the potential consumer of the deficiency. But there is, however, a problem about who is to decide if the practitioner is as good as she is supposed to be. Who is to "recall" the therapist and enforce the requirement that the adjustment is made? And most problematic of all, what are the criteria used to assess the therapist's work?

Health care providers do not like the term *quality control;* they prefer the phrase *competency assurance* instead. It is understandable that practitioners, especially those in private, independent practices, would see the word *control* in a pejorative sense. It connotes big brotherism and outside interference. "Competency assurance," on the other hand, is positive. It suggests to the consumer and the funding agencies that competency exists until proven otherwise and the public is assured, or guaranteed, of the fact. But in view of the problems about outcome and efficacy criteria, competency assurance is still a misnomer. There can be no assurance of competency without a specific definition of the *needed* skills in psychotherapy. As long as the results of therapeutic intervention can be attributed to a myriad of variables other than, or in addition to, the skills of the practitioner, there can be no assurance that the therapist was competent (Sharfstein et al. 1975).

What has been relevant in the past is that norms of psychotherapeutic behavior have been established by the different therapy professions. These norms were believed to be important, if not necessary, in contributing to the improvement of the client. The professions inculcated these normative behaviors in their practitioners primarily through professional education and socialization. Professional education differed from academic education in its emphasis on the actual doing of the professional task and integrating the theoretical and conceptual ideas with the desired behaviors. The socialization process occured through exposure of the entry-level professional to his more experienced peers. He was expected to emulate them and he was judged on his ability to approximate their behavior. Most mental health care providers, particularly in their earlier professional years, tended to work in organizations, agencies, hospitals, and clinics. In such facilities their work was scrutinized and "controlled." In this way the consumer was protected from incompetent or unscrupulous practitioners. The institutionalized use of supervision, internships, residency training, and other forms of apprenticeship afforded this protection (Granet et al. 1980). At least this is how it was in theory.

In practice it is difficult to be so sanguine. The uncontrolled, unsupervised practice of psychotherapy contributed to a long history of problems for the consumer, from misdiagnoses to inadequate treatment, from unscrupulous charlatans taking advantage of those in need of help to inept and poorly trained people inflicting their inadequacies upon the unsuspecting. The private practice model of service delivery was where such conditions were most likely to exist. Independent practitioners did not have peer group pressure to help them see when their work was not up to par. They made this judgment about themselves. They no longer received or felt they required supervision, instead feeling that it somehow demeaned or "infantalized" them. The opportunity for incompetence was far greater in private practice than in the institutional model.

However, it wasn't the abuses or instances of professional ineptitude that led to whatever improvements we now have. It wasn't the public outcry for protection from inadequate therapists either. What led to changes, to quality control, has been the growth of third-party funding for psychotherapy and other health care delivery systems. Those who are paying the bills want and deserve some way of knowing what they are paying for. They want to know that the practitioners they are paying are able at least to live up to the norms which were established for them. Government agencies which see that substantial funding takes place, as well as private insurance companies which do much of the paying, began pressuring the professions to upgrade their programs of quality control or competency assurance. The response has been for the professions to make many improvements. But they still have a long way to go. This is particularly true for the newer, nonmedical psychotherapies.

THE ALTERNATIVE TO SUPERVISION

The psychotherapy professions are in a period of transition. They are moving from a great deal of independence as private practitioners to greater conformity to their professional norms. As discussed in chapter 8, there are many problems with this transition, but it seems to be the only way of providing therapy for most people and protecting them at the same time. If the professions once depended on more supervision and peer pressure to maintain quality, they are now going to depend on better testing procedures, more stringent licensing and certification requirements, meaningful formal peer review mechanisms, and programs to determine whether the practitioner has kept current with recent scientific findings. Many private practice psychotherapists are finding that they belong to professions which do not have adequate quality control methods and thus they are ineligible for third-party funding. Some professions are finding that their work is not reimbursed by some insurance companies and government agencies unless they are supervised by members of those professions which *do* have visible and measurable quality control standards (Asher 1980).

Practitioners in private practice, regardless of profession, have the most to gain by instituting quality control mechanisms. Thus they should be at the forefront of efforts to encourage the development of the mechanisms. But those who work in institutional settings have something to gain too. Some institution-based therapists take comfort in the belief that as long as they forgo private practice and work in organizational settings or social agencies they will have secure jobs. But the agencies and institutions are becoming increasingly dependent on third-party payments to maintain their operations. They receive much of their resources from the same bodies which are insistent on quality controls in the private sector. This support will inevitably be contingent upon their personnel conforming to the same quality control standards as exist for independent practitioners.

For example, federally subsidized community mental health centers have employed thousands of nonmedical therapists in the past, including those trained in psychology, social work, nursing, counseling, personnel guidance, and sociology. But these clinics have been laying off many of these personnel. They replace them with personnel who belong to professions with insurance eligible credentials. The agency therapist whose qualifications do not conform to the standards set by the funding bodies may not have jobs much longer. For that matter, the organizations and social agencies who employ these personnel will have difficulty raising funds through citizen contributions and government grants because their staffs seem less qualified. Thus, it is in the interests of every psychotherapist, regardless of professional affiliation, whether in private or organization-based practice, to acquire the necessary credentials and to work toward the implementation of mechanisms for quality control.

There are eight major mechanisms now being used or proposed which are designed to keep professional psychotherapists up to prescribed standards. Not all the therapy professions have used all of them, and the degree of success in their use varies considerably. They are (1) formal training requirements, (2) competency examinations, (3) licensing and public regulation, (4) continuing education requirements, (5) periodic reexaminations, (6) peer review committees, (7) professional standards review organizations (PSROs), and (8) external quality controls. It is worthwhile to review each of these mechanisms and compare what the different psychotherapy professions are doing about each of them.

FORMAL TRAINING REQUIREMENTS

There is, of course, considerable variability among the psychotherapy professions as to the length, quality, and nature of their formal education requirements. While some professions require virtually no formal training at all, others require twelve years of education after high school. Psychiatrists must complete four years of medical school after four years of undergraduate preparation, and then undergo three or four years of intensely scrutinized internship-residency training. At the other end of the spectrum are those psychotherapists who haven't completed high school. They usually acquired their skills and knowledge as para-professionals or indigenous personnel, working with profession-als and observing how it is done, or picking up ideas on a trial and error basis. It seems there are as many claims of success being made on behalf of the less trained therapists as for anyone else. And it is difficult to argue that such claims are invalid. Some studies show that highly trained psychotherapists are no more successful in helping people than are those with little or no train-ing at all (Durlak 1979). Thus, it is difficult to justify extensive training for psychotherapists. It just *seems* that it is better to have more rather than less formal education in preparation for such a complex task.

But even more important, perhaps, than the length of the for-mal training is the nature and quality of that training. The estab-lished psychotherapy professions all have considerably different ideas about what constitutes good training. Consequently all of the professions are frequently changing the ways and emphases of their training programs. Psychiatry, for example, has been moving away from the requirement of internships and replacing it with an additional year of residency. This would have the ef-fect of giving new psychiatrists more extensive training in psy-chiatric theory and practice and less in general medical training. The change is hotly debated in medical and psychiatry circles and justified primarily on the basis of need for more training to as-similate all the knowledge about psychiatry that is currently available (Crowder 1981).

Psychologists have been having their own internal debate about the nature of their formal education. The present norm is for the aspiring psychologist to work in an academic setting through the four years or so that it takes to acquire the Ph.D. This is followed, for clinical practitioners, by an internship of one and sometimes two years, in an institutional setting in which their work is supervised. Because much of the training is under purely academic auspices, it is liberally sprinkled with many re-search and pedagogical requirements which many clinical and counseling psychologists find not particularly relevant.

Some psychologists are demanding that their profession offer two types of education and two contrasting degrees. The Ph.D. degree would be retained for those primarily involved in research and academic pursuits and the Psych.D. degree would be awarded to psychologists whose education and orientation is more clinical. The professional school movement grew stronger through the 1970s, following the American Psychological Association's Vail Conference on Professional Training in 1973 ("Five-Year Report" 1980). It was at the Vail Conference that the Psych.D. degree became institutionalized. Now there are over thirty schools of professional psychology in the nation, with the number expected to continue growing ("Development" 1981). Many psychologists oppose this change, however, because they are reluctant to give up the more familiar Ph.D. degree and they see it as increasing the trend of the profession toward fragmentation.

Changes are also occuring in social work education. Until recently most professional social workers terminated formal education when they received their master's degrees (M.S.W.). The degrees were granted by the eighty-three graduate schools of social work in the nation. All these schools use the professional school model of education in which there is a strong emphasis on experiential training. M.S.W. students spend nearly half their two years of graduate school in agencies performing social services under supervision. This system is beginning to change. In social work education the relative importance of the master's degree seems to be declining and that of the bachelor's and doctorate degrees is increasing. Social work is recognizing that there are many needed social services which can be performed by adequately trained undergraduate level workers (Barker et al. 1971). It is also recognizing that for the highly specialized kind of work it wants to do, including psychotherapy, the two-year program is too little. Accordingly most schools of social work have greatly expanded their doctoral programs. A few years ago a doctorate in social work was rare, but now more than half the professional schools have Ph.D. or D.S.W. programs, and the number of doctoral social workers has increased dramatically (Figueira-McDonough 1981). The same is true for undergraduates in social work. The National Association of Social Workers awarded full membership opportunities to B.S.W. workers in 1976, and most liberal arts colleges and universities now have majors for social work.

The relatively new profession of marriage and family therapy is also embarking on significant changes in its training program. Most of the practitioners in this specialization once came from the other psychotherapy professions, particularly social work, religious ministry, and counseling psychology. As the field is increasing in importance as a specialty of the established psychotherapy professions, it is also emerging as a distinct profession in its own right. At present the requirement for recognition by the American Association for Marriage and Family Therapy is a two-year master's level program which consists of courses oriented to family therapy issues, and a one-year clinical practicum under supervision. The programs which offer the master's degree in marriage and family therapy are mostly under the auspices of university departments of home economics, social sciences, and education, but it is expected that these programs will eventually become more autonomous (Everett 1979). The doctoral programs in marital and family therapy have not advanced very far as of yet (Nichols 1979). There are four major schools with doctoral programs, the same number as existed in the 1950s. The programs are located within sociology and family studies departments, and have a strong academic rather than professional orientation.

Nursing schools and theological seminaries are among the other professional institutions which are also changing their formal education requirements. They have greatly increased their course offerings and requirements in mental health subjects, and more of their graduates are engaging in independent fee-for-service psychotherapy. The *New York Times* reported that about 15,000 nurses have rejected the "traditional handmaiden-of-the-doctor role and are setting up independent practices as nurse practitioners." (*N.Y. Times* 1975). The training for these roles is at the master's level and occurs under strong supervision and peer review.

The upgraded educational requirements for psychotherapy practitioners probably lead to assurances of greater competence, but it is hard to tell. There is no way of knowing if the schools are training students adequately. All the academic and professional schools have accrediting bodies to certify that the training is as prescribed. But training by itself does not tell the consumer that the practitioner has the necessary skills. To determine if such skills are possessed the graduates of the training programs are often subjected to examinations or some form of scrutiny to determine if what they were taught has been translated into ability.

COMPETENCY EXAMINATIONS

Most professions do not rely solely on an individual's graduation from an accredited professional school as the criterion for her inclusion. That there will be examinations to test her competency for membership is taken for granted. For many professions this is the only way to regulate who its members are to be. Otherwise the educational institutions rather than the professions themselves would have that mandate. Competency examinations are usually developed *by the profession* and used in connection with the state licensing provisions as the requirement to practice that profession. Some professions, such as medicine, give overall competency examinations upon completion of formal training and then, after a period of time has elapsed, give special examinations, or boards, to certify specialists.

For example, the American Board of Psychiatry and Neurology (ABPN) certifies specialists in its field after they have completed state licensing requirements. The ABPN requires that only licensed physicians who have finished residency training in psychiatry or neurology can take its examination and then only after having at least two years experience in the field ("Annual Report" 1978). The examination is in two parts. The examinee must pass part 1, the written portion, prior to taking part 2, the oral exam. Part 2 includes actual patient interviews while being observed by examiners. If the examinee fails part 2, she must wait two years before trying again. Candidates become diplomates of the ABPN after passing both. The success rate for psychiatrists passing the examination is around 64 percent, with most of the difficulty coming in part 1 (Greenblatt et al. 1977).

The boards are seen by psychiatrists as being of utmost importance. Snyder says, "Practitioners may soon rely on certifying
and licensing boards to protect their right to practice in a federally regulated health care system" (Snyder 1977). The high failure rate is of some concern in psychiatry, but it also reflects the
seriousness of the examinations and the fact that they require
considerable study and substantial effort to master.

The other psychotherapy delivering professions have unique
forms of competency examinations after completing formal
training. For social workers there are two major test situations.
The Academy of Certified Social Workers examination is administered by the professional association, and other examinations
are conducted in conjunction with state licensing. However, as of
1980 only fourteen states which had licensing for social workers
had any type of entry examination, and some of these state examinations are mere formalities (Hardcastle 1977).

One recent study of the California examinations revealed that
while 25 percent of the applicants failed the exam, there was no
correlation between passing the exam and age, experience, field-
work, training and credentials of supervisors, or types of concen-
tration in the master's program. Only one thing seemed to matter
as a predictor of success in passing the test. If the applicant had
been in personal psychotherapy, she had a significantly better
chance of passing the exam than if she had not had therapy. This
suggests either that the examination had no worth as to actually
testing for competence, or that the education of social workers,
in California at least, is inadequate to assure desired clinical competence. It also implies that a worker would become more competent if she entered therapy than a social work school. The California system of examinations was the first in the nation, and
many look to it as the model for other states. It seems obvious
that much needs to be done in social work competency exams
for state licensure.

The ACSW certification test is given nationwide at regular
times each year under the auspices of the National Association
of Social Workers. It is a 175-question, four option, multiple-
choice exam developed with the help of the Princeton Educational Testing Service. Social workers are eligible to take the test

only after completing two years of paid full-time practice or 3,000 hours paid part-time after completing the MSW degree. Many have criticized the test as being too general, reflecting social work's attempt to be comprehensively knowledgeable about the full range of social and emotional problems and their treatment. The test has been attacked as being biased as to gender, race, and age. Successfully completing the test enables the social worker to declare herself certified by her professional association for competence. Because of the charges against the exam, however, certification can also be awarded on the basis of work experience and references from other social workers. Professional certification, however, has had little legal impact in any state and has not yet achieved recognition by the public or the other therapy professions as distinguishing the certified social worker from one who is not (Colten 1979).

Psychologists have a somewhat different type of problem in their own competency examination format. Every state requires that psychologists be licensed in order to practice their profession, and an examination is required to obtain that license. Psychologists have not had the problems social workers have experienced in developing competency examinations, and few if any charges about cultural bias or test deficiency have been made. Psychologists feel their main difficulty is with their specialty divisions. The divisions seem to engage in some sibling rivalry, with many of them striving for dominance or authority at the expense of other divisions. Psychologists see this rivalry mostly in their clinical and counseling divisions. The clinical psychology division consists of more than 15,000 members, or approximately one-third of the entire American Psychological Association membership of 45,000. Counseling psychologists number only about 4,500. Both groups struggle about whether to have separate licensing and separate examinations, or over how much of the exam will be devoted to the orientation of one or the other group (Goldschmitt et al. 1981).

Nurses have developed a nationwide examination to determine the competence of their incoming members and 100,000 new RNs annually take this test. Nurses take state board examinations to get their state licensing, and the tests are virtually identical nationwide. Some nurses have expressed dissatisfaction with the exams because they seem too general rather than reflecting the specialty or particular orientations of nurses. This is partly remedied by the ANA divisions on practice, in which nurses are tested for specialized competence, and by the thirteen nurse specialty organizations which have their own competency exams (HHS 1980).

The other psychotherapy professions have had considerable difficulty in establishing competency examinations. This is primarily because their members have dual affiliation, their primary allegiance being to other professions. For example, most of the members of the American Association for Marriage and Family Therapy, American Group Psychotherapy Association, and the American Personnel and Guidance Association also belong to other professional groups. Usually they also belong to one of the four professions described above. It is therefore difficult for these organizations to institute and require their members to take additional competency examinations. Psychotherapists who do not come from the four established mental health disciplines do not have a vigorous program of examinations to ascertain the competence of their practitioners.

LICENSING AND PUBLIC REGULATION

There has been little public support for legislation to license psychotherapists. Very few states grant licenses for psychotherapy per se, and even fewer have examinations or rigorously defined standards to use in awarding the licenses. Those who practice psychotherapy, if they are licensed at all, are covered under their affiliation with their other professions. All the states grant licenses to psychiatrists, psychologists, and nurses, and about half license social workers. Only several states have licensed any other professional groups which practice psychotherapy. One reason for the difficulty in licensing psychotherapists directly is, again, the difficulty in defining its practice. The purpose of licensing is to demonstrate to the consumer that the person is properly prepared to practice and is held to publicly defined criteria of qualifications and performance. When it is impossible to define or justify qualifications or performance, it is equally impossible to have a rational licensing policy. Licenses protect practice rather than title. The quality of practice is the thing to be publicly determined and regulated and not simply the name *psychotherapy*. Licensing would be worthless if it did not distinguish between who is and who is not competent to practice psychotherapy, which is perhaps why it has received so little public support (Hogan 1979).

The psychotherapy professions have been basically supportive of the movement toward universal licensing, however. The motivation is to protect their respective "turfs" as much as to protect the public from the incompetent. The professions which have licensing have been able to explain clearly what they do that is unique. Those with uncertain licensing usually have had trouble defining what is unique about their practice. Most professions recognize that licenses are no guarantee of the holder's competence and view them rather as one step, an important one, toward giving the public some measure of their background. One of the unintended consequences of the licensing requirements, as many professions are now discovering, is that they are changing the nature of professional education. Licensing and the accompanying examinations lead professional schools to gear their training efforts to more practical, how-to-do-it aspects of practice and away from the theoretical and conceptual foundations, which are also important ("Unintended Consequences" 1981). Another result is that licensing sometimes doesn't protect the client but only reduces the competitive marketplace factors, and thus increases costs ("How Licensing Hurts" 1977). Nevertheless, maintaining and enhancing licensing requirements will be important to the psychotherapy professions for the foreseeable future, particularly as long as the public assumes some of the financing for the provision of service.

CONTINUING EDUCATION REQUIREMENTS

Once a psychotherapist has completed her formal training, passed competency and certification examinations, and achieved licensing in her primary profession if it is required in her state, what evidence does she then have to show that she has not lost touch? Whatever the *original* indicators to demonstrate the therapist's knowledge and skills, these do not demonstrate that the therapist has kept up with advances in the field. There have been continued and rapid increases in the psychotherapy professions' knowledge in the past few years. It is therefore true that therapists must be continually in training for the duration of their careers.

If the career span is forty years or more, it is essential that this continued education be required and that the training be documented. Most of the therapy professions have been actively upgrading continuing education requirements. Their professional associations, or the specialty boards within the professional associations, have established minimum requirements for continued education. The incumbents are usually required to take a certain number of hours of approved training within a specified time period. Each discipline has determined its own requirements, but there is, as yet, no consensus about the ideal amount or type of education. For most psychotherapy professions about ten hours per year is the average.

Some professions have developed requirements which are so strong that they have become part of their state licensing qualification. Psychology, for example, has gotten ten states to institute requirements for continuing education, and twenty-four states have legalized continuing education requirements for psychiatrists (Simon 1980). These two professions have been actively promoting continuing education among their members even when no state requirement exists. The American Psychological Association in 1979 started a centralized program to evaluate and approve sponsors of continuing education for psychologists and to keep a record of the education units (CEUs) each member has obtained. The American Psychiatric Association requires that its members receive 150 hours of approved training every three years. Relicensing and recertification requirements for psychiatry will probably grow increasingly more difficult, and a requirement for taking recertification examinations will be satisfactory proof of obtaining the required credits in the three-year period.

Social work's continuing education requirements are not so stringent. As of 1980, only one state, California, has any legal requirement for continuing education. All licensed clinical social workers there must acquire ten CEUs per year. Several other states which have licensing are considering the imposition of CEU requirements as a prerequisite for renewing the social work license to practice, but have not yet done so. The other psychotherapy disciplines ask their members to account for and prove the continuing education units which they have obtained, but to date the system is essentially voluntary.

PERIODIC REEXAMINATIONS

The professional person is honor bound to continue her education and keep abreast of the knowledge and technologies of her field. It is professional negligence not to keep up (Holder 1973). However, unfortunate though it may be, not all professionals will voluntarily keep current. They must be compelled to do so. Professions attempt to keep their members current by requiring them to obtain CEUs and to take regular relicensing and recertification tests. This is necessitated by three current forces: expanding knowledge, public accountability, and government actions. Medical disciplines have discovered that the knowledge base is expanding so rapidly that there is only a five year "half-life" of knowledge (Robinowitz and Greenblatt 1980). In other words, the doctor must acquire half again as much knowledge every five years as she had acquired upon completion of her formal training, just to keep pace. In psychology the half-life is about ten to twelve years (Dubin 1972). Public accountability is becoming increasingly important as the professions are besieged by consumer advocates and interested citizens who want assurances of continued competence from those who serve the people. Federal and state governments and other third-party payers such as insurance companies are also beginning to demand evidence of the professional person's continuing competence as eligibility for payment.

The medical profession is ahead of the other professions in efforts to prove its members have kept current. All twenty-two specialty boards in medicine have now endorsed the principle of periodic recertification as a requirement for specialty competence (Robinowitz and Greenblatt 1980). Each specialty has its own requirements for recertification, but they all share certain common elements. Recertification comes up for each doctor every six to ten years depending on the specialty. Public listings of the doctor's dates of original certification and recertification are made through medical directories and the Who's Who *Directory of Medical Specialists*. The doctor must obtain the requisite number of CEUs approved by the specialty board in the time period. Then she takes written and oral examinations and has her work reviewed by her peers. The nature of the examinations varies considerably among the different specialties. For example, the surgery board employs surgeons to review the candidate's standing in her hospital and to review hospital records and issue review committee records. Then the candidate takes a test consisting of 200 multiple-choice items, pretested for content validity. Oral exams or essay tests may be available to those who did not pass the written portion. The internal medicine board and the neurology/psychiatry boards have developed extensive self-assessment examinations consisting of 400 multiple-choice questions and a set of patient management problems covering ten major subspecialty areas. This is used by doctors at their own initiative to determine for themselves what their current proficiency level is and how likely they are to prove this to examiners.

The other professions have not developed their recertification procedures nearly as much. Some even use the grandfather clause to enable experienced professionals to forgo any testing for continued competency. Their assumption is that experience is an adequate teacher and that the professional is keeping up simply by continuing to practice. Thus, any member of the profession who was admitted before a certain date is deemed up to date. It seems likely that grandfathering is due to pressure by the more experienced profession members who are fearful of failure on the exams. There can be no other justification for a profession to maintain such a policy.

One reason why professionals will be motivated to prove they have kept current through recertification tests is that they cannot be sure that their licenses to practice will be continued. Many states have started to adopt sunset laws which could end some professional licensing. Sunset legislation requires that the law simply end at a certain time if it cannot be shown that it has continued value. Licenses for professional practice might be greatly influenced by this trend. The profession's licenses could end under sunset laws if the members cannot demonstrate that the licenses were worthwhile. This means in essence that psychotherapy professions which desire continued state licenses would have to prove their efficacy before the sunset legislation expires, a task which has proved elusive for psychotherapy for decades. Yet such legislation pertaining to professional licensing now exists in 37 states, and some of these will be coming up for renewal in the near future (Grobe 1981). It isn't likely that the professions which provide for the physical care of people will be in much jeopardy of losing licensing through sunset laws, since they can demonstrate more tangible outcomes. But those professions which deal with less concrete phenomena, such as "happiness" and emotional well-being, may have more difficulty. If state licensing for these professions were to end, it would be all the more important for their members to prove their competence and currency by maintaining continuing education requirements and continually taking examinations sponsored by their profession.

PEER REVIEW COMMITTEES

Peer review is the way a profession evaluates the practice of one of its members. The evaluation is based on the assumption that there are generally accepted procedures and methods which the profession has found to be efficacious, and that all its members are expected to behave within their normative boundaries. If the individual is to represent the profession to the public and benefit from the privileges of membership, she is obligated to conform to those standards. Usually there is a range of behavior within those standards which the profession deems appropriate, and even then exceptions can sometimes be made if circumstances seem to warrant it. The standards cannot be too restrictive lest they stifle innovation, but they cannot be too loose or they have no value. Therefore, the member's practice is evaluated on an individualized basis to determine if deviation from accepted standards occurred, and if so, why. Appropriate behavior is usually determined by a comparison of the member's actions and results with the normative standards and predetermined criteria. Peer review is a cornerstone of the profession's accountability to the public, for it says to the potential consumer: "This profession practices this way, and if you are not treated this way we will determine why not."

There is nothing inherent in the peer review concept to suggest that it occurs only when the practitioner may have deviated from the profession's norms, although it is often perceived that way. Sometimes it is used to encourage members to upgrade their knowledge about a certain area, or sometimes to educate the member that there are now improved ways of doing something. But for the most part it takes place after a member's practices have come to the attention of the profession and there is a question about the appropriateness of those practices. In such a case a committee of one's colleagues objectively looks at a practice, compares it with what could have been done, and recommends actions either to the member or to the profession. Thus the profession is able to control its members and thereby be protected from public dissatisfaction about unacceptable behavior.

There are as many models of peer review as there are professions. Some professions have very formal systems for evaluating a member's practice, even with legally binding procedures, while other professions have very casual, informal, almost ad hoc systems which are not much more than personal chats with a "deviant" member. The more informal types have existed as long as the profession has, and in many instances they evolved into more codified procedures as the profession developed. Peer review became more formal as a result of many complaints which clients were making to the professions. The latter developed grievance committees which heard the complaints, discussed the matter with the member, and then made recommendations for action. The actions could range from officially censuring the member or terminating membership, through making suggestions for up-grading techniques or education, to burying the complaint in committee meetings. Grievance committees are the predominant model for peer review in most professions, but their focus tends to be on possible deviations from the profession's code of ethics. Less attention, if any, is paid to issues concerning the member's competence, knowledge, and practice abilities.

More progress toward formalizing peer review has been made in those professions which have tangible outcomes than where it is difficult to determine whether a practice leads to effective results or not. For example, when a local chapter of the American Dental Association receives many complaints that fillings keep falling from the teeth of one dentist's clients, it is clear that peer review is needed. On the other hand, if a profession has not sufficiently educated the public or itself as to what should be expected from a member, there is no clear answer about what to do with grievances. Thus, there is a tendency in those professions which have concrete results, visible practices, and specific, easily defined methods to have more formal peer review mechanisms than those which do not. Medicine, dentistry, law, nursing, accounting, pharmacy, social work, and psychology all have good peer review systems. Other psychotherapy professions do not.

Most of the peer review systems are centered around the adjudication of possible deviation from a code of ethics. This is, of course, only possible among those professions which have specific codes of ethics. One of the professions which has a strong code of ethics and an accompanying strong peer review mechanism is social work. As in most professions the process occurs at the local level, with the local chapter of the National Association of Social Workers administering the procedures. Each chapter has an ad hoc or standing committee on inquiry made up of appointed or elected representatives of the chapter (NASW 1973). Complainants and respondents may challenge the selection of any committee member. After a complaint has been reviewed, the chapter president acknowledges receipt within ten days and forwards the complaint to the committee. The committee decides whether the complaint meets necessary criteria. If it is accepted, the committee holds hearings, submits a written report, and makes recommendations. The chapter's board then implements recommendations. Barring appeal, the entire process should be completed within four months. When a member has been found in violation of the code of ethics, typical sanctions include temporary suspension from membership, formal conferences with the committee, written reprimands, and sometimes monitoring the member's practice for a specified time. Private practitioners may be required to accept supervision and waive fees received from clients for a specified time.

The most serious difficulty with the NASW adjudication procedure is that it really doesn't encompass any practice issues other than violations of ethics. While it is true that incompetence is unethical, it is difficult to envision a social worker being formally judged by her peers because she couldn't prove she had up-to-date knowledge or that she was unable to perform services which she should be able to perform. For example, if a worker had attended no course, seminar, or convention for twenty years, it is still unlikely that any peer review process would deal with the matter. If such a situation did occur, according to the current adjudication system, there would be no way of imposing sanctions on the worker unless some incident of malpractice were found to have occurred.

The other helping professions are fairly similar in their peer review designs, though there is some variability as to the frequency of implementation. Nurses and psychologists have developed strong codes of ethics too, but their practice utilizes specific tools and methodologies which can be judged by peers ("Ethical Principles" 1981). Consequently, their peer review mechanisms are implemented more frequently. The other professions utilize review much less, probably reflecting the looseness of their professional norms rather than members' devotion to professional proficiency.

Psychiatry uses its peer review mechanism in a much broader way than do the other professions which provide psychotherapy. It is concerned with a wider range of practice behaviors, since it is involved with medication, incarceration situations, and physical care issues. A wider range of actions is typically taken upon deviation from the norms. The peer review process generally attempts to minimize conflict and to create an atmosphere conducive to educating practitioners (Newman and Luft 1974). Private practitioners and organization-based psychiatrists meet at regular intervals to discuss cases, diagnoses, treatment objectives, and various means by which treatment is carried out. Larger psychiatric organizations develop systems in which reviewers are specially trained and selected because of their communication and diagnostic abilities, and attempt to help the psychiatric practitioner upgrade his knowledge and skills *before* any problems occur. The atmosphere is not considered punitive because if it were the doctor would become defensive and education and communication would be obfuscated. The doctor would be attempting to withhold or distort "bad" information and present only the actions which seemed to be within the approved range.

Many models of peer review in psychiatry have been reported, and they have a variety of unique characteristics and common features (Langsley and Lebaron 1974). Some are based on committees of doctors who accompany a psychiatrist on his hospital rounds, and some observe a psychiatrist interviewing patients. The major difficulties that psychiatry has in maintaining an adequate peer review system are "inadequate records, lack of agreement on diagnosis, the limited usefulness of psychiatric diagnosis, wide variations in the criteria for hospitalization and discharge, the complex nature of psychotherapy treatment process and problems in fitting all mental health care to the medical model" (Liptzin 1974). Psychiatry has not been at the forefront of efforts at quality assurance or peer review, but federal government interventions have been monumentally influential in enhancing its peer review process.

PROFESSIONAL STANDARDS REVIEW ORGANIZATIONS

The Professional Standards Review Organizations, or PSROs as everyone calls them, are another quality control mechanism and potentially the most powerful one of all. The PSRO is a federally financed and controlled program for determining if health care providers are doing their jobs in a cost-effective manner.

The organizations came into being in 1972 when Congress enacted amendments to the Social Security Act (Public Law 92-603). The federal government was spending billions of dollars for health care, particularly with Medicare and Medicaid, and wanted to know if it was getting its money's worth. The PSROs were set up to make that determination.

Several hundred offices were established in 203 local areas throughout the nation. Each one had full-time clerical and professional staffs. The Secretary of Health and Human Services was empowered by the act to select qualified applicants to supervise these local offices. The supervisors could be physicians or, if no qualified doctors were available, qualified laymen. Every local office became supervised by physicians as soon as it was established. At first the organizations concentrated their attention on hospital records to determine if any inpatient care that was funded by federal dollars was inappropriate. The professional associations which wanted its members to continue receiving federal money for their services were to provide the PSROs with norms and criteria for care. These norms would be compared with the actual care provided as indicated by the medical charts. For example, a Medicaid recipient might be a teenager diagnosed as "adjustment reaction of adolescence." If the patient were placed in a long-term inpatient care facility and given psychoanalysis five days a week, the treatment approach might raise PSRO eyebrows. If the health care provider repeatedly deviated from the prescribed norms in the diagnosis or treatment approach, the PSRO might institute sanctions. If the norms for treatment in one area deviated considerably from those of other localities, additional pressures might be brought to bear.

As originally conceived, the PSROs would first look into the inpatient federally funded physical care procedures and then broaden the scope of their influence. They would eventually scrutinize the outpatient health care providers, and include those who provide mental health services. The private hospitals and insurance companies were also using the PSROs to determine if their services conformed to the established norms. PSROs would be the major public overseer of the work of all health care providers, including private psychotherapy practitioners.

Many of the professional associations whose members are psychotherapists have been having considerable apprehensions about the burgeoning influence of the PSROs. They require norms, practice guidelines, and outcome criteria to determine if the service is worthwhile. But the therapy professions have not been very successful in developing or providing such information. The professions have been struggling for years to establish efficacy measures and have not yet been able to do so to a satisfactory extent. So it remains to be seen what will happen when and if the PSROs will continue to insist on such information.

When the Reagan Administration began looking for places to economize, one of the first things to be cut was the PSROs. In an effort to reduce the Social Security Administration's budget, much of the funding for the organizations was eliminated. It seems that the cut will give a reprieve to those who were uncomfortable with the federal quality control. But it seems more likely that the PSROs, or some form of them, will be reinstituted. The costs of medical care will become even more expensive, and if the federal government is going to pay most of the bill, it will want to give closer scrutiny to the providers. The associations and individuals which are involved in the business of psychotherapy might as well keep preparing for the day when federal overseers will be scrutinizing their work.

EXTERNAL QUALITY CONTROLS

In the future, psychotherapy and all other professions are likely to face more public scrutiny and increased regulation by society. External quality controls refer to the imposition of standards of professional conduct and expected outcomes by public or private agencies instead of by members of the profession itself. The consumer movement, the age of accountability, the increased importance of third-party payments for professional services all dictate its inevitability. The public and its elected representatives at all levels are calling for more legislation to control the practices of psychotherapists (Holden 1978). Private insurance companies and government funding bodies are looking more seriously at what they are paying for. At present, those professions which seem to put consumers at greater risk, such as medicine and law, are getting most of this attention. But whatever external quality controls are eventually imposed on them will serve as a model for the controls to be placed on other professions as well.

One example illustrates the possible future of professions in all states. In 1979 the Florida legislature established a new Department of Professional Regulation, which took over examining, licensing, and disciplining all the state's licensed professionals. The DPR has a 400-member staff who may be, but are not necessarily, members of any of the professions controlled. DPR regulations are oriented to protect the consumers rather than the professional. For example, every licensed professional's office must prominently display a sign which lists the address and toll free telephone number of the DPR agency, for those who wish to complain about any of the professional's practices. Professionals are required to report violations of one of their members and are given libel-action immunity when they do so. State agents are assigned to investigate every complaint, and the findings of the investigators are turned over to state attorneys. The attorneys evaluate the data, and if they and the DPR chairman agree that there is probable cause for disciplinary action, the matter goes before the state licensing board. The board then invokes whatever penalties are involved, from a reprimand or fine to license suspension or revocation. The law states that the file on the licensee ceases to be confidential ten days after probable cause for proceeding against the professional is determined. This law and the DPR are controversial in Florida, to say the least, but many professionals feel that they are a necessary means of weeding out practitioners who are incompetent or dishonest, and to upgrade professions.

Many professional associations which might fear public scrutiny or external quality controls such as exist in the PSRO or Florida systems can do something about it. They cannot stem the tide of public interest in their activities, and they should not want to do so. But they can be more rigorous in the development of their own peer review mechanisms. This would keep more complaints "in house" and out of lay control. If the standards and procedures for enforcement are reputable, there will be far less need and inclination for the public to intervene. If it is the consumer's well-being that is paramount rather than the professional's self interest, then external quality controls will be endorsed by the professions as well as the public.

WHAT HAPPENS WITHOUT "QUALITY ASSURANCE"?

Having surveyed the mechanisms used to maintain professional standards, we can now look at how such devices might influence private psychotherapy practice. As previously indicated, private practice might have more at stake in quality control issues than institutional forms of professional practice, at least directly. It is essential that the private psychotherapist be able to assure clients, third-party payers, and the public that her work measures up to established criteria. Institutional psychotherapists are immediately accountable to their employers, while the independent therapist is immediately accountable to the public. Accordingly, she is going to be scrutinized by her peers, by her clients, and by regulatory agencies much more carefully than is the institutional therapist.

If controls or assurances are deficient, then a number of serious consequences will inevitably result. If the professions are not somehow motivating their members to keep improving their skills and knowledge, there will be a decline in the quality of service that is offered to the public. There will always, of course, be a majority of professionals who are conscientious and honest without outside pressure. But there will also always be a minority of members of every psychotherapy profession who are not. These people would rather put off studying or returning to school. They would rather not be bothered unless it is demanded of them. If there were a decline in the quality of psychotherapy services offered, then the public would be at risk. The consumer would not be able to determine whose help to seek. He could be subjected to people whose experience, training, or ethics are questionable.

If the public were at greater risk, then there would be more cases in the public eye in which consumers were harmed by psychotherapeutic intervention. The public would come to see all psychotherapy, not just that practiced by the minority, as being dangerous or ineffective. Many who need the services of psychotherapists would be frightened off, and without needed help there is no telling what might happen to them or those in their environments. There would also be a diminution of public support for funding psychotherapy. If in the public eye it seemed to be a dangerous or ineffective treatment method whose practitioners had few institutionalized standards of conduct, it is hardly likely that paying for such programs out of the government treasuries would be popular.

If the sources of funding declined, both direct payments from consumers and public financial support, the psychotherapy professions themselves would face severe cutbacks. The practitioners themselves would not be supportive of their professions, since being so would be meaningless in such a scenario. Facing a declining role, the professions and their members would probably increase their competitive stance with respect to the other psychotherapists. The various professions would be jockeying for position, attempting to become the predominant provider of the remaining psychotherapy services. They would attempt to convince the public that theirs was the only profession capable of providing such services. This would result in increased fragmentation among the various psychotherapy professions. Fragmentation would lead to less cooperation among the mental health care providers. The mental health team concept would be threatened. There would be less exchange of ideas between the psychotherapy professions and a greater tendency toward stagnation. This would further reduce the effectiveness of psychotherapy practitioners.

In sum, the quality control or competency assurance measures that are taken by the professions or imposed on them by the public should not be seen as a threat or even as an inconvenience. Their absence would lead to far greater threats and inconveniences, far more risks to the consuming public, and far more negative consequences for the practitioners. If one is to consider a career as a private practice psychotherapist, one must recognize the importance of doing everything possible to enhance means of quality control. A career is only going to be productive and secure when such measures exist. It is the obligation of every private practitioner in psychotherapy to work toward enhancing these programs.

TEN

PROGNOSIS FOR THE BUSINESS
OF PSYCHOTHERAPY

PSYCHOTHERAPY, and especially the private practice of psychotherapy, has possibly reached its zenith in the 1980s. Certainly its influence has never been more prevasive or far reaching. The psychotherapy professions have been so successful in promoting and selling their ideas and methods that the demand for them seems insatiable (Harden 1981). The nation spends about 10 percent of its gross national product on health care, and a sizable proportion of that expenditure, over $2 billion, goes to the mental health industry ("Health Spending" 1981). More than 7 million Americans use the services of professional psychotherapists ever year, and 2 million of them are treated by private practitioners (NCHS 1979). As great as these figures are, they still do not count the million-plus Americans who receive treatment each year from the growing legions of lay therapists who have no special professional training but who nonetheless have successfully sold their own methods (Gross 1978). The figures do not count the untold multitudes who receive therapy, counseling, or their close approximation in non-therapy-based settings. Uncounted are the 60,000 educators trained as school guidance personnel, who are providing help to inestimable numbers of pupils. Thousands of clergymen who don't have a fee-for-service counseling business on the side are providing counseling to members of their congregations in larger numbers than ever before (Crabb 1978). Therapy is going on everywhere, in doctors' and lawyers' offices, in courthouses, in personnel departments, in police stations, and in an untold variety of other settings. The public as never before wants, expects, and demands psychotherapy.

Psythotherapy was an elitist privilege before it became so popular in middle America. Except for those who were institutionalized, only the wealthy could afford it, or even wanted to afford it, and they received it primarily from a few private practice therapists. The great majority of the population, most of us, dealt with our problems in other ways. We accepted that most psychic conflicts, except for outright psychosis, were the inevitable result of inescapable life experiences. Our conflicts would go away when our situations improved. We believed that the proper role of the psychotherapist was basically to help the insane or the very seriously disturbed people who could no longer take care of themselves.

But in the twentieth century these beliefs were challenged by some very persuasive and compelling people. We understood these people to be scientists, not philosophers, and we first thought their message was based on empirical analysis rather than speculation and inference. They told us how fragile our psyches were and how we could be seriously damaged if we did not experience suitable early environmental influences and freedom from childhood conflicts and traumas. The damage could be irrevocable unless psychotherapists could be called upon to restore the bruised egos and damaged psyches to their normal state. They frightened us. They warned us that one in ten of our children would have serious mental illness before they reached adulthood and that virtually no family in the nation would be entirely free from mental disorder. They said that happiness is normal and implied that unhappiness was abnormal. Any pain, suffering, failure, fear, or anxiety was seen as an illness rather than the inevitable product of being human.

The American ethos has never been confortable with any notion of passively accepting the continued existence of problems until, perhaps, they go away. Problems are to be solved. Problems of the mind and emotions, like all other problems, can be fixed. It is no wonder that the belief system of the psychotherapists was able to gain its strongest endorsement and following in the United States. Therapy was seen as the ultimate remedy, the way to fix any problem. So psychotherapy moved in the popular consciousness from the isolated provinces of the seriously disburbed and the wealthy to the crowded realm of everyman. Therapy became democratized. The public came to feel they needed it, deserved it, were entitled to it. The selling of psychotherapy was an unqualified success.

Success seems to breed success. The selling job was so thorough that the demand for psychotherapy services grew faster than anyone could have anticipated. In the 1960s the demand resulted in unprecedented support for public money to pay for therapy. Vast amounts were allocated for the training of new therapists, and even more was spent on establishing ubiquitous facilities for the care of the mentally ill. The federal government mandated and financed the development of the 570 community mental health centers that are the backbone of our publicly supported outpatient psychotherapy system. State governments expanded mental health care facilities to reduce the isolation problems endured by the staffs and patients of mental hospitals. The private insurance industry was pushed to include coverage for psychotherapy services, thus enabling private psychotherapy practitioners to offer their services to the middle class. More people than ever became psychotherapy consumers, which meant there were more people to proclaim the virtues of therapy and to convince their peers that they too could similarly benefit. The demand for psychotherapy was snowballing, and the bottom of the hill was nowhere in sight.

CAN THE DEMAND FOR PSYCHOTHERAPY KEEP GROWING?

The economic laws of supply and demand are just as relevant to the business of psychotherapy as to any other business. So far there has been a relatively stable and comfortable balance between the numbers of psychotherapists and the numbers of people who need, want, or can get psychotherapy. The balance has been lately maintained by the fact that the numbers of both keep steadily increasing at the same rate. It hasn't been uneven since the 1960s, when the demand for therapy services intensified with unexpected haste. That decade was a time of major social unrest and personal conflict. The nation was desperate for solutions, any solutions, whether they were proved to be effective or not. For awhile the gap between need and supply was so wide that the government was issuing gloomy projections and predicting dire consequences. But the nation mobilized to train thousands of new therapists, expand the professional schools, and encourage other professions to enter psychotherapy activity. The effort succeeded. There was a stabilization in the supply-demand system, with both sides rapidly and consistently expanding.

But now it seems that a new imbalance between supply and demand is imminent. The snowball is reaching the bottom. It must be obvious to any objective observer that there are limits to everything that is ever in demand. The manufacturers of large, energy inefficient automobiles can readily attest to that fact. When the demand finally levels off adjustments have to be made. There must be a reduction in the available supply on hand, or some way must be found to spur the demand to ever greater heights. So far, like most members of the business community, psychotherapist business persons have been counting on the continued demand pressure. They have not faced the inevitability that at some stage the demand will be reduced.

To understand why the demand for psychotherapy services has reached its apogee one must consider the factors which caused it to increase in the first place. If there are shifts in these factors, it seems likely that there will be reduced pressure for more psychotherapy. There are five interrelated trends and cultural phenomena in the United States which are the major contributors to the increased demand for service, each of which seems to be already in retrenchment. The trends are (1) demographics, (2) the culture of narcissism, (3) the creation of more individual therapy consumers, (4) the creation of more institutional consumers, and (5) the effect of third-party financing.

First, the growth in the demand for psychotherapy services has been strongly correlated with the growth in the population. The more people there are, the more people there are who are likely to want therapy. Furthermore, those most likely to be seeking the services of the psychotherapist have tended to be younger, more affluent, and better educated. Not coincidentally, this segment of the population has had the greatest growth at the time the demand for more services has increased fastest. But this group, the one most likely to be consumers of psychotherapy services, is changing. Its members are becoming older. They are approaching stable, comfortable, less conflicted middle age. The generation which is succeeding them, the people who would be expected to exert the present and future demands on the psychotherapy industry, is smaller. Already there is a considerable decline in school enrollments and a reduction in demand for child care facilities and the consumer goods most often purchased by or for younger people (NCHS 1980). If more people meant more demand for services, then less demand is likely to follow fewer people. This is a trend with which therapy will have to deal.

The second trend which has influenced the demand for psychotherapy services has to do with the *kind* of people our culture has lately produced. If more of the people desire psychotherapy, whether they really need it or not, there will obviously be greater demand pressures. Clearly this desire has never before been felt by so many. Many Americans are preoccupied as never before with *self*. We want to know everything we can about ourselves, what makes us tick, why we feel the way we do, and what we can expect to feel like tomorrow. We want to know why we aren't as happy or self-actualized as we think we should be. All the psychotherapy professions, particularly the new therapies, the ones which tend to indulge this self-preoccupation, have been the beneficiary of this interest. People are also seeking, in unprecedented numbers, the services of everyone who claims to have answers about what makes human beings what they are. But the evidence is mounting that the public preoccupation with self is on the wane. Cultural values and interests have always shifted gradually from one generation to the next, and there is no reason to think that the culture of narcissism is exempt. If the trend is beginning to reverse itself, if fewer people are preoccupied with self, there will be fewer people who seek the services of those who would teach about self. More people may stop frequenting psychotherapists just to learn about themselves and go only when treatment of illness is needed. Given the large numbers of people who are in therapy but who have no serious emotional disturbance, this trend could substantially reduce the numbers of psychotherapy hours which are now being filled (Gelwin 1981).

The third factor which influences the demand for therapy services is also seeing some reversals. It has to do with faddism, or what some would call the "lemming effect." If something appears to be a good and desirable thing, more and more people seem to want it. This is especially true if not everyone can get it. When psychotherapy began to spread throughout the nation, when private therapists and mental health clinics were in virtually every community in America, there were fewer people who were not exposed to someone who had been treated by a psychotherapist. Virtually everyone began to see firsthand what became of those who went into therapy. It no longer seemed such a strange phenomenon. Few people would be willing to admit, even to themselves, that a considerable expenditure of time, money, and effort was completely wasted. They more likely would feel they benefited and that they made a good decision to go for treatment. They are more likely to tell their friends about their good decisions than about their bad ones. Inevitably the good word spread. Everyone has anxieties at times and psychotherapy has convinced people that such conditions might be symptoms of deeper and more severe problems. Or as Jerome Frank indicated, psychotherapy and its mental health industry may be the only form of treatment which appears to create the illness it treats (Frank 1973).

But is this another trend that might be reversible? If the selling of psychotherapy has been largely based on the premise of its necessity and effectiveness, then it is very important that this perception be maintained. If potential psychotherapy consumers begin to question the need for and effectiveness of therapy, their numbers could be significantly reduced. Momentum seems to be building in this direction. More people than ever are questioning the premise. Hundreds of efficacy studies have been and are being conducted, and their results, so far, have not been encouraging for psychotherapy (U.S. Congress 1980). Such findings have not yet reached the public consciousness, and they are still inconclusive. But when the potential consumer begins to be exposed to such questions, and when third-party payers decide that there is no proof of therapy's worth, its support can easily diminish.

The fourth trend which has influenced the demand for psychotherapy is the expansion of its services from helping individuals to helping institutions. After convincing people that they could benefit, psychotherapists moved into the business community, government, and social organizations. The National Training Laboratory and its competitors were at the vanguard of this movement, but now there are psychological consultants by the thousands who are advising organizations on how to improve morale and staff efficiency. The movement has successfully convinced many of the largest organizations in America, including its armed forces, that their personnel can become more productive if psychological methods are utilized. Large numbers of psychiatrists, psychologists, social workers, nurses, and educators were hired or consulted with this objective in mind. This too has increased the demand for more therapists.

Can this trend be softening like the others? So it would seem. Government is becoming increasingly conscious of the need for conserving taxpayers' dollars, so it is looking for places to cut costs wherever possible. Businesses too are faced with money problems and are looking for ways to economize. These institutions look at expenditures which are not proving to be cost-effective. The effect of employing psychological consultants will be scrutinized very closely. If employee productivity increases after the adoption of the therapist's methods, then the consultant appears to have been a sound investment. But if productivity remains static or declines, the value of the therapy techniques in the organization setting is challenged.

Many companies and organizations are getting mixed results. But one thing is not mixed. The nation's total productivity, its gross national product, has been leveling off for the first time in its history at the very time when businesses and organizations have been using psychotherapy consultants. This is certainly not to imply that such methods have caused the leveling. There are too many other factors which account for the business slowdown, and the psychological consultants are such a small part of the overall economic picture that their influence would not be measured on the GNP anyway. But the point here is that *perceptions* about psychotherapy's usefulness lead to greater demand for it, and if businesses and organizations do not perceive that it is helpful they will call off their support. Business conditions do not auger well for the continued demand for therapists.

The fifth and final trend which has contributed to the growing demand for psychotherapy services has been the expansion of third-party financing. The strongest surge in demand for therapy always follows increases in help from government or private insurance companies. When they first began to pay for psychotherapy services in the 1960s, this development was accompanied by the largest and most rapid increase in demand the helping professions have ever encountered before or since. Insurance coverage led to demand pressures on private practice therapists, and government-financed clinics and hospitals made therapy possible for everyone. If the trend toward increased financial assistance continued, it could be expected to result in an increase in demand for therapy services. But the third-party payers are showing signs that they will be reducing their contributions in the near future. The publicly funded clinics are seriously considering raising their fees and reducing the amount of subsidization. They are cutting back on personnel and engaging in all around belt tightening.

In the private sector the trend is even more serious. Insurance companies have begun cutting back on their amounts of mental health coverage. Most are raising the deductibles, reducing the length of therapy time covered, and reducing the percentage amount they will pay relative to the client's contribution. For example, one major health insurance company recently paid 80 percent of the therapist's bill indefinitely after the client paid the first $50. But then it reduced its psychotherapy benefit to 50 percent of the therapist's bill, limited the coverage to fifty sessions per year, and increased the deductible to $100. Other companies are becoming even more parsimonious about the amounts they will pay. The effects of these reductions are obvious. They will lead to a softening of demand for therapy services.

Clearly then, the five major trends which led to increased therapy demand are changing. Unless they reverse themselves soon, the result will be fewer potential therapy consumers. There will also be a return to the supply-demand imbalance. A new labor crisis will occur, only this time there will be a therapist oversupply rather than a shortage. Unless demand pressures return, an unlikely prospect for the foreseeable future, there must be a commensurate reduction in the numbers of therapists, or at least a slowdown in their increase. Otherwise, many therapists will be dealing with another set of problems, such as unemployment, income reduction, feelings of uselessness, declining prestige, and underutilization. The question is, what is happening to the numbers of therapists and the numbers of those who aspire to become therapists?

SUPPLY SIDE ECONOMICS IN PSYCHOTHERAPY

The major premise of the Reagan administration economic policy is that inflation and economic upheaval can be controlled if the supply of goods and services is greatly increased. If incentives are given to increase the available supplies, then inflationary pressures will diminish. Psychotherapists have experienced their own version of supply-side economics for the past twenty years, but it has taken that long for the results to be noticeable. In the 1960s thousands of new doctors, nurses, psychologists, social workers, counselors, and health care personnel were trained. Hundreds of new training facilities, medical schools, and teaching hospitals were built. Extensive financial aid was given to students who wanted the training in order to become psychotherapists.

The results of this effort are now apparent. There are enough therapists and counselors (NCHS 1979). Most of the therapists in direct practice were trained during this mobilization. Most of the nation's 25,000 psychiatrists, 25,000 psychologists, 100,000 social workers, and 60,000 school guidance workers received their formal education through this effort. The training extended into other occupations too. Clergymen were spending more of their theological school time learning about how to provide emotional as well as religious guidance because their schools were being awarded grants for such education. Policemen, firemen, probation officers, lawyers, and many other occupational groups were training in these methods because of education grants.

But now that the schools have been built and the education has become available within them, it seems that continued support for training is being questioned. Government calculations show that the goals of the manpower effort have been reached. The need now is to stop the growth in labor supply. Consequently, student training grants in the mental health field are becoming scarce. Funding for the training programs is being cut. Government is reducing subsidies of professional schools and requiring that some quotas be placed on the numbers of students admitted. The U.S. Congress has made it more difficult for foreign doctors and other professionals to enter this country to practice because of the increased difficulty in finding jobs for them (HHS 1980). Further efforts are being made to discourage Americans from going abroad to get medical or other professional education with the intention of returning here to practice. Most mental health clinics have ample staffing and long lists of applicants for new jobs. Private practitioners are becoming increasingly aggressive in their efforts to keep their schedules filled.

In the face of such pressures to put a lid on the number of people who would enter the field, it is surprising to see that so many are still working to become psychotherapists. The numbers of therapists keep growing in spite of the difficulty in finding jobs. But psychotherapy practice is very attractive to young people, and the jobs, once obtained, hold great appeal. It is meaningful and comfortable work. The practitioner is accorded, whether deserved or not, an aura of wisdom, power, and compassion. The work pays well, at least in some of its professions, and it appears to the aspirant to be steady and secure employment. The attractions of entering a psychotherapy profession still seem very great.

If the demand for therapy services is peaking and possibly will decline in the near future, and if the labor needed to fulfill this demand is nowhere near peaking and is possibly even increasing, it seems likely that those about to enter the psychotherapy careers will face many obstacles. They may be entering the field at the worst possible time, just before the bubble will burst.

THE DAY THE BUBBLE BURSTS

The "day the bubble burst" is an expression usually reserved for October 24, 1929, Black Thursday, when the stock market plunged and threw the nation into a decade of economic depression. There are some significant parallels between what was happening in business at that time and what is happening now in the business of psychotherapy. Before the stock market crash there was an era of unrestrained optimism and ever increasing consumer pressure for more goods, more services, and more stock purchases. The trend was feeding on itself, with people buying stocks in the expectation that they would continue to rise, and the effect of their purchases was to push prices ever upward. As long as the common perception was that increased demand would lead to increased prices there was no problem. Then came Black Thursday. Eveyone suddenly realized there were limits to demand. Something like this can happen again in the psychotherapy professions, though it seems unlikely to happen on one dramatic day. It will probably take years for the bubble to burst. But it can happen when there are very many more therapists than there is demand for them, when many therapists find they must leave the work for which they trained and which they struggled to enter. It will happen if the insurance companies decide they can no longer pay for therapy services that aren't proved effective and if government funding is cut back to cover only treatment of the seriously disturbed. It can also happen if the public perception about psychotherapy is no longer so positive, if it no longer sees therapy or counseling as the only answer. The competitive struggle within the therapy professions for the dwindling demand for their services would intensify, and the powerful mental health lobby and industry would begin to lose its impact.

After the bubble bursts, considerable adjustments will have to be made. The 1929 economic crash did not eliminate business or the stock market, and in the long run it led to many business improvements. So too there will be upheavals in the business of psychotherapy, but it will not cease to exist. Individual careers will be ended and perhaps entire methods of therapy will become obsolete, but other careers and methods will continue. There will always be a need for psychotherapists, though probably a diminished one. There will probably be many improvements in the system of delivering services. Therapies which have proved themselves will thrive, and those which cannot demonstrate effectiveness will be on the wane. Therapists whose skill and training are deficient will be economically expurgated from psychotherapy delivery, resulting in less risk of harm to the remaining therapy consumers. In sum, even though precarious days seem to lie ahead for many psychotherapists, after the inevitable adjustments are made the professions can be more meaningful and helpful for those in need. This adjustment period will be hastened by two influences which are gaining momentum and whose effect on therapy is just beginning to be felt. They are the efforts to improve the system of third-party financing and the efforts to prove what is and what is not effective about psychotherapy.

THE EFFICACY OF PSYCHOTHERAPY

As indicated above, a major reason for the demand for psychotherapy is the prevailing belief that it is a good thing to experience. People believe in therapy. They believe in its effectiveness. When they obtain therapist's services, they come to feel better. Naturally they attribute this improvement to the therapy, and they extol its virtues to their friends. But many researchers are questioning whether it is the therapy or something else which accounts for the "improvement" (Eysenck 1972).

Numerous studies have been conducted in recent years comparing groups of applicants for psychotherapy services. The studies typically match the individuals in two groups on many relevant variables and then permit the members of one group to enter therapy while getting the other group to wait (Frank 1979). The studies usually reach the same conclusion: those who have waited for therapy and never received it seem just as well off at specified times thereafter as those who received treatment. The same conclusion is usually reached when comparing groups who experience different types of therapy: there is no difference in outcome. In fact some studies suggest that nonprofessional therapists are just as effective as therapists who are professionally trained (Durlak 1979).

The explanation offered by the many critics of psychotherapy seems plausible. It is called "spontaneous remission," the tendency of most people's emotional discomforts to go away with the passage of time. People have an inherent adaptive capacity to recover from life crises and emotional disturbances regardless of the kind of care they receive, or even if they get no care. Obviously spontaneous remission does not apply to everyone. Many of the seriously disturbed, the psychotics and manic-depressives, will require professional assistance to become able to function effectively. But this is a relatively small proportion of the number of consumers of psychotherapy services. For most people it is possibly the effect of time on human nature which accounts for much of the success attributed to therapy. More studies and objective inquiries are needed and are being conducted to determine what needs are not going to be met by spontaneous remission and what needs can only be filled by the psychotherapist. Answers to this question must be found before long, because those who pay for psychotherapy will have less inclination to do so (Hilts 1980).

It is ironic that the major efforts at answering the question about psychotherapy efficacy are coming from the consumer and the third party. It seems that the burden of proof is on the people who pay rather than those who provide the service. The therapist's argument might sound like this: "How do you know we are not effective? I have many former clients who will tell you they have been helped. Prove I'm not worth it." Some therapists' arguments might sound like this: "Well, of course, those studies show there is no effectiveness. But they were studying the wrong treatment method. Mine is the only method that works. I have many success stories for proof." But why should the consumer or payer have to prove that the treatments are worthless? Why shouldn't the therapist have to prove that they are worthwhile?

Government regulations concerning other forms of treatment have been changing. At one time it was only necessary that the producers of various treatment methods or medications had to demonstrate that the product or method was not harmful to the consumer. But now the burden of proof is shifting. Producers are being asked to demonstrate not only that the product won't hurt the consumer but also that it will live up to the claims. So far public regulations do not apply these same standards to the providers of psychotherapy. But how long can the government, the third-party payer, or the consumer be expected to continue using services in the absence of such standards? Eventually someone is bound to say, "The emperor has no clothes." The one most likely to say it will be the third party.

THE THIRD PARTY

Government and private insurance companies are now paying more than 80 percent of the costs of all the mental health care in America (HCFA 1979). The mental health industry is very dependent on such support, and its lobby has considerable influence as well as much motivation to see that these funds are not reduced (Fisher 1981). Continuing payments will be justified by the lobby presenting pictures of seriously disturbed people being released from mental hospitals for lack of money. The third parties will be deluged with statistics describing the millions of emotionally disturbed children, families, and aged who could not get by without psychotherapy. But the government economists and insurance company actuaries may no longer be persuaded. Already they are taking note of a curious phenomenon in the mental health care delivery system. They note that the apparent nature of people's problems seems to change every time the third party alters the kind of coverage it provides (Enoch and Sigel 1979). When coverage is extended for longer periods, then it seems to take longer for clients to work through their disturbances. If payments were only given for people who were diagnosed as depressed, then the nation's incidence of diagnosed depression would probably increase. If the only therapy method that would be completely covered were behavioral modification, then hordes of therapists would probably become behavioral therapists. As events of this nature continue, the third party is likely to reduce its support despite the lobby.

But reduced third party support may be not all bad. The psychotherapy professions are troubled by the involvement of third parties, not only because of the continued imminent risk of cutbacks but because the influence of these bodies on the way treatment is provided. Sometimes this influence is seen as deleterious to the therapy and exposes the client to needless risks and inconveniences.

Four examples illustrate how this is so. First, many needed social and "indirect" health services are not reimbursed by insurance companies. Funding organizations and insurance companies are properly concerned with *health* care, and services such as family therapy or marital counseling are not eligible for coverage per se. These services are not going to be reimbursed by insurance companies unless it can be demonstrated that such intervention is necessary for the mental health of the client. The second example involves time. When third party payers impose limits on the amount of treatment time for which they reimburse, they possibly encourage the overuse of short-term therapy, even in those situations where it doesn't serve the client needs. If a client is rushed through therapy, problems may recur and be painful and more expensive for all.

The third example is in regard to the use of group therapy. Group treatment methods often are used by agencies and health care providers because insurance companies will not pay the larger fees charged for individual appointments. Group therapy is a valuable treatment method, but the decision to prescribe its use must be made on the basis of therapeutic rather than financial considerations.

Finally, the need to conform to insurance company requirements usually means that many of the preventative and less traditional forms of mental health services are given up at the expense of the more traditional medical model fee-for-service programs. The emotionally disturbed adolescent whose best mental health therapy might have been peer group recreational activities instead must sit in an office with a therapist and discuss his problems in the abstract, if his treatment is to be reimbursed through insurance coverage. A depressed person may benefit more from an educational and physical fitness program, but since insurance will not cover such activities the traditional psychotherapeutic interview might be conducted instead. The insurance companies are not particularly sympathetic to or interested in these considerations, or attuned to the fact that less traditional forms of mental health treatment may be more effective. Their structures require that treatment be in quantifiable terms. Third-party payers are unwilling to pay for outreach programs or community prevention efforts or anything that looks like recreation or education. In other words, the most serious countertherapeutic consequence of third-party reimbursement is the way it alters the methods employed for mental health care.

Insurance reimbursement also nullifies or distorts the competitive or marketplace aspects of service provision, more often than not to the disadvantage of the newer or nonmedical therapies. If all the professions were competing equally to provide services to all consumers, then there would probably be a place for them all. The consumer would be able to choose who would provide for his health care needs on the basis of what is important to him and not according to criteria prescribed for him by a third party. Consumers would then gravitate to those individual health care providers who seem to be effective and successful in meeting the needs of their clientele, or at least in convincing the public of their effectiveness in doing so. Insurance payments have distorted the marketplace and effectively restricted consumer choices.

If the insurance company says psychiatry is the only profession to provide reimbursable mental health care, then individuals who belong to other disciplines, no matter how skillful or effective they are, will be in a disadvantageous economic position. Decisions about which discipline to reimburse, and amount of reimbursement, are probably based more on economic and political considerations than on any which are conceptually valid. Those professions which lobby the insurance companies the most effectively and which have the greatest political clout are more likely to be in an advantageous position with the insurance companies, regardless of which group has the potential for providing the best and most economical services for the clients.

Another problem of insurance reimbursement is that the mental health care providers are vulnerable at any time to changes in the criteria used for making third-party reimbursements. Many mental health care providers enter private practice when their professions become eligible for third-party payments, but when the insurance programs are then cut back, the professionals are left in an economically precarious position. Mental health care payments are highly subject to the vicissitudes of social and economic conditions and are the most likely of all the health care services to experience cutbacks. Financial coverage for mental health care has always been shortchanged by public and private health insurance programs, compared with physical health care provisions. According to figures of the American Psychiatric Association, total benefit payments spent on mental health care are only 7 percent of the total health care outlay in the nation (APA 1977a). About 20 percent of all persons who have hospitalization insurance still lack benefits for mental health care. Moreover, when benefits for mental illness are covered in the policy they are usually more restrictive than those for physical illness. This is true in most private insurance plans, many federally funded programs, and was even true in Medicare. Until recently, outpatient Medicare psychiatric benefits were limited to an annual maximum of $250 or 50 percent of "reasonable charges," whichever is less, after a $50 deductible was paid. No such restrictions or deductibles were imposed on the Medicare recipient for physical health care needs. Clearly, despite assertions to the contrary, government and private insurance carriers are still biased against mental illness and mental health care.

Any changes in such payments, whether increases or cutbacks, are sensitive to and influenced by public economic and political shifts over which the private psychotherapy practitioner has almost no control. The insurance model for reimbursement is precarious and unsatisfactory and subjects many career psychotherapists to considerable financial risk.

FUTURE CAREERS IN PSYCHOTHERAPY

In view of so many career problems facing psychotherapists in the near future, what can the person who wants to be a therapist, or who wants to remain one, do to enhance her chances? The aspiring therapist will have to confront more obstacles than any of her predecessors met, and she may experience fewer rewards for her effort. She will be confronted, as we have seen, with difficulties in finding employment. If she gets a job in an organization, hospital, clinic, or social agency, it is likely that her pay will be relatively lower than that of previous generations of therapists. If she opts to work in private practice she will encounter immense pressures from third-party payers to prove she is worth being reimbursed. If she belongs to some therapy professions she will not be reimbursed by insurance companies or government, no matter how skillful she is. She will be faced with growing public disaffection for her methods and intensified competition from her colleagues. To become a therapist she will have to compete with many other intelligent, capable, and highly motivated people in order to gain admission to the dwindling positions in professional schools. Once in school, she will have to finance the education on her own, with little help from government training grants or even from student loans. Once she is practicing she may be subjected to growing doubts about whether her services are really needed. A career in psychotherapy appears to be a challenging prospect.

Nevertheless there will be those who are highly motivated for this career, so much so that they are willing to endure and overcome these and many more obstacles. No doubt they will be an elite generation of therapists, with uncommon abilities and dedication to their art and craft. Their presence in the field will be welcomed and will serve to upgrade all the psychotherapy professions. There will be fewer of them but they will be more capable, given the obstacles they will have had to overcome. Such people deserve to be protected from as many of the pitfalls as possible along the way. Toward this end, here is a list of actions which the psychotherapist or aspiring psychotherapist might consider taking.

Enter the Field at the Right Time.   Now is not a propitious time to attempt to become a therapist. Not only are the afore-mentioned obstacles there to be overcome, but there is no assurance that there will be a job when the training is completed. Social conditions which will reduce public support for psychotherapy are just beginning to be felt. The trends will get worse before they get better. Entry into psychotherapy will probably be easier and more fulfilling after the necessary adjustments are made, after the supply and demand balance is restored. When this restoration occurs, therapists will be doing more meaningful work, serving those who are truly in need rather than those who are merely indulging themselves in narcissistic preoccupations.

Enter the "Right" Profession.   Some professions of psycho-therapy are better than others, from a career viewpoint. If the aspirant decides to become a member of the profession which is in a disadvantageous position in the competitive marketplace of therapists, it will be more difficult for him to remain a therapist. The right professions are those which seem to have the greatest public support for their continued existence. These are the ones which will receive insurance coverage and government funding after the other professions have been excluded. These are the professions which have the strongest public regulation of practice and the strongest political influence. Certainly psychiatry is to be included in this group, as is clinical psychology. Nursing has strong public regulation and its large numbers give it significant political influence. Social work has less public regulation and seems to be declining in its ability to get independent third-party funding. These are the four "establishment" mental health care providers, and their positions are all probably less precarious than the newer professions. The new field of marital and family therapy seems to be having trouble getting recognition as an independent professional entity, as is sex therapy, dance and music therapy, and some of the newer therapies. People in educational guidance might have difficult times outside the school setting, and cutbacks in the schools suggest this is a risky field to enter. The aspiring therapist will want to find that profession which is compatible with his own values and interests, so the wrong profession for him is any one which deviates from them very much. It is impossible, beyond these caveats, to determine which the right or wrong professions will be in the future. No doubt new methodologies and techniques will be discovered by members of professions which aren't even considered now, but which will cause them to be considered the best choice.

Get the Best Possible Education in a Professional School. Too much needs to be known for any psychotherapist to acquire it all in the few years of his professional training. Professional education, at its best, will only be an introduction to the vast amount of available information needed to be a skilled therapist. Accordingly, the new psychotherapist must utilize the training time he has to the best possible advantage. He should begin to refine his skills as he becomes exposed to a solid theory-based foundation of knowledge. He should try to determine which are the best possible professional schools and seek to be admitted to one rather than just settling for a professional degree. Mere possession of such a degree in the future will be no guarantee of a position as a therapist.

Work Toward Improved Professional Standards. Whatever profession one finally decides to enter, there will always be room for improvement in its standards. Standards give the public the deserved assurance that the members are capable of doing what is claimed for the profession. But some of the psychotherapy professions are rather deficient in the standards which they have instituted or which they are supposed to enforce. For example, a profession should require tests of any applicant to its ranks. Some therapy professions automatically confer membership on anyone who was able to complete formal training. This assigns the role of doorkeeper to the professional school rather than to the profession itself. But the therapist does not represent his school to the consumer. He represents his profession. Furthermore, the professions are not doing all they could do to insure that the professional member has remained current in his field. The major means of doing this is by requiring that each member obtain continuing education credits within specified time periods. Periodic reexamination is also necessary to improve professional standards. Psychiatry and psychology both have rather rigorous standards for continuing education. In some states their licensing is contingent upon it. Other professions delivering psychotherapy have little continuing education requirements and even less enforcement. They use the honor system with their members, believing that the therapists will keep current of their own volition. This may be true but it is not reassuring to the public or to the consumer. Professional standards are essential and the aspiring or experienced psychotherapist should do everything in his power to enhance the standards of his profession.

Endorse the Public Regulation of Practice. Funding from third parties will not be conferred upon those professions and individuals who are not subjected to licensing and certification. If a profession does not have licensing for the practice of psychotherapy, and most do not, then the member of that profession would do well to expend considerable time and effort toward getting it. Many professions have tried and found that it was difficult because they could not define what is unique about the work they do. If their work is not unique, if other occupations are to be permitted to do it too, then no license can be granted. Each profession which hopes to have licensing will find it necessary to define the unique aspects of its work to the licensing boards. Failure to do this eventually will result in decreased public support and probably an end to the financial support of insurance carriers. This is important not just for those in private practice; organization-based therapists are finding that their agencies are becoming increasingly dependent on third-party payments. They will not hire therapists who are not eligible to receive reimbursement.

If Possible Avoid Dependence on Third Parties. This, of course, is not possible, but the therapist who is completely dependent on such reimbursement is very vulnerable. This is true whether he is paid directly by the third party while he is in private practice, or when the third party pays his employer who in turn pays him. As we have seen, there are many uncertainties about the future of third party payments. The therapist could belong to a profession which is suddenly excluded from coverage.

It is conceivable that all professions could face serious cutbacks. The therapist who has become the least dependent upon this form of payment will be in the best position to survive the resulting economic hardships.

Specialize and Offer Unique Services.   The therapist who is known for his expertise and interest in meeting a special human need will be in a better position than the therapist who attempts to treat all conditions using eclectic methods. Unless he has something unique to offer, he will be in a highly competitive situation, struggling with other professionals to see a reduced number of clients. If his work is unique he will have much less difficulty of this sort. To develop a unique skill and interest, it will be necessary for the therapist to devote most of his time and attention to a narrower range of interests and methods than he might like. Of course, he will lose something important and valuable in doing so. But he will gain depth in the field of his specialization and probably find that the unique service which he provides is important and valuable to a select group of consumers. If many therapists take this approach, some of them will discover innovative and effective means of serving their clientele that they might not have discovered had they remained generalists.

Enter Private Practice Cautiously.   The psychotherapist who enters private practice faces more obstacles than the organization-based therapist, as we have seen in previous chapters. The trends and social conditions which are determining that there will be a decline in the demand for therapy services will have a particularly strong effect on the private practitioner. The private worker will feel the economic cutbacks faster than will the organization based therapist. A diminution of public support for the methods of psychotherapy will be felt by the private therapist long before it is experienced by the organization. Private practice has considerable rewards, and for some it is the only way to practice therapy, so such people should not avoid private work. They simply should exercise caution and realistic expectations about their choice.

Use Sound Business Practices.   Much of this book has been concerned with business practices in delivering therapy services, particularly in outpatient private therapy. When the expected decline in demand gets closer, some will be tempted to deviate from these principles, to gain short-term advantages. Members of other professions where there is greater supply than demand have been guilty of avoiding sound practices. The cost to them personally and to their professions has been great. The short-term advantage that comes from this is eventually nullified. If the helping professions are faced with members who engage in such behavior, they will lose some of their credibility.

Be Competent.   The therapist who merely attempts to get by, who doesn't keep abreast of the developments in his field, who doesn't seek to expand his range of knowledge, who remains uninvolved with his profession's effort to maintain high professional standards, is missing a great amount of satisfaction in his chosen profession. Despite the questions raised about the efficacy of the profession, the practitioner who comes in daily contact with clients and helps them to find themselves as more fulfilled human beings is extremely fortunate. Having such experiences every working day makes the obstacles and frustrations and threats of economic collapse seem easily endurable. But having such experiences presupposes that the worker is conscientious about his commitment to being competent. The commitment involves hard work, study, working with peers to keep skills refined, and dedication to keeping up. The commitment is to being the best possible therapist that one can be.

CONCLUSION

Many aspiring private psychotherapy practitioners might feel apprehensive about their career plans after reading this book. They have been confronted in these pages with many examples of the difficulties which they will face in their chosen field. They have been exposed to the dangers, the obstacles, and the future risks which might be in store for them. But the intent of these caveats has not been to discourage hopes or cause anxiety. Nor has it been to dissuade capable people from entering the field. Psychotherapy needs new people, new ideas, and new ways of helping those with real needs. Its private practice sector needs dynamic young men and women who are motivated to serve their fellow humans honestly and conscientiously. There will always be room for people of this type, even as it becomes more difficult for others to succeed.

But it is important, now more than ever, that the psychotherapy professions attract the right kind of people. There is no longer any room for those who think this is a career filled with easy money, high prestige, and few problems. Those who attempt to enter the field with such thoughts only harm themselves as well as clients, the public, and other psychotherapists. The only way to keep people with such illusions from entering the field and bringing about this harm is to describe the inevitable hazards and realistic frustrations of private psychotherapy practice.

If such facts are revealed, then those who do enter the field will have looked objectively at the advantages and disadvantages and will not be dissuaded. Those who become private practitioners will be willing to expend the effort required. For their efforts they will find that they have entered one of the most rewarding occupations a person could ever hope to have. They will find themselves in jobs which are tremendously gratifying. Private psychotherapy practice is an occupation which offers many challenges and opportunities, and the kind of fulfillment that can only come through helping those truly in need. It offers considerable variety, bringing one into daily contact with many different types of people, interesting people, people who share one's deepest thoughts and highest ideals. It offers economic well-being for those practitioners who are willing to work hard. It offers freedom from the increasingly burdensome bureaucratic entanglements which seem omnipresent to most modern Americans. It is not a job for everyone. It is a job which is available to fewer people than in the past. But those who are to be included are fortunate indeed. Each of these people will be an important asset to the field of private practice, to the business of psychotherapy.

BIBLIOGRAPHY

ABPN. 1978. "Annual Report of the American Board of Psychiatry and Neurology." *American Journal of Psychiatry* 131(11):1195–1199.

ABPN. 1980. "Annual Report of the American Board of Psychiatry and Neurology." *American Journal of Psychiatry* 133(11):1246–50.

Allison, James and Klaus Hartmann. 1981. "A Note on Choosing a Service Provider from Telephone Listings." *Journal of Community Psychology* 9(1):78–80.

American Psychiatric Association. 1977. *As the Nation Moves Toward National Health Insurance What About the Mentally Ill?* Washington: APA.

American Psychiatric Association. 1980a. *The Diagnostic and Statistical Manual III.* Washington: APA.

American Psychiatric Association. 1980b. *Quick Reference to Diagnostic Criteria from DSM-III.* Washington: APA.

American Psychological Association. 1977. *Standards for Providers of Psychological Services.* Washington: American Psychological Association.

Arieti, Silvano, ed. 1979. *American Handbook of Psychiatry.* 7 vols. New York: Basic Books.

Asher, Janet. 1980. "The Coming Exclusion of Counselors from the Mental Health Care System." *The CEU Clearinghouse*, pp. 3–19. College Park, Md: The Maryland Foundation.

Ayers, George, Charles Mindel, Linda Robinson, and Johnny Wright. 1981. "Fees in a Human Service Agency: Why Do Clients Pay?" *Social Work* 26(3):245–48.

Bahn, Anita. 1965. "Survey of Private Psychiatric Practice." *Archives of General Psychiatry* 12(3):295–302.

Ball, Robert. 1978. *Social Security: Today and Tomorrow.* New York: Columbia University Press.

Barker, Robert. 1971. "Research Findings Related to the Education of Baccalaureate Social Workers." In Robert Barker and Thomas Briggs, eds., *Undergraduate Social Work Education for Practice.* Washington: Government Printing Office.

Barker, Robert and Thomas Briggs. 1968. *Differential Use of Social Work Manpower.* New York: National Association of Social Workers.

Barker, Robert and Thomas Briggs. 1969. *Using Teams to Deliver Social Services.* Syracuse: Syracuse University Press.

Barker, Robert, Thomas Briggs, and Dorothy Daly. 1971. *Educating the Undergraduate for Professional Social Work Roles.* Syracuse: Syracuse University Press.

Baumback, Clifford and Kenneth Lawyer. 1979. *How to Organize and Operate a Small Business.* 6th ed. Englewood Cliffs, N.J.: Prentice-Hall.

Bergin, Allen and Sol Garfield. 1971. *Handbook of Psychotherapy and Behavioral Change: Empirical Analysis.* New York: Wiley.

Berne, Eric. 1955. "Group Attendance: Clinical and Theoretical Considerations." *International Journal of Group Psychotherapy* 5(3):321–34.

Bernstein, Barton. 1977. "Privileged Communications to the Social Worker." *Social Work* 22(4):264–69.

Bernstein, Barton. 1978. "Malpractice: An Ogre On the Horizon." *Social Work* 23(2):106–12.

Bernstein, Bianca and Conrad Lecomte. 1981. "Licensure in Psychology: Alternative Directions." *Professional Psychology* 12(2):200–7.

Billingsley, Andrew. 1964. "Bureaucratic and Professional Orientation Patterns in Social Casework." *Social Service Review* 38(4):400–7.

Birdwhistell, Ray. 1970. *Kinesics and Context: Essays on Body Motion Communication.* Philadelphia: University of Pennsylvania Press.

Borenzweig, Herman. 1977. "Who Passes the California Licensing Examinations?" *Social Work* 22(3):173–77.

Borenzweig, Herman. 1981. "Agency vs. Private Practice: Similarities and Differences." *Social Work* 26(3):239–41.

Brager, George and Sherman Barr. 1967. "Perceptions and Reality: The Poor Man's View of Social Services." In George Brager and F. Purcell, eds. *Community Action Against Poverty,* pp. 72–80. New Haven: College and Yale University Press.

Brammer, Lawrence. 1968. "The Counselor Is a Psychologist." *Personnel and Guidance Journal* (September 1968), pp. 29–36.

Brasch, Phyllis. 1980. "A Helping Hand from the Boss." *Parade* (June 8), pp. 6–8.

Briar, Scott. 1966. "Family Services." In Henry Mass, ed., *Five Fields of Social Services: Reviews of Research,* pp. 9–50. New York: National Association of Social Workers.

Bromberg, Walter. 1975. *From Shaman to Psychotherapist*. Chicago: Regnery.

Bruce, Martin. 1962. "Managing for Better Morale." *Small Marketers Aids Annual* no. 4, pp. 59–60. Washington: Small Business Administration.

Bry, Adelaide. 1976. *est. 60 Hours That Transform Your Life*. New York: Harper and Row.

Buttrick, Shirley. 1972. "Innovative Ideas in Social Service Delivery." *Social Welfare Forum, 1972*. New York: Columbia University Press.

Castendyck, Elsa and Anne Fenlason. 1936. "The Confidential Nature of Social Case Records." *The Family* (March).

Claiborn, W. L. and J. S. Zaro. 1979. "The Development of a Peer Review and Professional Helpers." *Psychological Bulletin* 36(2):80–92.

Cloward, Richard and Irwin Epstein. 1965. "Private Social Welfare's Disengagement from the Poor." In Mayer Zald, ed., *Social Welfare Institutions*, pp. 623–44. New York: Wiley.

Consumers Union. 1978. *Report on Life Insurance*. New York: Consumer Reports Pamphlets.

Consumers Union. 1980. "Individual Retirement Accounts: Costs, Benefits, Problems." *Consumer Reports* (January), pp. 40–48.

Coulton, Claudia. 1979. *Social Work Quality Assurance Programs: A Comparative Analysis*. New York: National Association of Social Workers.

Crabb, L. J. 1978. "Moving the Couch into the Church." *Christianity Today* 22(9):17–19.

Crowder, D. R. 1981. "The Internship Year in Psychiatry." *American Journal of Psychiatry* 138(8):964–67.

"Development and Current Status of Professional Psychology." 1981. *Professional Psychology* 12(3):377–83.

Dickson, Paul. 1978. *The Official Rules*. New York: Dell.

Directory of Social and Health Agencies of New York City, 1981–82. Centennial edition. 1982. New York: Columbia University Press.

Dubin, S. S. 1981. "Obsolescence or Lifelong Education: A Choice for the Professional." *American Psychologist* 81(6):486–98.

Durlak, J. A. 1979. "Comparative Effectiveness of Paraprofessional and Professional Helpers." *Psychological Bulletin* 36(1):80–92.

Elkin, Meyer. 1975. "Licensing Marriage and Family Counselors: A Model Act." *Journal of Marriage and Family Counseling* 1(3):237–51.

Enoch, Louise and George Sigel. 1979. "Third Party Reimbursements:

Countertherapeutic Considerations." *Psychiatric Opinion* 16(7):8–16.
"Ethical Principles of Psychologists." 1981. *American Psychologist* 36(6):122–31.
Everett, Craig. 1979. "The Masters Degree in Marriage and Family Therapy." *Journal of Marital and Family Therapy* 5(3):7–14.
Eysenck, Hans J. 1965. "The Effects of Psychotherapy." *International Journal of Psychiatry* 1(1):97–168.
Eysenck, Hans J. 1972. "Factors Influencing the Outcome of Psychotherapy." *Psychological Bulletin* 78(4):403.
Fanning, John. 1975. "Protection of Privacy and Fair Information Practices." *Social Welfare Forum, 1975*, pp. 115–20. New York: Columbia University Press.
Figueira-McDonough, 1981. "Doctoral Programs in Social Work." *Journal of Education for Social Work* 17(2):76–84.
Fisher, Kathleen. 1981. "Final Budget Bill Called Success for Mental Health Lobbyists." *Clinical Psychiatry News* 9(9):1.
"Five Year Report of the Policy and Planning Board: 1980." 1980. *American Psychologist* 81(6):547–50.
Fleming, J. G. 1974. "The Patient or His Victim: The Therapist's Dilemma." *California Law Review* 62(10):1025–68.
Frank, Jerome. 1973. *Persuasion and Healing: A Comparative Study of Psychotherapy*. Baltimore: Johns Hopkins University Press.
Frank, Jerome. 1979. "The Present Status of Outcome Studies." *Journal of Consulting and Counseling Psychology* 47:310.
Freeman, Alfred and Harold Kaplan. 1967. *Comprehensive Textbook of Psychiatry*. Baltimore: Williams and Wilkins.
Fretz, Bruce and David Mills. 1980. "Professional Certification in Counseling Psychology." *The Counseling Psychologist* 9(1).
Freudenberger, Herbert. 1975. "The Staff Burnout Syndrome in Alternative Institutions." *Psychotherapy* (Spring), pp. 73–82.
Freudenberger, Herbert. 1976. "Burnout: Occupational Hazard of the Child Care Worker." *Child Care Quarterly* (Summer), pp. 26–95.
Friedman, Milton. 1962. *Capitalism and Freedom*. Chicago: University of Chicago Press.
Ganserhoff, N. 1977. "Clinical and Legal Issues in the Family Therapy Record." *Hospital and Community Psychiatry* 28(6):911–13.
Garfield, Sol. 1981. "Psychotherapy: A Forty Year Appraisal." *American Psychologist* 36(2):174–83.
Garfinkel, Irwin. 1975. "Demogrants and Health Insurance: What We Can Afford and What We Value." *The Social Welfare Forum, 1975* New York: Columbia University Press.

Gelwin, David. 1981. "Psychotherapy in the 80s." *Newsweek* (November 30), pp. 70–73.

Gibson, R. M. and M. S. Mueller. 1977. "National Health Expenditures, Fiscal Year 1976." *Social Security Bulletin,* pp. 3–22.

Goldensohn, Sidney. 1977. "Cost, Utilization, and Utilization Review of Mental Health Services in a Prepaid Group Practice Plan." *American Journal of Psychiatry* 134(11):1222–26.

Goldschmitt, Marvin, Robert Tiplan, and Ralph Wiggins. 1981. "The Professional Identity of Counseling Psychologists." *Journal of Counseling Psychology* 28(2):158–67.

Good, Lawrence, Saul Siegal, and Alfred Bay, eds. 1965. *Therapy By Design.* Springfield, Ill.: Charles Thomas.

Goodman, Nathaniel. 1960. "Are There Differences Between Fee and Non Fee Cases? *Social Work* 5(4):46–52.

Goodman, Nathaniel. 1971. "Fee Charging." *Social Work Encyclopedia,* pp. 413–15. New York: National Association of Social Workers.

Granet, Roger, Thomas Kalman, and Michael Sachs. 1980. *American Journal of Psychiatry* 137(12):1443–46.

Green, Ronald and Gibbi Cox. 1978. "Social Work and Malpractice: A Converging Course." *Social Work* 23(2):100–5.

Greenblatt, Milton, Jean Carew, and Chester Pierce. 1977. "Success Rates in Psychiatry and Neurology Certification Examinations." *American Journal of Psychiatry* 134(1):1259–61.

Group for the Advancement of Psychiatry. 1975. *The Effect of the Method of Payment on Mental Health and Practice.* Report 95. New York: GAP.

Grobe, Susan. 1981. "Sunset Laws." *American Journal of Nursing* (July 1981), pp. 1355–57.

Gross, Martin. 1978. *The Psychological Society.* New York: Random House.

Gruber, Alan. 1973. "The High Cost of Delivering Services." *Social Work* 18(4):33–40.

Hall, Edward. 1966. *The Hidden Dimension.* New York: Doubleday.

Hamilton, Gordon. 1946. *Principles of Social Case Recording.* New York: Columbia University Press.

Hardcastle, David. 1977. "Public Regulation of Social Work." *Social Work* 22(1):14–20.

Harden, Blaine. 1981. "Shrink City: The Psychiatric Industry in Washington." *Washington Post Magazine* (November 22), pp. 20–30.

Harsham, Philip. 1979. "Don't Let Your Retirement Plan Loaf On You." *Medical Economics* (May 28), pp. 99–100.

Hartman, Barbara and Jane Wickey. 1978. "The Person Oriented Record in Treatment." *Social Work* 23(4):269–99.

Hauser, Philip. 1974. "Mobilizing for a Just Society." *Social Welfare Forum, 1974*, pp. 3–22. New York: Columbia University Press.

Health Care Financing Administration. 1979. *Health Care Financing Trends* 1(1). Washington: Government Printing Office.

"Health Spending Rises in U.S." 1981. *American Medical News* (November 20), p. 4.

Henry, William, John Sims, and Lee Spray. 1971. *The Fifth Profession.* San Francisco: Jossey-Bass.

Herrington, B. S. 1981. "APA Expresses Reservations on Competition Bills." *Psychiatric News* 16(21):1.

Herrman, Robert. 1980. "Consumer Protection: Yesterday, Today and Tomorrow." *Current History* 78(457).

Hess, Allen, ed. 1980. *Psychotherapy Supervision: Theory, Research and Practice.* New York: Wiley.

HEW. 1973. *Medical Malpractice: Report of the Secretary's Commission on Malpractice.* Washington: Department of Health, Education, and Welfare.

HEW. 1974. *PSRO Manual.* Washington: Department of Health, Education, and Welfare, Office of Professional Standards Review.

HEW. 1980. *National Data Book, 1980.* Publication ADM 80–938. Washington: Department of Health, Education and Welfare, Alcohol, Drug Abuse and Mental Health Administration.

Hilts, Philip, 1980. "Psychotherapy to be Put On Couch by the Government." *Washington Post* (September 29), p. 1.

Hofstadter, Richard, 1944. *Social Darwinism in American Thought.* Philadelphia: University of Pennsylvania Press.

Hogan, D. B. 1979. *The Regulation of Psychotherapy.* Cambridge: Ballinger.

Holder, A. R. 1973. "Failure to Keep Up as Negligence." *American Journal of Psychiatry* 224(11):1461–62.

Holden, C. 1978. "Senators Hear Case for Psychotherapy." *Science* 201:794.

Houghkirk, Ellen. 1977. "Everything You've Always Wanted Your Clients to Know but Have Been Afraid to Tell Them." *Journal of Marriage and Family Counseling* 3(2):27–35.

"How Licensing Hurts Consumers." 1977. *Business Week* (November 28).

Howe, Elizabeth. 1980. "Public Professions and the Private Model of Professionalism." *Social Work* 25(3):179–91.

Hynan, Michael, 1981. "On The Advantage of Assuming Techniques of Psychotherapy Are Ineffective." *Psychotherapy: Theory, Research and Practice* 18(1):11–13.

Internal Revenue Service. 1982a. *Tax Guide for Small Business.* IRS Publication 334. Washington: Government Printing Office.

Internal Revenue Service. 1982b. *Mr. Businessman's Kit.* Washington: Government Printing Office.

Jackson, Eugene. 1981. "All Things Change: Including Nursing." *Nursing 81* 11(11):9–14.

Johnson, Frank. 1975. "Court Decisions and the Social Services." *Social Work* 20(5).

Justman, Richard. 1979. "Let's Be More Professional About Professional Courtesy." *Medical Economics* (May 28).

Kahn, Alfred. 1969. *Theory and Practice of Social Planning.* New York: Russell Sage Foundation.

Kane, Rosalie. 1974a. "Look to the Record." *Social Work* 19(3):412–19.

Kane, Rosalie. 1974b. *Interprofessional Teamwork.* Syracuse: Syracuse University Press.

Karger, Howard. 1981. "Burnout as Alienation" *Social Service Review* 55(2).

Kauffman, Herbert. 1980. "Do Your Collections Measure Up?" *Medical Economics* (April 28), pp. 88–89.

Keefe, Thomas, 1978. "The Economic Context of Empathy." *Social Work* 23(3):460–66.

Kerson, Tobe, 1978. "The Social Work Relationship: A Form of Gift Exchange." *Social Work* 25(1):326–27.

Kilgore, James. 1975. "Establishing and Maintaining a Private Practice." *Journal of Marriage and Family Counseling* 1(2):145–48.

Kiplinger, Washington, ed. 1980. *The Kiplinger Tax Letter* (May 9).

Kirchner, Marian. 1979. "New Quality Controls on Your Practice: How Soon, How Tough?" *Medical Economics* (June 25).

Krutch, Joseph Wood. 1948. *Henry David Thoreau.* Boston: Houghton-Mifflin.

Kurzman, Paul. 1976. "Private Practice as a Social Work Function." *Social Work* 21(5):363–69.

Lampman, Robert. 1975. "Contemporary Trends in Social Welfare Expenditures." *The Social Welfare Forum, 1975.* New York: Columbia University Press.

Langsley, Donald and George Lebaron. 1974. "Peer Review Guidelines: A Survey of Local Standards of Treatment." *American Journal of Psychiatry* 131(12).

Langsley, Donald. 1978. "Comparing Clinic and Private Practice." *American Journal of Psychiatry* 135(6):702–6.

Lantz, James and Beverly Lanahan. 1976. "Referral Fatigue Therapy." *Social Work* 21(3):239–41.

Lasser, J. K. 1982. *Your Income Tax*. New York: Simon and Schuster.

Lebensohn, Zigmond. 1978. "Private Practice of Psychiatry: Future Roles." *American Journal of Psychiatry* 135(11):1359–62.

Lesse, Stanley. "Caveat Emptor: The Cornucopia of Current Psychotherapies." *American Journal of Psychotherapy* 33(3).

Levin, Arnold. 1976. "Private Practice Is Alive and Well." *Social Work* 21(5):356–62.

Lindenberg, Ruth. 1958. "Hard to Reach: Client or Casework Agency?" *Social Work* 3(4):23–30.

Liptzin, Benjamin. 1974. "Quality Assurance and Psychiatric Review." *American Journal of Psychiatry* 131(12:1374–77.

Lubove, Roy. 1965. *The Professional Altruist*. Cambridge: Harvard University Press.

Luborsky, Lester and H. Bachrach. 1975. "Comparative Studies of Psychotherapies." *Archives of General Psychiatry* 32(10).

Lunde, Anders S. 1981. "Health in the U.S." *Annals of the American Academy of Political and Social Sciences* 453(1):28–69.

Maas, Henry. ed. 1966. *Five Fields of Social Service: Reviews of Research*. New York: National Association of Social Workers.

Magaro, Peter, Robert Gripp, and David McDowell. 1978. *The Mental Health Industry*. New York: Wiley.

Manley, Mary. 1981. "Clinical Privileges for Nonhospital Based Nurses." *American Journal of Nursing* 81(10):1822–25.

"Manpower Data Bank Frequency Distributions." 1975. Washington: National Association of Social Workers.

Maslach, Christina. 1976. "Burned Out." *Human Behavior* (September), pp. 16–19.

Masters, William and Virginia Johnson. 1970. *Human Sexual Inadequacy*. Boston: Little Brown.

McCann, Charles and Jane Cutler. 1979. "Ethics and the Alleged Unethical." *Social Work* 24(1):5–8.

McKane, Maureen. 1975. "Case Record Writing With Reader Empathy." *Child Welfare* 54:593–97.

Meltzer, M. L. 1975. "Insurance Reimbursement: A Mixed Blessing?" *American Psychologist* 30:1151–64.

Mendelson, F. 1981. "Long Term Psychotherapy Coverage Under National Health Insurance." *Social Security Bulletin* 18(1):76–85.

Merke, Sharp, and Dohme. 1982. *The Merke Manual*. Rahway, N.J.: Merke, Sharp and Dohme.

Miller, Roy, and Gordon Black, Paul Ertel, Gordon Ogram. 1974. "Psychiatric Peer Review: The Ohio System." *American Journal of Psychiatry* 131(12).

Mueller N. S. and P. A. Piro. 1976. "Private Health Insurance in 1974: A Review of Coverage, Enrollment and Financial Experience." *Social Security Bulletin* 39(3):3–20.

Nagelberg, Steven, Arthur Schwartz, Barry Perlman, Martin Paris, and John Thornton. 1980. "Providers and Receivers in the Private Psychiatric Medicaid System." *American Journal of Psychiatry* 137(6):690–94.

NASW. 1977. *NASW News* 22(6).

NASW. 1980a. *Manual for Adjudication of Grievances*. Rev. ed. Washington: National Association of Social Workers.

NASW. 1980b. "The Code of Ethics." *Social Work* 25(3):185–86.

NASW. 1982. *Register of Clinical Social Workers* 3d ed. Washington: National Association of Social Workers.

NCHS. 1978. *Health Resources Statistics*. 1977–78 ed. Washington: National Center for Health Statistics and USDHHS.

NCHS. 1979. *Health Resources Statistics*. 1978–79 ed. Washington: National Center for Health Statistics and USDHHS.

NCHS. 1980. *Health United States 1980*. Washington: National Center for Health Statistics.

Newman, Donald and Lorraine Luft. 1974. "The Peer Review Process: Education versus Control." *American Journal of Psychiatry* 131(12):1363–66.

"New York Psychiatrists to Use PR Firm for Image Problem." 1980. *Psychiatric News* (April 18), p. 24.

New York Times. 1980. "Nurses Demand Increased Responsibility." (March 25), B12.

New York Times. 1981. "Litigations Rise in U.S." (July 5), D8.

Nichols, William. 1979. "Doctoral Programs in Marital and Family Therapy." *Journal of Marital and Family Therapy* 5(3):45–61.

Noll, John. 1974. "Needed—A Bill of Rights for Clients." *Professional Psychologist* (May), pp. 3–12.

Noll, John 1976. "The Psychotherapist and Informed Consent." *American Journal of Psychiatry* 133(12):1451–53.

Olbrisch, M. E. 1977. "Psychotherapeutic Interventions in Physical Health" *American Psychologist* 32(10):541–44.

Osmond, Humphrey. 1957. "Function as a Basis of Psychiatric Ward Design." *Mental Hospitals* 8(4):44–49.

Owens, Arthur. 1979. "Is A Management Consultant Worth the Money?" *Medical Economics* (April 16).

Owens, Arthur. 1980. "Look What's Happening to Professional Courtesy." *Medical Economics* (February 4), pp. 140–51.

Patti, Rino. 1974. "Organizational Resistance and Change: The View from Below." *Social Service Review* (September), pp. 367–83.

Physicians Desk Reference (PDR 1982) 1982. 36th ed. Oradell, N. J.: Medical Economics.

Piliavin, Irving. 1968. "Restructuring the Provision of Social Services." *Social Work* 13(1):34–41.

Pins, Arnulf. 1971. "Changes in Social Work Education and Their Implications for Practice." *Social Work* 16(2):5–15.

Piven, Frances Fox and Richard Cloward. 1971. *Regulating the Poor: Functions of Public Welfare*. New York: Random House.

Pope, Kenneth, Henry Simpson, and Myra Weiner. 1978. "Malpractice in Outpatient Psychotherapy." *American Journal of Psychiatry* 32(4):593–96.

"Recent Problems with Champus Settled." 1981. *The Family Therapy News* 12(4):4.

"Regulations Imperil Medical Records." 1981. *Psychiatric News* 16(14):1.

Resnick, Reuben and Harry Balter. 1934. "Withholding Information from Law Enforcement Bodies." *Social Service Review* 8(4):668–77.

Richmond, Mary. 1921. "Why Case Records." *The Family* 21(7).

Robinowitz, Carolyn and Milton Greenblatt. 1980. "Continuing Education and Continuing Certification." *American Journal of Psychiatry* 137(3):291–92.

Rosenberg, Charlotte. 1980. "Which Malpractice Reforms Protect You Best?" *Medical Economics* (April 28), pp. 149–55.

Roth, Loren. 1979. "A Commitment Law for Patients, Doctors and Lawyers." *American Journal of Psychiatry* 136(9):1121–28.

Roth, Loren and Alan Meisel. 1977. "Dangerousness, Confidentiality and the Duty to Warn." *American Journal of Psychiatry* 134(5):508–12.

Roth, Loren, Jack Wolford, and Alan Meisel. 1980. "Patient Access to Records: Tonic or Toxin?" *American Journal of Psychiatry* 137(5).

"Savings Revolution, The." 1981. *Time* Magazine pp. 58–61.

Satir, Virginia. 1964. *Conjoint Family Therapy*. Palo Alto: Science and Behavior Books.

Schaeffer, Phyllis. 1981. "Psychiatrist Still at Low Risk for Malpractice Suit." *Clinical Psychiatry News* (September), p. 1.

Schultze, Charles. 1977. *The Public Use of Private Interest*. Washington: Brookings Institution.

Schumacher, E. F. *Small Is Beautiful: Economics as if People Mattered*. New York: Harper and Row.

Schwartz, William. 1970. "Private Troubles and Public Issues." *The Social Welfare Forum, 1970*. New York: Columbia University Press.

Schwartz, Harry. 1980. "Two Decades that Altered the Character of Medical Practice in America." *Medical Tribune* 21(17).

Seabury, Brett. 1971. "Arrangement of Physical Space in Social Work Settings." *Social Work* 16(4):43–49.

Seabury, Brett. 1976. "The Contract: Uses, Abuses and Limitations." *Social Work* 21(1):16–23.

Sears, Roebuck Catalogue, 1902 Edition. 1969. New York: Crown Publishers (p. 447).

Selvini-Palazzoli, Mara, Luigi Boscolo, Gianfranco Cecchin, and Guiliana Prata. 1980. "The Problem of the Referring Person." *Journal of Marital and Family Therapy* 6(1):3–10.

Serban, George. 1981. "Sexual Activity in Therapy: Legal and Ethical Issues." *American Journal of Psychiatry* 35(1):76–85.

Sharfstein, Steven. 1978. "Will Community Mental Health Survive in the 1980s?" *American Journal of Psychiatry* 135(11):1363–66.

Sharfstein, Steven, Carl Taube, and Irving Goldberg. 1975. "Private Psychiatry and Accountability." *American Journal of Psychiatry* 132(1):43–47.

Sharfstein, Steven, Carl Taube, and Irving Goldberg. 1977. "Problems in Analyzing the Comparative Costs of Private versus Public Psychiatric Care." *American Journal of Psychiatry* 134(1):29–32.

Sharfstein, Steven and Harry Clark. 1980. "Why Psychiatry Is a Low Paid Specialty." *American Journal of Psychiatry* 137(7).

Shear, Beatrix. 1973. *The Malpractice Problem for Non-Physician Health Care Professions as Reflected in Professional Liability Rates*. Publication no. S73–88. Washington: Department of Health, Education, and Welfare.

Shireman, Joan. 1975. "Client and Welfare Opinions about Fee Charging in a Child Welfare Agency." *Child Welfare* (May), pp. 331–40.

Simmons, Janice. 1981. "Issues Raised by Tarasoff Case Confusing to Psychiatrists, Courts." *Clinical Psychiatry News* 9(10):1.

Simon, Carol. 1980. "Continuing Education: Is the Push for It Slackening?" *CEU Clearinghouse*, College Park: The Maryland Foundation.

Slavson, S. R. 1947. *The Practice of Group Psychotherapy*. New York: International University Press.

Slovenko, Ralph, 1966. *Psychotherapy, Confidentiality and Privileged Communications*. Springfield, Ill.: Charles Thomas.

Slovenko, Ralph. 1973. *Psychiatry and Law*. Boston: Little, Brown.

Snyder, Bruce. 1977. "Neurology in the Psychiatry Boards." *American Journal of Psychiatry* 134(11):1267–69.

Social Workers Professional Liability Insurance. 1978. New York: American Professional Agency.

Sommer, Robert. 1959. "Studies in Personal Space." *Sociometry* 24(1):247–60.

Sommer, Robert. 1962. "The Distance for Comfortable Conversation." *Sociometry* 25(1):111–16.

Sommer, Robert. 1965. "Further Studies in Small Group Ecology." *Sociometry* 28(4):337–48.

Sommers, Anne. 1977. "Accountability, Public Policy and Psychiatry." *American Journal of Psychiatry* 134(9):959–65.

Spitz, Henry and Susan Spitz. 1980. "Co-therapy in the Management of Marital Problems." *Psychiatric Annals* 10(4).

Spotnitz, Hyman. 1972. "Comparison of Different Types of Group Psychotherapy." In Harold Kaplan and Benjamin Sadock, eds., *Sensitivity Through Encounter and Marathon*. New York: Jason Aranson.

Stickney, Stonewall. 1968. "Schools Are Our Community Mental Health Centers." *American Journal of Psychiatry* 124(4):1407–14.

Szasz, Thomas. 1970. *The Manufacture of Madness*. New York: Harper and Row.

Tarasoff v. Regents of University of California. 1976. *California Law Reporter* 14 551 P2d, 334.

Theobald, Robert, ed. 1966. *The Guaranteed Income*. Garden City, N. Y.: Doubleday.

Thomas, Lewis. 1981. "Medicine Without Science." *Atlantic Monthly* (April), pp. 40–44.

Thompson, James. 1980. "Burnout in Group Home Houseparents." *American Journal of Psychiatry* 137(6).

Titmuss, Richard. 1968. *Commitment to Welfare*. New York: Pantheon.

Torrey, E. Fuller. 1969. "The Case for the Indigenous Therapist." *Archives of General Psychiatry* 20(3):365–72.

Torrey, E. Fuller, 1974. *The Death of Psychiatry*. New York: Penguin.

Trent, Chester and William Muhl. 1975. "Professional Liability Insurance and the American Psychiatrist." *American Journal of Psychiatry* 132(12):1421–24.

Turner, Francis. 1978. *Psychosocial Therapy.* New York: Free Press.

"Unintended Consequences of Requiring a License to Help." 1981. *American Psychologist* 36(1):13–21.

U.S. Congress, Office of Technology Assessment. 1980. "The Efficacy and Cost Effectiveness of Psychotherapy." Background Paper no. 3. *Implications of Cost Effectiveness Analysis of Medical Technology* Washington: Government Printing Office.

U.S. Master Tax Guide. 1982. Chicago: Commerce Clearing House.

Van Hoose, William and Jeffrey Kuttler. 1977. *Ethical and Legal Issues in Counseling and Psychotherapy.* San Francisco: Jossey-Bass.

Weed, Lawrence. 1969. *Medical Records, Medical Education and Patient Care: The Problem Oriented Record as a Basic Tool.* Cleveland: Case Western Reserve University Press.

Wilensky, Harold. 1970. "The Professionalization of Everyone?" In Oscar Grusky and George Miller, eds., *The Sociology of Organizations,* pp. 484–90. New York: Free Press.

Wilensky, Harold and Charles Lebeaux. 1958. *Industrial Society and Social Welfare.* New York: Russell Sage Foundation.

Williams, Arthur. 1975. "Setting Up a Rural Private Practice." *Journal of Marriage and Family Counseling* 1(3):277–80.

Wolberg, Lewis. 1976. *The Technique of Psychotherapy.* 3d ed. New York: Grune and Stratton.

Zilboorg, Gregory and G. W. Henry. 1941. *A History of Medical Psychology.* New York: Norton.

Zurcher v. *Stanford Daily.* In *Decisions of the United States Supreme Court: 1977–78 Term,* pp. 262–65. Rochester, N.Y.: Lawyers Cooperative Publishing Co.

INDEX